Holding Your Ground

Holding Your Ground

*An action guide
to local conservation*

ANGELA KING
and
SUSAN CLIFFORD
for
Common Ground

Foreword by
David Bellamy

WILDWOOD HOUSE

First published in Great Britain in 1985
By Maurice Temple Smith Ltd
Revised and reprinted in 1987
By Wildwood House Ltd
Gower House, Croft Road, Aldershot, Hants GU11 3HR

King, Angela, 1944-
  Holding your ground : an action guide to
local conservation.
  1. Environmental protection—Great Britain
—Societies; etc.
  I. Title   II. Clifford, Susan
  304.2   Td171.5.G7

Published with
financial support
from the
Countryside
COMMISSION

Pri

Contents

Common Ground

Common Ground was established in 1983 with two main objectives: to promote the importance of our common cultural heritage—common plants and animals, familiar and local places, local distinctiveness and our links with the past; and to explore the emotional value these things have for us by forging practical and philosophical links between the arts and the conservation of nature and landscapes.

Holding Your Ground is the first of Common Ground's many projects to celebrate and to promote the value of the commonplace at the local level. It has led to *The Parish Maps Projects* which is encouraging people to chart the wild life, landscape, buildings, history and cultural features which *they* value in their own surroundings. By displaying the maps publicly there is a better chance that others will respect and protect things that have meaning and importance for local people.

Trees, Woods and the Green Man is drawing people from all sides of the arts to generate new plays, music, poetry, sculpture. The aim is to heighten our awareness of the cultural and spiritual as well as the environmental importance of our trees and woods.

The New Milestones Project is encouraging a new generation of village and countryside sculptures involving artists and crafts people with local communities in celebration of their locality. The purpose of the sculptures is to encourage us to see our surroundings in a new light and to discover things we had not noticed before.

Common Ground has no membership. It is a small limited company and charity, relying on grants and donations to continue its work of enabling people to give active expression to their affection for the commonplace and everyday in town or country.

Common Ground
45 Shelton Street
London WC2H 9HJ

The authors

Susan Clifford grew up on the Notts/Derby border. She worked in Scotland during the 1960s in landscape and planning consultancies. In 1970 she became a full-time lecturer in rural and natural resources planning, first at the Polytechnic of Central London and since 1975 at the Bartlett School of Architecture and Planning, University College, London. From 1974 to 1981 she was on the Board of Directors of Friends of the Earth. She is a cofounder of Common Ground and works voluntarily for the organisation in her spare time .

Angela King comes from Dorset. From 1967 to 1971 she worked as a dress designer and fashion buyer in New York, but she returned to England in 1971 and joined the newly forming Friends of the Earth to become its first wildlife campaigner. She took a leading role in the start of the Save the Whales and Endangered Species campaigns. In the second half of the 1970s she worked to try to save the otter in Britain, latterly as joint coordinator of the Otter Haven Project. In 1980 and 81 she worked on reports on wild life habitat loss for Earth Resources Research and the Nature Conservancy Council. She has written articles and booklets on whales and otters and two publications for children. A cofounder of Common Ground, she now works as its full-time coordinator.

Acknowledgements

We are extremely grateful to the Countryside Commission for giving us a 75 percent grant to research and write this book and for their cooperation and help throughout. We should particularly like to thank Terry Robinson for his patience, enthusiasm and guidance.

While the Countryside Commission supported the research and writing of this book, and advised on some points, it did not exert any editorial control. Therefore, the views expressed are those of the authors, and do not necessarily reflect the views of the Countryside Commission.

We should also like to thank Ford Motor Company Limited, British Petroleum Company p.l.c., and two charitable Trusts for their financial help.

Many people have given us helpful advice on various drafts. Our thanks go to Sue Wright who contributed considerably to the section on local councils and to the following for their comments on different sections: Dave Baldock, Mark Bowden, Angela and Paul Brassley, John Clark, Roger Deakin, David Goode, Saskia Haslam, John Hudson, Robert Hutchison, Liz Kessler, Brian Lymbery, Duncan Mackay, David Pedley, Chris Rose and Charles Secrett.

We are most grateful to all the parish councils, local groups and individuals who have sent us information about their activities and are only sorry we could not include them all.

Particular help and information have been gratefully received from Colin Booty, RSPCA; Ruth Colyer; Dorset, Hertfordshire and West Sussex County Planning Departments; Lyndis Cole and Mark Lintell of Land Use Consultants; Richard Mabey; Ian Scott; Paul Carnell,

Northants Rural Community Council; Bevan Craddock, Staffordshire Rural Community Council; James Derounian, Devon Rural Community Council; Eric Carter, FWAG; Philip Oswald, NCC; Heather Mayall, WI; Mike Kirby, Countryside Commission; and from far too many rural community councils, county planning departments, county archaelogists, community arts officers, parish clerks, county naturalists' trusts and conservation organisations to mention individually.

We thank NCVO for circulating requests for information to the rural community councils and the Nature Conservancy Council for obtaining information for us from their regional offices.

We should like to thank the following people for the use of their photographs. Chris Baines, pages 16 and 208; Ian Anderson, page 94; Countryside Properties Plc, Essex, page 103; and Ron Frampton, page 239. The remainder of the photographs are by Susan Clifford and Angela King who are very grateful to Michael Clifford for his patient work in reproducing them.

Robin Tanner has been kind enough to allow us to use the line drawing of the gate details from his and Heather Tanner's book *Wiltshire Village* (1939 and Robin Garton 1983) on page 182. The letter-cutting on the stone 'Common Ground' was by Richard Grasby.

Special thanks are due to Tony Foster for his painting for the cover and to David Bellamy for writing the Foreword.

To Stephanie Burton go heartfelt thanks for deciphering difficult handwriting and for typing the many drafts, to Marinetime for the use of their photocopying machine.

Our greatest thanks must go to Oliver Baines, Cornwall Rural Community Council, and to Tony Long at CPRE for their very full comments, advice and sustaining enthusiasm, and to Vivienne Sweet, Tom Greeves, Joanna Morland and Neil Sinden for their hard work and moral support.

The breadth of ground which we have tried to cover has led us to new interests and new friends – we thank them all and hope that you find the guide useful and stimulating. Any deficiencies we should like to hear about, any errors are our responsibility alone.

Foreword

Every day my post bag includes at least ten letters which casually ask the same question, can you help?

Each one is a plea from the heart of some one person or group of people who desperately want to avert the destruction of part of their local heritage, their Common Ground which has meant so much to them throughout their lives.

Sometimes, it is a single tree, a meander in a small stream, a dry stone wall, a patch of primroses, a village pond. At other times it is much larger; recently every child from a small school in Scotland wrote asking me to help them save their local broadleaf woodland, the last left in the area.

Perhaps it was all summarised in a letter from a Welsh miner. It told of his young days when he could emerge from a long shift down the pit to refresh himself with wildflowers and goldfinches in the hedgerows, tiddlers in the pond, butterflies in the field and brown trout in the streams. Then there was a vibrant living unofficial countryside which still kept the black valley and the lives of its people green. Now, he complains, I take my grandchildren out into a sterile valley, sterile of work, sterile of wildlife, sterile of any hope.

The letters tear me apart. What can I do? In some cases I can be of direct help, in most cases all I can do is write a formal letter and say there are local or national bodies to go to.

Now at least I can ask them to read this book, for in its pages is the know-how, the expertise, the methods by which any community however large or small can take steps to save its Common Ground.

Please, please buy and read this book for it is the voice of the people who know and understand that there is a real future here in Britain.

David Bellamy
Bedburn, July 1984

Introduction

The purpose of the guide

We hope this book will give basic information on how to look after your locality and the reasons why conservation at the local level is important.

We believe it is vital to conserve our cultural heritage as a whole and to make connections between landscapes, wild life, ancient monuments and buildings.

The prevailing interest is in rare animals and plants, spectacular landscapes and grand buildings – the cream of our heritage which has national importance but with which most people have little contact. We feel that the 'experts' have monopolised the discussions and decisions about our environment, and because they have concentrated on the special things, the everyday surroundings of most people have been devalued by default. In our view it is imperative for people to maintain their contact with the past and with the natural world not as a means of escape at weekends and holidays but in everyday practical ways. Vernacular buildings, ordinary landscapes and their creatures chronicle our unwritten history and in their subtle variety embody the spirit of our everyday culture; here lies their specialness.

Science has tended to devalue the spontaneous response of the senses to nature, landscape and place – yet even the most hardened field biologist will sometimes admit that the real reason for wishing to conserve something is because he 'likes' it, though he may not be able to say quite why. We support those who take courage and express attachments to or care for particular places in writing, drama, poetry and painting and translate these sentiments into practical action. The emphasis of the book is on ways of influencing everyday changes, preventing the insidious nibbling away at cultural and local individuality, rather than with fighting major schemes such as motorway building, the construction of airports and reservoirs. Our concern is mainly with rural areas, but many of the ideas for projects can be translated for use in cities. We have tried to give a lead to other more detailed sources of information, support and help since our preoccupation is to give a wide ranging view of conservation. We thought it important to include examples and case histories of parish, local group and individuals' initiatives to show the kinds of things which have been done and which can be achieved, in the hope that others will be encouraged to embark on similar projects. Wherever possible we have quoted people's experiences directly to ensure that their enthusiasm comes across. Throughout the book we have tried to stress the cultural importance of our surroundings and have included a chapter on some ways in which locality can be celebrated by using the arts.

How to find your way around the book

In the first chapter, 'Personal Landscapes', we try to show how important the locality is to our feeling of well-being – the security of 'the home range', the value of familiar places with their distinctive history and natural history, not just as a backdrop to our common culture but part of its very fabric. We follow this with a practical look at the broad choices we have for looking after buildings, landscape and wild life before taking specific subjects such as historic landscapes, trees and woods, plants and animals and buildings, and exploring the reasons for conserving them, and how to conserve them using official routes as well as spontaneous and domestic ways. We give lists of further reading, people and organisations to contact. Information on particular statutory agencies occurs at the end of relevant chapters.

Subsequent chapters give ideas and advice on ways of combatting pollution from farms, celebrating the locality organising others, some clues on how to find your way around parish, district and county councils,and how to raise money or get physical help.

A list of national organisations and their addresses is followed by a section on designations – AONBs, SSSIs, etc.

Reprint 1987

1987 will be regarded as a turning point for the British countryside. The often destructive scale and speed of change we have seen in merely half a lifetime is likely to pale into insignificance beside what is about to happen. With a planning system under threat, impatient developers, pressure for change of agricultural subsidies and proposals for massive conifer afforestation, *Holding Your Ground* becomes all the more vital as people look for imaginative ways of using the land as well as creating new economic and social patterns.

An appreciation of nature and our cultural heritage is not enough. We must have an *active* commitment to its conservation. There is no excuse for inaction, we each have a responsibility to care for our own place to ensure that its character and distinctiveness is enhanced, not eroded by change.

1
Personal Landscapes

We shall not cease from exploration
And the end of all our exploring
Will be to arrive where we started
And know the place for the first time.

T.S. Eliot, 'Four Quartets'

It seems only natural that we should value most what we are in contact with every day – local and familiar places, commonplace birds and animals – yet the reverse is often true. We appear to place a higher value on rare animals and plants and spectacular views and far-flung places. Of course both are important because they fulfil different needs. But the everyday places desperately need our attention – partly because they are changing so fast, and not always for the better, and because there is tremendous benefit to be gained from a personal involvement with one's own locality. As Fraser Harrison wrote in *Second Nature* (1984, edited by R. Mabey, S. Clifford and A. King):

The ordinary places and objects that make up our everyday landscape, our personal countryside, stand as living monuments to our continuing survival and feeling response to the world. Without such monuments, and they are not necessarily a rural monopoly, our sense of identity begins to crumble and warp. We need little, low, unspectacular corners which can carry special resonances for us alone. These local views and familiar landmarks, these commonplace flora and fauna, are the more valuable for being easily accessible... they can be seen, touched and understood in the course of our daily round... All this complex intermingling of our emotions and their reflection in nature makes possible the birth of a powerful sense of rootedness and meaning in a world which otherwise yields little but confusion and futility. By conserving the mass of precious detail in our parishes, we conserve ourselves.

Local distinctiveness

At a time when regional and local distinctiveness are disappearing so fast, it is important to try to retain the local character of a place whenever possible. Fifty years ago it could be said that there were real regional and local differences in the landscape and in villages and towns. In the pursuit of progress we have swept away the past with such impatience and voraciousness that we are beginning to lose identity with our surroundings. Houses, street lamps, bridges, shop fronts, front doors have become standardised. Ubiquitous building materials are used in preference to local stone or brick, and there is little evidence of new regional or local building styles emerging as a modern counterpoint to the old. The recent revival of interest in the crafts could be used to great effect to recreate local character, redolent of our own times.

Geology, altitude, aspect and climate combine to determine what trees and flowers grow in particular places and hence what insects and other animals will occur. The planting of 'exotic' trees in the countryside has, along with the replacement of deciduous woodlands by non-native conifers, Dutch Elm disease, the removal of hedgerows and hedgerow trees, the spread of barbed wire and electric fencing, done much to reduce regional and local individuality.

Land drainage and the wide application of herbicides and fertilisers has also reduced diversity on a massive scale. Never before in our history have we had the means with which to alter our environment to such an extent.

Yet it is to the enduring and subtly distinct aspects of our environment that we are drawn and through them we feel our allegiance to 'home'.

Homing in

Where does the concept of 'home' begin and end? It can vary from the physical structure we live in, to the place where we were brought up, to our road, village, parish, county or even country – especially when we are away from it. 'Oh, to be in England now that April's there.' Most of us have allegiance of some sort to a 'home range' or 'territory'. It may start in childhood as Michael Barker describes:

No-one possesses so intimate a familiarity with its own locality as a child. The tiny garden of a modern estate house can be a huge, mysterious, seasonally ever-changing place to a small child.

Later his environment widens to take account of such features as the number of paving stones between the front gate and the corner shop, the short cuts along back alleys which to an uninitiated adult might seem lengthy detours, where deep puddles form after a night of rain, the pavement undulations which can confound an unwary tricyclist, and so on.

(What is a Local Study?, *Heritage Education News*, Spring 1983)

The poet John Clare as a child had developed his own notion of space: he 'imagined that the world's end was at the 'orizon and that a days journey was able to find it'. In his essay, 'An Affection for Cathedrals', William Golding describes the pull of his familiar territory:

Driving home across the downs, I was now prepared for the invisible barrier, and heard a distinct 'Ping!' as I passed through it, the barrier was the exact point where Salisbury and Winchester influences were balanced. Like a space probe passing from moon's gravity to earth's gravity I was now hurrying faster and faster towards my own experiences of *mana*. I do not live in the close; but I was going home, and I was going home to the Cathedral.

And in *Freedom of the Parish* Geoffrey Grigson describes where his loyalties lie:

Don't we all need to be emotional property owners? Each bird and each mammal knows the frontier of its territory as if it were marked by a red line on the map which accompanies the title deed, as if there were frontier guards and barbed wire. So, in a way, it has been with ourselves and the Country Parish. The Parish, I say, and not the village. Urban writers fall in love with a countryside and then make the mistake of describing it as though villages, and not parishes were the units of loyalty. A village is only the capital of a country in miniature. It is this little country, this parish, which bounds our emotion, and is the territory of that pack or tribe into which we are born.

It is the *size* of the parish which makes us feel happy with it as our home range. Grigson describes the parish as 'the smallest unit of a familiar and valuable environment'. Other factors which make it important are its *familiarity*. We love our home range because we know it, or parts of it, intimately. The parish may not hold anything which is remarkable in regional or national terms, but its specialness to its inhabitants is that they are a part of its history and future; its views are their views and its culture is a part of their very being. In Wales these ideas are themselves a commonplace – 'cynefin' and 'bro' (words for which the English have no literal translation) imply more than the physical locality and its landscape, they describe deeply felt ties of familiarity, identification and belonging.

Place and culture

Obviously change does have to occur. We need food, new houses, factories, hospitals and so on. But we also have to hold on to the character and essential fabric of our everyday surroundings for our own cultural identity and psychological wellbeing – not just the 'cream' of our natural or built environment which is inaccessible to most people. As Gillian Tindall said in her book about Kentish Town, London, *The Fields Beneath*: 'We are very ready today to concede to people's need for "meaningful human relationships", yet we fail almost entirely to realise that other relationships, with places, objects, views – other supports for the human psyche – may be just as profoundly important, and that, if these are denied, the resulting impoverishment of the person may have deep and lasting consequences.'

It is difficult to see a place, a landscape, without sensing its ghosts: ghosts of the imagination – the Heathcliffs, Judes, Peter Grimeses, David Copperfields, Toads and Ratties; ghosts of legend and the ghosts of local characters past. Dorset is beautiful enough in its own right, but knowing that Thomas Hardy lived there and wrote about it; that Gustav Holst, inspired by Hardy's writing, wrote the music 'Egdon Heath'; that Constable painted Weymouth Bay adds further dimensions to the mystery and enjoyment of the place.

More domestic ghosts exist – smugglers, highway men, ladies walking on the moor; every locality has it stories of past 'larger than life' characters. Legends too form a significant part of our relationship with place – the countless tales of black dogs, giants dropping stones to form hills, notorious young lords making pacts with the Devil. The associations with magic, with gods of nature, with mythical creatures – all of these can enrich our feelings about places, add questions and dilemmas about our relationships with the natural world.

The reasons why we value our surroundings are many. They could be described as personal, cultural, aesthetic and scientific. But increasing emphasis has been placed on the so called scientific reasons for wishing to save something, usually because a plant, animal or landscape is rare or 'special'. If this argument is used too often the decision makers will not take seriously our parallel cultural desire to conserve the *common* plants and animals, *vernacular* buildings. It is imperative therefore that we do not let our rationale for nature conservation in particular become too biased towards such evaluations, otherwise we will end up with little pockets of nature reserves surrounded by land empty of animals and plants except monocultures of wheat, barley and conifers. These reserves, in any event, will gradually disappear as they cannot exist in isolation.

Every piece of land is *unique*. The geology, the form of the land, the place where it is, the production processes it supports – agriculture, mining, building; the investment it represents and receives; its ownership and the rights over it; the social relationships it encourages, the politics it sustains – all are apparent in the landscape before us. Almost every corner of our land has been made by man's activities; although the geology and topography of course dominate, the fine grain of the landscape has been socially constructed. Every piece of land shows not just the present, but overlays of past activities and relationships, and, like old documents, paintings, literature, buildings and dialect, holds many keys to an understanding of our past, our present and the evolution of our culture. To study the landscape is to study our forefathers and to understand ourselves. To preserve it in aspic is to deny our present needs and to cheat posterity: to protect it from wanton misuse and degradation is to cherish our heritage and culture.

Rapidity and scale of change

Man-made change has enriched the landscape. Why worry, then, at our current generation's activities – merely another overlay? Change there must be, but the fears now are for the scale, the type and the rate of change – unprecedented in all human history – capable not just of adding to the mosaic, but of oblitrating all that has gone before.

At one time, perhaps, we unconsciously expected the countryside to provide us with a kind of stable reference point. We looked upon it as something which was changeless and which would compensate us, to some degree, for the changes which were taking place so rapidly in our towns and cities. But in the past forty years our landscape has been increasingly unable to fulfil this role: an agricultural revolution has taken place in the countryside. Parts of it – particularly in East Anglia and the Midlands – have changed out of all recognition as a pattern of mixed farming has been superseded by arable farming. The most obvious loss has been that of hedgerows and of hedgerow trees. 140,000 miles of hedgerows have been grubbed up since 1945. Almost half of our deciduous woodlands have been cut down over the same period. In addition 95 per cent of our old hay meadows, 80 per cent of our chalk and limestone grassland and 50–60 per cent of our lowland heaths have also been destroyed in that time. With them most of the farm ponds have been filled in, our wetlands drained and 30 per cent of all upland grasslands have either been afforested or 'improved'.

Wild life habitats have not been the only sufferers. Field monuments – the mysterious remains of our forbears in the form of round and long barrows, hill forts, standing stones and so on – have also been vandalised. 'The lack of comprehensive survey makes it difficult to quantify the destructive effects of agriculture in the last fifty years. In 1970 it was estimated that the earthworks of 300 deserted medieval villages had been destroyed between 1500 and 1950, and the same number between 1950 and 1970; a further 20-30 disappearing each subsequent year.' (Baker, *Living with the 'Past*). In 1982 alone 145 listed buildings were demolished in England and a further 1,627 were partly demolished.

What has this catalogue of destruction to do with us? It hasn't happened in a vacuum, but in *somebody's parish*. To what extent are we aware of what is happening in our localities and to what extent can we control the forces of change and temper them to the requirements of our communities? As Richard Mabey has said – *The Common Ground*, 'Conservation begins precisely where the pain and destruction of modern development are most keenly felt – in the parish, that "indefinable territory to which we feel we belong, which we have the measure of".'

What should be protected and who should decide?

What people value in their localities will differ from place to place. We cannot make sensible decisions about influencing change unless we know what we have, and who cares about it.

The people who live or work in a place obviously know it better than council officials who might be based thirty miles or more away. By carrying out surveys and parish appraisals, local communities can demonstrate to district and county councils what they value and the direction in which they would like to go. Parishes are a manageable size, as history has shown, and the parish council is an important, if neglected, tier of local government. Parish councils should be given more power, not less, but should first make full use of the powers they possess.

The extent to which we determine the future of our parishes, our localities, is largely up to us. Although there is a general move towards centralisation, and power is being removed from ordinary people, the opportunities we have to alter our surroundings are enormous. Local groups and parish councils have the ability to do a whole host of things to benefit local people. As the examples in this book will show, there is a tremendous amount which is going on at the grass roots which we hope will give courage and inspiration to others to follow.

TO
OLD ROAD
TO
TO HAWORTH
HEBDEN
BRIDGE
HAWORTH
KEIGHLEY
HEBDEN
BRIDGE

2

Five main ways of conserving buildings, landscape and wild life

Individuals, parishes and local groups are in a unique position to conserve buildings, landscape and wild life – it is very wrong to think that this is solely the province of the local authorities, statutory bodies, the farming community or national conservation groups. A tremendous amount can be done at the local level. Here we outline broad approaches and examples – the detail you will find in later chapters.

There are five major ways to help in conservation locally:

1. Landscape and wild life survey and action;
2. Arrangements for management and access;
3. Leasing land and buildings;
4. Purchasing land and buildings;
5. Habitat creation.

1. Landscape and wild life survey and action

In order to enhance your own locality to protect it from neglect and from unacceptable or ill-considered change, you could embark upon a landscape survey, or even a landscape plan for practical activities. Better still, you could combine a landscape (including buildings) and wild life habitat appraisal.

Your objectives could include: an examination of the types and conditions of the parish's buildings, landscape and wild life habitats; an identification of changes which have occurred or which may occur in the future; a plan to enhance and conserve them (page 251). You need also to be constantly vigilant for changes in the use of farmland and to vet all planning applications.

Moss Valley Wildlife Group

Back in September, 1981, when I enrolled on an evening course on the natural history of the Moss Valley, little did I envisage how this would develop. From an evening class introducing the natural history of the area, we have developed into a pressure group to protect the wildlife of the Valley.

At first the class proceeded like any other evening class; but then the bombshell of the Sheffield Green Belt Enquiry was brought to our notice by our class tutor. From then on the seeds were sown. At extremely short notice, the class members assimilated knowledge on the natural history of the Valley from various sources, and the likely consequences of further housing development in or near the Valley. This material was then presented at the Public Enquiry. Personally I expected us to have only a minimal impact, but the Inspector took account of the wildlife interest of the Valley in his recommendations. Moreover, the importance of the Valley for wildlife was brought to the notice of the planning authorities. In respect of the Green Belt Enquiry, the Group has been extremely successful, thus proving the impact that a small determined group can have. I quote from the proposed modifications to the Green Belt Plan in response to the Inspector's recommendations:

> Extend the boundaries of the Green Belt and Area of County Landscape Value to include the objection site... Extend the Areas of Natural History Interest in the Valley to include all sites containing habitats of natural history interest lying within the amended Green Belt. The final plan will include an assurance that in the Moss Valley the City and County Councils will adopt wildlife conservation as the principal consideration in any management or improvement work undertaken in that area and an undertaking to consider appropriate wildlife management in the Moss Valley in conjunction with Derbyshire County Council and other intested parties in the future.

The Group has also been successful in persuading other parties to take an interest in the Valley, in particular Sheffield City Museums, who are to undertake a survey of the area. Sorby Natural History Society, the Derbyshire Naturalists' Trust and others have shown an interest in the

Valley. The Group has also begun to make contacts with farmers and landowners, and our aim ils to continue to protect the Valley's wildlife and, in the long term, to enhance it. The dangers to it are manifold, some obvious (airguns, egg collectors, motor cyclists, etc.), others not so obvious (e.g. agricultural improvements). We have won the first battle, but not the war.

The Group is carefully moving forward to the next stage, collecting information on the Valley and identifying the most important sites, and considering positive conservation measures, e.g. barn owl and bat boxes.

(Mr and Mrs Egan, *The Moss Valley Wildlife Group*, June 1983)

2. Arrangements for management and access

In some circumstances parish councils can either persuade the local authority, Nature Conservancy Council or National Parks Authority to enter into a management agreement under section 52 of the Town and Country Planning Act 1971 or enter into formal or informal agreements themselves.

'A management agreement consists of an agreement between 2 or more parties to voluntarily adhere to an agreed course of action or inaction usually in return for some form of compensation, consideration or practical assistance.'(Feist, *A Study of Management Agreements*, Countryside Commission, 1978.)

Section 39 of the Wildlife and Countryside Act 1981 makes it possible for local authorities to make management agreements with landholders for the purpose of conserving or enhancing the natural beauty or amenity or promoting its enjoyment by the public.

Many informal agreements and understandings such as permissive access exist: e.g. allowing the hunt to go over private land, access to ramblers, etc. It may be counterproductive to try to formalise an understanding which works very well, as landholders (or their protective agents) may be reluctant to sign away their 'rights' in case it reduces the value of their land.

The best kind of arrangement is when both parties

benefit from it, otherwise one party may feel 'beholden' to the other. The Rattery Firewood Syndicate (see p67–9) is a good example of reciprocal benefit. Landholders are often pleased to have stiles, gates and footpaths maintained in return for access across fields, through woods and so on.

Formal or informal access and management arrangements could apply to the following:

> access to nature reserve, ancient monument, wood, etc.; creation of new footpaths/farm trails/local history walks; maintenance and/or management of meadow, wood, ancient monument, barn, pond, etc; grazing access for stock for certain months of the year; access for photographic/artistic projects; access agreements for specified days/times of day/month; access agreements for specific occasions – festivals, bonfire night, beating of the bounds; creation of amenity areas/picnic sites and their management; access and/or management of land owned by statutory bodies – e.g. British Rail; Regional Water Authorites.

Otford Parish Ranger

The Council wishes to employ an
OTFORD RANGER
to improve and maintain the
local environment. The
successful applicant will be
required to work on his/her
own intiative, under direction,
on a part-time basis.

This advertisement appeared in Kent local papers in March 1984. Otford Parish Council had resolved to appoint a ranger initially part-time to work about 10 hours per week in winter and up to 20 hours per week in the summer. The ranger is to be responsible to one council member and will carry through environmental policies agreed by the council. These will be based upon a major report on Environmental Conservation in the parish produced by Mr Gardiner – a coopted member. The tasks will include things like open space, hedgerow and footpath maintenance and importantly the ranger will be asked while out and about to encourage the flow of ideas, suggestions and general liaison between the parish council and local people.

The county and district councils will help in training and other areas and the parish council will raise the salary of the ranger through the rates.

Heckington Village Trust
Rather than see the old station buildings (dated 1858) demolished, the Trust reached an agreement with British Rail to create offices for local groups and a public meeting room. British Rail gave help, advice and encouragement, and the Trust raised money by coffee mornings and sponsored walks. Much of the cleaning and painting was done by local volunteers.

3. Leasing land and buildings

For wild life, landscape and building conservation, management is best carried out over long periods, so long leases should be negotiated when possible. Landholders may be more willing to lease land at a peppercorn rent than to sell it or to enter into some form of joint management arrangement.

Local authorities and statutory bodies will often agree to lease land and buildings, but in the context of a village or town may not be willing to give up all prospect of development in the long term. Even on a short lease much can be achieved.

Plants Brook Community Nature Park
Plants Brook Community Nature Park is an area of about 9 acres of willow carr, marsh, a pond and dry grassland at Walmley in Sutton Coldfield near Birmingham. The site is surrounded by housing on three sides but on the other adjoins a 17-acre site containing three disused reservoirs.

It was an application to fill the reservoirs with domestic and industrial

Plants Brook, Sutton Coldfield: now a community nature park

waste that gave rise to the nature park. In fighting the proposals to tip rubbish residents became interested... to take over the site to prevent further deterioration. The help of the Urban Wildlife Group was enlisted and proposals for a community nature park were drawn up. The plans for the park are aimed at enhancing the value of the site for wildlife and as an amenity for local people.

In February 1982 the Birmingham City Council who own the site gave the Urban Wildlife Group a 5 year lease for the site for a peppercorn rent to allow its development as a Community Nature Park. The site is managed by a committee made up of local residents, councillors, naturalists from the Urban Wildlife Group and a representative of the Education Committee.

Over the past year £2,000 has been raised towards the project, rubbish has been cleared, trees planted, footpaths made, ponds cleared, notices put on site and a small car park made for school minibuses. All the work has been undertaken by local people who have turned up for regular workdays.

Future plans include a circular walkway through the wetland area of the site. This will increase the value of the park for educational visits by allowing access to the marsh and pool side.

(Ian Kemp, Urban Wildlife Group, Birmingham)

4. Purchasing land and buildings.

This provides ultimate protection and control (although

land and buildings are always vulnerable to compulsory purchase for development for roads etc.).

Since 1895 the National Trust has been buying land and property, or acquiring them by gift; over half a million acres of coastline, moor, parkland and farmland are now owned and managed by this large charity for the nation. Areas of great beauty, wildness and cultural significance are thus protected. The Nature Conservancy Council, local authorities, the county naturalists' trusts, The Woodland Trust, the Royal Society for the Protection of Birds and many civic societies buy land and buildings in order to protect them.

Increasingly rural parishes and urban boroughs are buying land and managing it for wild life and amenity. It provides a focus for community activity, and brings cooperation, and enjoyment. Every parish should look for land it can buy, especially if it lies at the heart of the village or is a threatened wild life habitat, such as an ancient wood, old meadow or ancient monument site. Small areas can be of considerable importance to the parish but too small for the county or national bodies to consider buying. Why build a new village hall when an old barn needs restoration? Loans are available from buildings preservation trusts for the conversion of old buildings for re-use.

Perranzabuloe Preservation Society

The railway through Perranporth was closed over 20 years ago and the land has gradually been sold off. A 2 acre area of old line and embankment covered now in undergrowth and sycamore still remained in British Rail ownership. No planning permission existed, but the possibility of development was always present. A small group of local people formed the Perranzabuloe Preservation Society with the idea of purchasing the land for the town. Within a year they have raised the £8,000 required from local people, donations from the Parish Council and District Council and others. The offer of this sum was accepted by British Rail after the land had been put out to tender, the cost of building land being substantially more per acre in this area. It is hoped to improve access without making any undue or drastic changes, so that everybody can enjoy it. The use and management will be overseen by the Perranzabuloe Preservation Society and the Gardens Trustees – a long established local body registered as a Charity, which maintains and cares for the open spaces and recreation areas in the town. The Gardens Trustees made a generous donation towards the purchase of the land. (Dr F.H.N. Smith, Perranporth, Cornwall, 1984)

5. Habitat creation

If your intention is to enhance derelict or waste areas, the conservation process can be wholly positive, retrieving for wild life, landscape and amenity purposes an area of land degraded by industrial or other neglect.

But beware that the area is not, despite a dishevelled appearance, full of history and wild life interest, as well as a terrific play area, without your help. Much damage has been done by filling old quarries, small hollows, disused railway lines and gravel pits with rubbish and the creation of tidy landscaped areas from a rich though perhaps untidy 'wasteland'.

As well as restoring derelict sites, new habitats such as meadows and woods can be created in town and country. Although they should in no way be regarded as substitutes for our dwindling ancient meadows and woods, they can compensate a little for their loss, make us realise what we are missing in urban areas, and bring a little of the countryside to the town. Above all, it is exciting to create something out of nothing and to watch new plants and animals colonise these habitats as they become established.

Statutory agencies

At a broad level many people and institutions have duties to protect buildings, wild life and habitats. Many government and local government organisations have responsibility for looking after landscape and wild life in town and country – the difficulty, as usual, is finding the right person with the duty and power to respond to particular circumstances. The Department of the Environment (DOE) has a strategic overview of the planning system and other environmental matters and the Secretary of State makes final decisions on contentious development.

County and district councils have many responsibilities and powers (see Chapter 16). The three main government agencies with broad countryside responsibilities are the Countryside Commission, the Nature Conservancy Council and the Historic Buildings and Monuments Commission for England.

Countryside Commission

The Countryside Commission was created by the Countryside Act 1968 replacing the National Parks Commission which had existed since 1949. It is independent but receives a grant from the DOE (£13.2 million in 1984/5). About 100 staff are employed and governed by the 13 or so Commissioners who are appointed by the Secretaries of State for the Environment and Wales. There is a separate Countryside Commission for Scotland.

The Countryside Commission has interests over the whole countryside; it provides advice and finance for the conservation of natural beauty and 'the provision and improvement of facilities for enjoyment of the countryside and access for open air recreation'. Much work is achieved through collaboration with voluntary bodies, local authorities and private landholders. Seven distinct kinds of activity are achieved: promotion of understanding of countryside issues; research; experimental work exploring new ideas in conservation and management; policy advice; technical advice; designation of scenic areas (Areas of Outstanding Natural Beauty and National Parks) and long-distance footpaths; and grant aid for conservation and recreation purposes to public voluntary bodies and landholders.

The Countryside Commission has a main office in Cheltenham and eight regional offices. Much information is available – practical advice, policy statements, how to apply for grants and footpaths, tree planting etc. The Commission believes staunchly in the interdependence of conservation and recreation and is becoming increasingly interested in helping promote understanding and activity at the parish level.

The Countryside Commission is working with other national

bodies to monitor landscape changes, is continuing to discourage massive afforestation in upland areas, and taking a firm line on development ideas which threaten landscape and conservation. The regional offices can offer advice and information and may grant aid local initiatives (see page 294-6)

Nature Conservancy Council (NCC)

The Nature Conservancy Council was established by Act of Parliament in 1973 'for the purposes of nature conservation and fostering the understanding thereof'. It receives its main grant-in-aid from the DOE (£15 million in 1984-5) but can also accept funds from the private sector for specific projects.

Policy decisions are made by its governing body, the Council, whose chairman and members are appointed by the Secretary of State for the Environment and include naturalists, scientists, politicians, landholders, farmers and foresters. There are also statutory advisory committees for England, Scotland and Wales.

The NCC's work can be considered under five headings:

Site Safeguard: *the establishment of National and Marine Nature Reserves and notification of Sites of Special Scientific Interest to conserve prime examples of Britain's wild life and geological features;*

Species Protection: *advice to Government on the protection of species of wild birds, other animals and plants under Part 1 of the Wildlife and Countryside Act 1981;*

The Wider Countryside: *advice on nature conservation to local authorities and others;*

Research: *commissioning and carrying out the research and survey required to enable these tasks to be done adequately;*

Information and Advice: *through literature, interpretation on National Nature Reserves, use of the media etc.*

The NCC has its main headquarters in Peterborough, Scottish headquarters in Edinburgh, Welsh headquarters in Bangor and fifteen regional offices covering the whole of Great Britain. There are nearly 200 National Nature Reserves.

The first point of contact for individuals is with the regional office. (See telephone directory for address.)

Historic Buildings and Monuments Commission for England
(HBMC)
The Commission was established by the National Heritage Act
1983 and came into operation in April 1984. It amalgamates the
Ancient Monuments Board and the Historic Buildings Council. It
manages and maintains monuments in the care of the Secretary of
State for the Environment; makes grants for the preservation of
buildings, monuments, land and gardens of outstanding historical
interest; coordinates and finances rescue archaeology; and advises
on listing, scheduling and taking monuments into care, and the
'lively and imaginative presentation of those monuments'. The
Department of the Environment supports the Secretary of State for
the Environment in his responsibilities for policy, confirmation of
listing and scheduling and the exercise of all planning functions.

The Ancient Monuments Boards for Scotland and Wales have
functions similar to those of the HBMC.

3
Historic Landscapes and Ancient Monuments

The farmer ploughs up coins in the wet-earth-time
He sees them on the topple of crests' gleam
Or run down furrow; and halts and does let them lie
Like a small black island in brown immensity,
Till his wonder is ceased and his great hand picks up
                    the penny
Red pottery easy discovered, no searching needed . . .
One wonders what farms were like, no searching needed.

Ivor Gurney, 'Up There'

HISTORIC LANDSCAPES

Very little of the British landscape is natural – the centuries of man's endeavours to tame and use the land have resulted in a constructed landscape. New dimensions are added to our understanding of its simple beauty once we learn to read the subtle clues endowed by the humps, bumps, hedgerows and field patterns which are our link with the social and economic pursuits of our long-dead ancestors. Overlay upon overlay of hard work lies waiting to be understood; the potential excitement of this as history and the basis for speculation about our culture and roots is enourmous. The lives of ordinary people are only occasionally written about in historic literature: the land, if only we can read it, gives a much broader view. Fragile local history may now only remain in the secrets of the landscape.

Scheduled Ancient Monuments such as old hill forts, long barrows and standing stones have some degree of protection under the law, but much of our landscape holds less obvious archaeological and historic interest and has no protection save that of caring owners.

In his classic book, *The Making of the English Landscape*, W. G. Hoskins shows how our forbears have created, with or despite nature, the diversity and richness of our landscape. Celtic fields, ancient mines, Roman villas and roads, the creation of our village pattern in Anglo-Saxon times, the clearing and taming of woodland, marsh and moor, the villages abandoned after the spread of the Black Death in the fourteenth century, the building of country houses and the making of parks, the new fields of the great Enclosure Acts of the 1700s and 1800s the spread of the industrial landscapes of water and steam power, the extension of roads, canals and railways and the fossil clues of countryside in our towns – all these things Hoskins explores with us. Anyone who cares for landscape and history cannot fail to be fascinated and excited at the insights and the questions this book raises.

Why conserve historic landscapes

The overlays of social and economic history embodied in our landscape are part of our cultural heritage.

'Roots' are of psychological importance to many people.

History and geography are particular to place and individual landscapes are not reproduced elsewhere; each is unique.

For most periods of the past material remains are the only record of human endeavour.

The removal of hedgerows and walls, deep ploughing of ridge and furrow, tumuli and other archaeological remains, the tidying of old quarries and building over unknown graves are robbing us of layers of common cultural history at a far greater scale and rate than ever before.

Past social, economic, spiritual and artistic relationships between people and environment as seen in the landscape offer endless routes for educating our sensitivities.

Historic landscapes add to the interest and mystery of the countryside and are often valuable visual components in the landscape.

Many people are fascinated by historical exploration for its own sake.

Increased leisure and the tourist trade make the value of sites even greater; visitors to archaeological sites, field monuments and more subtle historical landscapes may bring such needed local economic impetus.

How to protect historic landscapes

Know what there is Using W. G. Hoskins as your mentor, trace parish and manorial boundaries, old trackways, hedgerows and walls, field markings and patterns, vegetation changes, flood patterns, farm building patterns, village architecture and shapes, quarries and old industrial buildings, ancient woodland and old coppices, churches and old parkland.

Derbyshire: field patterns

Use old and new OS maps, aerial and old photographs, field observation (shadows and vegetation colour/growth changes), walk and talk with farmers and local people, search public record office maps and documents, local planning authority and archaeological surveys and reports.

Look for patterns – parallel hedges, straight roads.

Look for anomalies – large churches with small villages, names which do not describe what now exists.

Look for one pattern overlaying or cutting through another.

Try to reconstruct maps of the parish at different times in history – e.g. Roman, medieval and early 1800s, mid 1800s (before and after enclosure).

Take particular features, like quarries, commons or transport routes, and research their ages and origins.

Add to *parish information* and add to *parish treasures* (see pp.265-6) or *parish map* (see pp.267-9); take photographs.

Bring up for discussion at local and parish council meetings.

Talk to local landholders – excite them with any new information about their land.

Persuade your district and county councils to add the information to their own information on historic landscapes and archaeological sites. Attempt to interest them into making positive use of legislation to *protect* sites you feel most vulnerable.

Write a guide to the historic landscapes of your locality.

ANCIENT MONUMENTS

Ancient monuments, or field monuments if they are situated in the countryside, form a part of our historic landscapes. Some are so slight that they are only visible from the air in crop marks and shadows, some still deeply etched like Maiden Castle hill fort.

Each age has brought change, but during the last forty years there has been an unprecedented rate of destruction of field monuments. The revolutionary improvements in agricultural techniques, from machinery to chemicals, have permitted both deeper cultivation and extensive drainage schemes and the cultivation and afforestation of hitherto unproductive land such as heathland, chalk downland and upland moors. All this has resulted in a catalogue of destruction on a scale which no other generation has witnessed, let alone permitted.

The Historic Buildings and Monuments Commission for England and the Ancient Monuments Boards for Scotland and Wales have neither the money nor the staff to adequately protect all the 13,000 or so Scheduled Ancient Monument sites let alone the further half-million monuments which probably deserve protection. The problem is compounded by the grants liberally given by MAFF to farmers to plough land which has not been cultivated for many generations.

In Wiltshire alone 250 of the 640 scheduled Bronze Age barrows which existed in 1954 had been destroyed or badly damaged, and a further 150 had suffered significantly, within ten years. Between 1950 and 1970, 300 medieval village earthworks are thought to have been destroyed (the same number as in the previous 350 years!). Up to 30 may disappear each year. Building development claims some of these, but the majority are suffering beneath the deep plough. Some have the protection of the law, most do not.

Why protect ancient monuments?

To the reasons given for historic landscape protection generally should be added:

– It is often the least resilient and most vulnerable sites which yield most information to careful study.

– We have a duty to hand on a respectable proportion of our cultural heritage to posterity – a representative sample must be conserved.

Ways of conserving them

Statutory methods: scheduled ancient monuments

Monuments considered to be of national importance become legally protected once they are included in the central *Schedule* maintained by the Department of the Environment (Ancient Monuments and Archaeological Areas Act 1979).

For this purpose a 'monument' can include any building, structure or work (above or below ground), cave, excavation or remains of any of these.

There are some 13,000 'scheduled' monuments, mostly enclosures, barrows and other earthworks. Some sites of outstanding importance are further protected by being taken into 'guardianship' by the State. These include principal castles and abbeys and a handful of prehistoric sites like Stonehenge. Many other site types – ancient hedgerows, trackways and deer parks, for instance – are rarely protected at all. The sites which are most at risk are probably those which have not yet been discovered. Artefact scatters and chance finds are constantly appearing, many of which may indicate the position of otherwise totally 'invisible' but nevertheless important sites. The National Trust owns many archaeological sites which are therefore given a high degree of protection.

Copies of the Schedules for your area may be found at: The County Sites and Monuments Record at the County Planning Department or County Museum; the District Planning Office; the Historic Buildings and Monuments Commission, and in the Reports of Royal Commissions on Ancient and Historical monuments for England, Wales and Scotland in your local library.

Landholders are notified of scheduled ancient monuments in their ownership, and if any action to demolish, destroy, damage, remove, repair, alter, add to, flood, cover up the monument or excavate it is intended they will need to apply for *Scheduled Monument Consent*. If the work done without consent results in damage to the ancient monument, the landholder is liable to a maximum penalty of two years' imprisonment and an unlimited fine.

However, if the landholder intends to continue to plough over the monument and if ploughing in this way has been carried out for five years, then he is given *Class Consent* and does not have to apply for Scheduled Monument Consent. But if he wants to plough deeper, under drain the land, plant or uproot trees, he will need Scheduled Monument Consent.

Ancient monuments are often remote from public access and public view and enforcement of the law is very difficult. Part-time Monument Wardens report on the state of scheduled monuments to the Inspectorate of Ancient Monuments. There are not enough of them – but they are an official presence at least.

The act of scheduling also presents problems, for although scheduling affords some protection, the unscheduled sites are degraded in value as a consequence and are often destroyed with impunity. Unscheduled sites increase in importance with the destruction of scheduled monuments.

The Ancient Monuments and Archaeological Areas Act 1979 has been interpreted as being exclusively concerned with 'buildings' as opposed to other man-made features such as parish boundary banks. So far few man-made historic landscape features have been scheduled under the Act and the only protection they have received is by chance if they lie within nature reserves, or are subject to management agreements negotiated with local authorities or the Nature Conservancy Council. Some county councils have included historic landscapes within conservation area boundaries (see example of River Wey Water Meadows, Hampshire, p.32).

Excavation Consent from the landholder and DOE is needed for archaeological excavation on a scheduled ancient monument. Archaeologists have differing views, but excavation inevitably means destruction of at least some layers of the past. So nowadays it is usually only carried out as a last resort. There are embarrassing examples of barrows and other sites pillaged by Victorian archaeologists, the sites ruined, the findings lost. Conservation-conscious archaeologists prefer to leave a site untouched rather than make arbitrary decisions about which age to explore and which to destroy. They argue that things are safer in the ground, – that less destructive ways of exploration will be developed.

Use of metal detectors It is an offence to use a metal detector on a 'protected place' (scheduled site, site owned by the Secretary of State or local authority, in a designated area of archaeological importance) without the *written* consent of the Secretary of State. If an object of historical or archaeological importance is removed (even if permission to search has been granted) the penalties are much greater.

Found objects Any object found on someone else's land belongs to the owner, and permission is needed to take it away. If the object is of gold or silver you must report it to the local coroner who will hold a Treasure Trove Inquest – it may be the property of the Crown.

Access is usually given to any monument owned by the Secretary of State unless it would damage the site. The scheduling of an ancient monument on private land does not mean that the public have access to it. Permission must be sought from the landholder to visit ancient monuments on private land.

Grants The Secretary of State and local authorities can give grants to landholders to enable them to provide public access to ancient monuments on their land. Management agreements and grants to help owners and occupiers to look after ancient monuments are available from the HBMC.

Areas of archaeological importance In order that a site may be properly excavated if threatened with development, the Secretary of State or local authority may designate an area as being of 'archaeological importance' and nominate an 'investigating authority' for the area which must decide if it wishes to carry out an archaeological investigation before development starts. If it does, it is given 4½ months in which to do it.

How can we look after them?

1. *Consult the Schedule* – Find out if you have any scheduled monuments in your locality from the county archaeologist, district council — Royal Commission on Ancient and Historical Monuments list — or in your local library. Try to discover as much as you can about them — why they are scheduled, etc. Are there any monuments which you think should be scheduled?

2. Build up a good relationship with the *county archaeologist.*

3. Join your local *archaeological society.* Try going to evening classes on archaeology which will help you to

History in the landscape: Fontmell Magna, Dorset

become better informed. Read all you can in your local library/museum/record office such as old documents and records of the parish.

4. Ask permission to look at ancient monuments which are on private land. Ask the landholders about their history and what form of protection/*management* they are given.

5. *Volunteer* to help with their *maintenance and restoration*.

The River Wey Water Meadows

The valley of the River Wey in Hampshire, sometimes no wider than 30 feet, has an old system of water meadows originally flooded by controlled sluices and a complicated system of carriers (leats) up to two miles long, small aqueducts and other constructions.

The Bramshaw and Liphook Preservation Society has been doing research, walks and physical work along the valley in an attempt to restore both the water meadows and the engineering works. The society is concerned to restore but not fake the often puzzling system, and it is hoped that collaboration with the interested landowners will result in reciprocal benefit, permitting control of local water flow once more.

The derelict meadows are interesting in their own right and the society is well aware that a balance must be sought between drainage of land for restoration and conservation of the wetland ecology which has now developed.

The land is largely in private ownership, some falls within a Conservation Area, and there are three scheduled ancient monuments (one being the Liphook Aqueduct) owned by the Parish Council. The society would like the Department of the Environment to schedule the area of water meadows and constructions as a field monument. They are also attempting to create the River Wey Trust to look after ten miles of river valley. Much local interest has been generated and the society hopes to involve more people.

Grants of around £5,000 have helped with contract labour and materials, and more than 1,000 hours of voluntary work have gone into the maintenance of the Liphook aqueduct alone.

6. Encourage a school or parish group to *adopt an ancient monument*. The group could be encouraged to write a guide or to document it with photos or paintings which could be exhibited to raise funds for the maintenance of the monument.

Perran Round, Rose

Perran Round is a scheduled ancient monument, originally constructed during the Iron Age as a fortified farm, complete with earth rampart approximately 8 feet high and surrounded by a ditch about 6 feet deep. The total site area is roughly a quarter of an acre, and the inside diameter is 130 feet.

During the Middle Ages the Round was adapted and used as a 'Plen an guary' or open-air theatre for the enactment of Cornish miracle plays.

The area leased to the parish council had become neglected and overgrown. A group of villagers, forming themselves into Rose Village Community in the summer of 1983, approached the council and the landholder with thoughts of restoration, and with the encouragement and involvement of both a management committee of ten people was set up.

Rescue Archaeology on hearing this initiative offered advice and help in the form of an MSC group to clean and clear the bramble and undergrowth, and fence the site. When this is completed they will hand the job of maintenance back to the management committee. A small but beautiful and historic site will soon be available for the benefit of the people of Rose once again.

Traditionally the Round was used for many years by the people of Rose as a preaching pit for its Church and Sunday School Anniversary Services, as well as for children's Tea Treats and occasional village fetes. It is hoped that when the Round is cleared these traditions will be revived, and that it will also be used for the staging of some traditional Celtic festivals. The Gorsedd of the Bards of Cornwall is to be held in the Round in September 1985.

(Roger Glanville, Local History Group, Rose, Cornwall, 1984)

7. Encourage your *parish council to purchase* any site of archaeological interest within its boundary. Burwell in Cambridgeshire bought the site of its castle in 1983 and is now considering how best to manage it and provide interpretative facilities.

8. *Field survey work* The kinds of things which can be done in local survey work can provide modest or ambitious projects needing few or many people with or without expertise:

– Field by field survey (written, drawn or photographic), noting carefully the position and type of all artefacts found, recording significant changes in the colour and texture of soil and vegetation as well as odd bumps in the ground and deviations made by hedgerows ditches and walls.

– Recording of all field monuments – their positions, sizes, profiles and relationships.

– Compare findings with aerial photographs (check local library, district and county planning office or local flying club).

How to stop people from damaging scheduled ancient monuments
Farmers on their own land If you see someone doing obvious damage to a site which you know to be protected, ask the person if he knows what he is doing. In many cases these things are done through simple ignorance. It is often the farm worker who is doing the ploughing, or whatever, and he might be unaware that the site is important. However, if the person is doing deliberate damage or will not desist from the work he is doing then take photos if possible. Postive proof of destruction is needed in order to prosecute.

People using metal detectors Find out whether they have *written* permission from the DOE. (Permission from the landholder alone is not enough.) If not, then ask them to leave; get names and addresses if possible. Take car registration numbers, and take photos. For further information on the use of metal detectors on scheduled ancient monuments ask your local metal detector club/local museum/the Town Hall and the HBMC.

Motor-bike scrambling Ask if they have permission from the landholder. Ask them to leave. Take photos. Take registration numbers.

In all cases contact the county archaeologist immediately, also the landholder and the local police. If necessary raise the issue through the letters column of the local newspaper and at the next parish council or district council meeting.

References and further reading

The best books mentioned below for general background as well as detailed encouragement are those by Baker, Hoskins and Muir. Steane and Dix is very helpful on fieldwork techniques. *Current Archaeology* is a very useful easily read journal.

Information abounds on how to minimise damage from agricultural operations. Especially useful leaflets have been produced by ADAS/ MAFF (leaflet 764, 1981) *Farming on ancient monuments* (which includes a section on 'Chance Finds – A code of Practice'), available from MAFF Publications, Tolcarne Drive, Pinner, Middx HA5 2DT; Hertfordshire County Council, *Field Monuments – A Farmers' Guide* (1977), and the *Countryside Conservation Handbook* (a useful collection of loose-leaf pages) Leaflet No. 8 'Protecting Ancient Monuments and Historical Features' which is available from the Nature Conservancy Council. *Users of Metal Detectors – Advice about Scheduled Ancient Monuments* by the DOE, 1982.

The Historic Landscapes Steering Group under Peter Brandon and Roger Millman based at the Department of Geography, Polytechnic of North London, Holloway Road, London N1, have produced many papers on identifying, recording and managing historic landscapes – contact them for details.

The main legislation is Historic Buildings and Ancient Monuments Act, 1953. Ancient 'Monuments and Archaeological Areas Act 1979. National Heritage Act 1983.

Baker, D., *Living with the Past – The Historic Environment*, 1983. (Available from 3, Oldway, Bletsoe, Bedford MK44 1QG.)

Gelling, M., *Signposts to the Paast*, 1978.

Groube, L. M. and Bowden, M. C. B., *The Archaeology of Rural Dorset: Past, Present and Future*, Dorset Natural History and Archaeological Society, Monograph 4, 1982.

Hampshire County Council, *Man and Landscape*, Hampshire's Countryside Heritage Series, No.8, 1984.

Hayfield, C. (ed.), *Fieldwalking as a method of Archaeological research*, Directorate of Ancient Monuments and Historical Buildings Occasional Papers No. 2, 1980 (HMSO).

Herts Association of Local Councils. *Landscape Action in Hertfordshire*, (The Survey and Management of Archaeological Sites), 1981.

Hoskins, WG., *The Making of the English Landscape*, 1955, paperback 1970.

Hoskins, WG., *Fieldwork in Local History*, 1982.

Hoskins, WG., (ed.), Various County Volumes of the Making of the English Landscape.

Lowenthal, D. and Binney, M. (eds), *Our Past Before Us. Why do we save it?* 1981.

McDowell, RW., *Recording Old Houses: A Guide*, Council for British Archaeology, 1980.

Muir, R., *Shell Guide to Reading the Landscape.*, 1981.

Muir, R., *History from the Air*, 1983.

Shire Archaeology Series, e.g. *Deserted Villages; Medieval Fields*. Available from: Shire Publications Ltd, Cromwell House, Church Street, Princes Risborough, Aylesbury, Bucks.

Steane, JM. and Dix, BF., *Peopling Past Landscapes – a handbook introducing archaeological fieldwork techniques in rural areas*, Council for British Archaeology, 1978.

Wilson, DR., *Air Photo Interpretation for Archaeologists*, 1982.

Wood, ES., *Collins Field Guide to Archaeology*, 1972.

4

Open country, commons, footpaths and bridleways

There once were lanes in natures freedom dropt,
There once were paths that every valley wound;
Inclosure came and every path was stopt;
Each tyrant fix'd his sign where paths were found;
To hint a trespass now who cross'd the ground.
John Clare, 'The Village Minstrel', 1821

ACCESS TO THE COUNTRYSIDE

We do not have the freedom of the countryside, and as you see from John Clare's sad poem our rights to roam have long been eroded. All of our land is owned by someone; the degree of access which we have over it is dependent upon ancient rights, the goodwill of some landholders, vigilance of others, and the continuous campaigning for increased rights.

Of the land which is owned by the state, the areas owned by the Forestry Commission have been most opened up for public use, and some water authorities have encouraged considerable recreational use of land and water. The land between high and low water mark along our sea shore belongs to the Crown and, with a few exceptions, we enjoy access along it when the tide is out.

Local authorities run over 150 country parks close to towns and ranging in size from less than 20 to 4,500 acres, offering all kinds of recreational possiblities from sitting in the car watching the birds to walking, sailing and riding. They may be, as with Shipley Park in Derbyshire, on areas reclaimed after coal working, or they may be in the estates of old houses as at Rufford in Nottinghamshire. The National Trust owns more than half a million acres much of which is open to the general public.

In these ways our access to the wider countryside has been increased. But many of our ancient rights of way and traditional access to open country continue to be eroded – many farmers and grouse moor owners feel that there is a conflict between their activities and those of the wandering public. In their booklet, *Agreeing on Access*, the Country Landowners' Association (CLA) suggest that many public footpaths are 'unused relics of a bygone age' and that resources should be 'spent on paths that are of real use to walkers and riders'.

Many people fear that increased accessiblity to a place will bring about its degradation and the loss of the very features which people have come to see. Fears are often based upon prejudice. There are now many ways of 'organising' people in the subtlest ways to safeguard crops, wild life and landscape. The Countryside Commission and CLA give Access Awards to landholders who have opened up their land for greater public access. Many landholders successfully combine farming with the provision of recreation, and many negotiate Access Agreements with local councils and other bodies.

Kemsing Downland and Woods

Kemsing Parish Council bought 85 acres of farmland and woodland on the lower slopes of the North Downs (in an AONB) in 1976 at a cost of £35,000 in order to 'ensure that desirable features were preserved'. The previous year 20 acres had been purchased by a development company with the purpose of fragmenting them into over 200 'leisure plots'. Funds were raised by means of an Appeal, a loan of £19,000 from the Public Works Loan Board over a 10-year period and an additional precept for £5,000 in 1975.

Development on the leisure plots was prevented by the District Council making an Article 4 Direction (of the General Development Order) which had the effect of preventing the plot owners from erecting buildings, putting up fences or parking cars and caravans on the plots without planning permission.

36 of the 85 acres have been made into a nature reserve. It is managed by the Parish Council with assistance of the Kent Trust for Nature Conservation, 'with the aim of providing an area of beauty and quiet for people to walk in and enjoy, where the downland flora and fauna are preserved in all their variety'. There has been much local enthusiasm for the reserve and a very informative illustrated guide book was published by the Parish Council in 1980. 'The areas outside the reserve are let to a local farmer under an Agricultural Tenancy Agreement, although Green Hill (about 40 acres) is grazed and the public enjoy considerable freedom to walk on the Hill.'

(Mrs Rosemary Banister, clerk to Kemsing Parish Council, Kent, 1983)

Traditional (de facto) access exists over moorland, hill and coast in Britain where either the landholder does not mind or where prevention of access is difficult. But even in national parks there is little free legal access. Ancient rights once lost are hard to re-establish. 1982 saw the 50th anniversary of the mass trespass on the moors of Kinder Scout; in 1932 ramblers from Manchester and Sheffield were imprisoned for their direct action in asserting their need for freedom to walk.

Planning Authorities were encouraged to secure access to open country under the 1949 National Parks and Access to the Countryside Act. This defined 'open country' as 'mountain, moor, heath, down, cliff or foreshore', (woodlands, rivers and river banks were included later). All 'open country' should have been mapped by the local authorities and attempts should have been made to secure access agreements or orders to purchase land. Not many such agreements have been made except notably in the Peak District National Park. Worse, much downland and moor has since been ploughed and therefore falls out of the definitions.

You should ask to see the Open Country Map prepared by the local authority and make suggestions for additions of woodland and river. You may try pressing for access agreements with local landholders.

COMMON LAND

Swamps of wild rush-beds and sloughs' squashy traces,
Grounds of rough fallows with thistle and weed,
Flats and low vallies of Kingcups and daises,
Sweetest of subjects are ye for my reed,
Ye commons left free in the rude rags of nature,
Ye brown heaths beclothed in furze as ye be,
My wild eye in rapture adores every feature,
Ye are dear as this heart in my bosom to me

John Clare, 'The Village Minstrel', 1821

What is it?

Something like 1½ million acres of common land exist in England and Wales in all kinds of situations from small village greens to thousands of acres of upland.

In towns everyone has access to the commons, but in the countryside (except in particular cases) the commons are not public property nor do we have any rights over them except to walk the public rights of way. The rights of common are generally restricted to people living nearby who have registered those rights.

The town and country commons are leftovers from the feudal system. Local people enjoyed rights of grazing, fishing, gathering wood or peat over the poor parts of the land owned by the Lord of the Manor. The most rapid erosion of commons and rights came during the enclosures of the eighteenth and nineteenth centuries. Acts of Parliament allowed Lords of the Manor to fence land and only small amounts of common were left for local needs. The 1866-1898 Metropolitan Commons Acts and 1876 Common Act resulted from the concern that important local social and economic resources were being lost – these and the Law of Property Act 1925 gave urban commons to the people.

In an attempt to sort out the complexity of the remaining commons the Commons Registration Act of 1965 demanded the registration of all common land and all rights by 1970 – failure to register meant that common rights ceased. This has been described as the 'greatest enclosure act of all time'. The intention was to safeguard remaining commons. It gave no one the duty but everyone the right to register village greens and common land. Many landholders objected and many people failed to register or had lapsed rights refused, legal costs were great and many simply could not afford to 'stand up for their rights'. Many cases are still pending.

You may consult the Register of Commons kept by county council (county archive, planning, parks or surveyors department). Information on the rights of commons may also be held by the parish council. The County Commons Registration Officer wil help with complaints, questions and recording of commons.

Why should we protect it?

The rural commons are often very important for smallholders and large farmers for grazing stock. They are invariably highly attractive areas for recreation. Many have been managed in the same way for generations and the landscape and wild life are of considerable historical and ecological interest. Traditional patterns of use are needed to support the wild life and maintain the landscape.

How can we look after it?

In some places the ownership of the common has fallen to or been bought by the county, district or parish council. Here common rights may be augmented by by-laws and much more liberal access may be allowed. Agreement and practical cooperation between the Lord of the Manor, local residents, parish council or local societies is another way of ensuring good management and access. It is recognised in all situations that management is the key to maintenance of the common for people and wild life.

Stelling Minnis Common

Stelling Minnis Common is situated about 8 miles due south of Canterbury, just east of the Roman road known as 'Stone Street' (B2068), running between Canterbury and Newingreen. It consists of approximately 125 acres of mostly flat land with bracken, grass, thorn scrub, wild flowers and various kinds of hardwood and attractive wild fruiting trees. Although regarded as 'Common Land', it is in the ownership of the Trustees of the Late Lord Tomlin, who enjoy the title of 'Lord of the Manor'. The right of the general public and residents of Stelling Minnis is 'to take air and exercise'.

With the encroachment of 'civilisation', the regular and sustained grazing by hooved animals, which was once a feature of the area, has ceased. This has allowed the rapid and uninhibited growth of bracken, undesirable thorn scrub and bramble, resulting in large areas of the Common being 'lost', and to the decline of wild flowers and desirable trees. There are now few parts of the Common available to the local community on which to exercise their right.

The Common is administered by the Conservators, five local residents appointed by the Lord of the Manor. The Conservators act for the Lord of the Manor to the benefit of the Common, but have no access to funds, apart from a nominal annual grant to cover necessary postage and administrative costs.

In the latter part of 1979, the Conservators called a meeting, open to the residents of the villages of Bossingham and Stelling Minnis which adjoin the Common. At that meeting it was apparent that a genuine desire existed within the local community to act together to improve the Common. It was felt very strongly that steps should be taken to enable local people to enjoy the possibilities that exist for both young and old to walk and to ride over larger areas; to enjoy the wild flowers, shrubs and trees. As a result of that meeting, a Steering Committee of local residents was formed which decided, in conjunction with the Conservators, basic aims and priorities. At a subsequent meeting on 12 March 1980, again open to the public, a chairman and other officers were elected and the society known as the Friends of Stelling Minnis was formed.

The basic premise of the Friends is that both the social and environmental life of the villages will be improved if real and positive steps can be taken to restore the Common to the area of natural beauty that it once was, resulting in free movement over the area as a whole. The Friends of Stelling Minnis know that the nature of the work needing to be done is such that most of it can be achieved by voluntary effort, and indeed, the steps taken so far prove this to be the case. Whilst the aim is to cater for the needs of the human population, due regard must and will be given to protecting the natural habitat of the birds, insects and animals that abound there. To this end the Conservators commissioned a report from the Kent Trust for Nature Conservation. The report contains many features, detailing various tree species to be found and some fairly rare shrubs, but in short it shows that a careful and planned maintenance programme can improve the area for flora, fauna and villagers alike.

As the Conservators have no access to finance, and limited time available, it is the intention of the Friends to concern themselves in particular with raising money and organising the voluntary effort. Much of the work, and future maintenance, can be done by enthusiastic volunteers, but help will be needed from local contractors.

From these small beginnings stems the confidence that the Friends of Stelling Minnis can go on to a wider still involvement of the local community and thus to achieve a real improvement in environmental and social life. A massive voluntary effort is needed, but in the early stages machinery must be hired to do the very heavy work. For this funds must be raised locally, but having restored the Common to its natural beauty a continuing effort from the whole community will be required over the years to ensure that the great benefits achieved are never 'lost' again. (The Secretary of the Friends of Stelling Minnis, Kent, 1983)

FOOTPATHS AND BRIDLEWAYS

What are they and why should we protect them?

Took a walk in the fields saw an old wood stile taken away from a favourite spot which it had occupied all my life the posts were overgrown with ivy and it seemed so akin to nature and the spot where it stood as tho it had taken it on lease for an undistrubed existence it hurt me to see it was gone for my affections claim a friendship with such things...

John Clare's 'Journal', September 1824

For most of us the 'way in' to the countryside close to our homes or in far-away places has been along the footpaths, bridleways and lanes.

The disused railway line taking you all the way out of town, the canal towpath, the path from village to village, and the criss-cross of lines, their purpose long forgotten but

A Cornish Stile

their pleasures still abundant, all give you the chance to know more closely the corners of your 'territory'. The paths provide a means of movement but they have many values in their own right. If the scale of the parish 'feels right' then the footpath is surely fitted to that scale. The variety it offers underfoot, in taking sheltered routes by the hedges or striking out unashamedly across a field, in meandering through the woods and by the stream, in the details of stile and gate, are all part of that very richness that the locality offers.

A simple line hardly impinging upon nature – the path – is the oldest mark to be made upon the landscape by man. History written in a single line – the link with all the feet that have trodden the same trail gives the humble path another significance to us. Those windy tracks across the moors linking village with village and valley with valley, those ridgeway paths – routes for salt traders, pilgrims, drovers, the paths to the cider house, 'deadmans lane' (the way the coffin was carried to church), the lovers lanes, the smugglers lanes, the path to the gibbet at the edge of the parish – are all part of the rich cultural tapestry of our countryside.

Our pattern of footpaths both illustrates and symbolises rights of passage created by generations of ordinary people going about their everyday business. That footpaths are an inheritance to be cherished simply for their commonplace qualities and because they are everywhere may seem odd – but for those who are landless and for those who care about the whole of the countryside, that intricate network of common paths provides the only vital popular link with land and place. To lose a footpath is to lose an ancient right hard won and to let down both our forbears and our children.

Something like 120,000 miles of tracks, footpaths and bridleways exist, but, as the Ordnance Survey maps note, their existence does not imply a right of way.

Rights of way should be mapped and continuously updated by the county highways officer. The *Definitive Rights of Way Map* may be consulted at the county highways department, at the district council, or the local library; or the parish clerk may have a copy. In Scotland there is no legal duty to prepare these maps but many counties have compiled information.

Public rights of way are defined as highways – you have no other right than to walk along footpaths, and to walk or ride horses or bicycles along bridlepaths. Picnicking and tadpoling are allowed at the landholder's discretion. Although trespass is not a criminal offence a landholder may sue for unauthorised entry. The legal costs could be expensive and if any damage is proved you would be called upon to pay compensation.

Byways open to all traffic (BOATs) are those known to have vehicular rights. They are part of the reclassification of roads used as public paths (RUPPs) called for in the Wildlife and Countryside Act 1981. Conflict between motorcyclists and walkers – as along the Ridgeway – stems from this designation.

The way to the coast path Cornwall

There may be footpaths and bridleways along which the landholder allows you to go, but which he does not intend to dedicate for public use – these are *permissive paths* and the right to use them may be withdrawn at any time. The Countryside Commission has been responsible for the creation of new *recreational paths* and *long-distance footpaths* like Offa's Dyke, the Pennine Way and the West Highland Way. The Forestry Commission has opened many Forest and Nature Walks, including one in Grizedale which has the added attraction of sculpture produced by a variety of artists who have spent some months in this Lake District Forest working with natural materials.

How can we look after them?

Final responsibility for rights of way lies with the county highways authority, although district or parish councils may have powers to remove obstructions of vegetation, wire, locks, etc. Anyone may remove an obstruction to allow passage, but you may not go out with the express intent of removing that obstruction. Bridges are the responsibility of the county but stiles and gates must be kept safe and passable by the landholder. A grant of 25 per cent is available from the county council, but because maintenance is frequently lacking, local authorities and voluntary organisations often do this work. Any maintenance work to be done by volunteers must be arranged with the council and landholder. Signposting from roads is the duty of the county – many are still working on this.

The parish councils have various powers related to paths – but they have no duties. They may maintain paths, erect lights, create new footpaths; they may veto the county council closure of paths; they may prosecute anyone obstructing a public right of way; they may bring proceedings for failure to restore a ploughed path; they may signpost paths. Some parishes hold parish walks and produce maps and guides.

The Hertfordshire Federation of Rights of Ways Societies has suggested that each parish nominate a councillor to be responsible for rights of way, that the definitive rights of way map be displayed prominently in each parish together with names of responsible officers and that rights of way be signposted and maintained to a better standard.

The public has a duty to keep to paths, close gates, keep dogs on leads near to stock, damage no crops, leave no litter, start no fires. The landholder has a duty to keep footpaths open and stiles safe. In fields (but not on open hills) non-dairy breeds of bull *with* cows and heifers may now be legally grazed where public rights of way pass but a farmer is liable to prosecution if he places *any* animal which he knows to be dangerous in a place frequented by the public. Ploughed paths must be reinstated two weeks after the ploughing began.

The Open Spaces Society and the Ramblers' Association have done much nationally and locally to support public rights of way. Detailed information help can be obtained from them. The Ramblers' Association Rights of Way Charter reads as follows:

1. Definitive maps of rights of way should be comprehensive and up to date.
2. Footpaths should be adequately signposted and waymarked.
3. Paths should be kept in good repair and kept free of obstructions.
4. Paths should be restored after ploughing.
5. Paths affected by housing development should be retained as 'walk ways' through new estates.
6. New Rights of Way should be created to improve the network of paths in the countryside.
7. Adequate national and local funds should be made available to ensure that local authorities' statutory duties are complied with.

Walk or ride your footpaths and bridleways, report obstructions to the parish and county council (there may be a footpaths officer – if not, someone in the highways department has responsibility). Ensure that the county or parish is putting up signposts. Encourage more signposts and way marking by land holders too. If you believe the public paths are not included on the definitive map, ask how to get them included – their absence may not mean all is lost.

Rodney Stoke Parish Footpath Volunteers (Somerset)
Volunteers get together to walk the paths and keep them clear; these walks are social occasions and have developed into natural history walks too. Any organised clearance brings people together with their own tools and covered by the parish council's insurance. They may produce a detailed footpath map of the area, with landmarks and field boundaries. No formal organisation or running costs have been needed and as a series of social events it has proved simple and enjoyable.
(Community Council of Somerset)

Improvements to Wood Lane, Pirton, mid-Hertfordshire

The Public bridleway between Pirton and Pegsdon, 1½ miles long, probably forming one of the parallel tracks of the Icknield Way, has been very well used for many years by both walkers and riders.

The central section is in constant use by a local farmer who trims the hedges and overgrowth each year. This has produced a very attractive open 'highway' with chalk grassland verges and banks, excellent for butterflies and other wildlife.

The south-west section, however, past Tingley Field Plantation, has been very overgrown for several years, but is this year being cut back by the farmer. The north-east section, near Pirton village, was also severely overgrown by blackthorn/elm scrub to such an extent that the width had been reduced from some 25–30' to about 2'.

Pirton Parish Council approached the Highway Authority for assistance in clearing it. Highways replied, indicating that it would cost £3,000 or more to do the work! Highways then approached the Herts/ Barnet Countryside Management Service to see if the Service could do anything. Countryside Manager Christine James agreed to help and organised two Sundays in October 1983 when volunteer rangers would turn up to help people from the village to do the clearance.

The Countryside Management Service, its volunteers and about sixteen people from the village all turned up and managed to clear 150– 200 yards of the route on the first Sunday. The exercise was repeated the following Sunday very successfully and a further section cleared. By this time the village was both motivated and conversant in the clearance techniques so that on the subsequent four Sundays, they took the matter into their own hands, borrowed tools from the Countryside Management Service and completed the job. Altogether half a mile of very dense scrub was cleared.

An adjacent farmer/owner is to maintain the cleared area by mowing when required.

(Herfordshire County Council Countryside Section, 1984)

Footpath Heritage Competition

The Gloucestershire Group of the Ramblers' Association holds an annual competition to encourage parish and town councils in the vicinity to improve their public footpaths, bridleways and green lanes, 'thus encouraging their increased use . . . Community effort is particularly looked for and account is taken of parishes with small populations and limited resources'. The Footpath Heritage Trophy – a handsome eight foot high ironwork sculpture depicting a stile, signpost and tree – made by Gloucestershire craftsman Michael Roberts is presented to the winning parish.

References and further reading

The main Acts relating to footpaths are:
   Wildlife and Countryside Act 1981
   Countryside Act 1968
   Highways Act 1980
   National Parks and Access to the Countryside Act 1949.

The Ramblers' Association produces many useful leaflets including guidance notes on *Path Surveys*, *Waymarking*, *Path Clearance* and *Producing a path guide or map*. Advice on the law can be gained from them and the Open Spaces Society. They have jointly published *Rights of Way. A Guide to Law and Practice* by Paul Clayden and John Trevelyan (1983), which is an essential reference book for all parish councils and groups. *Footpaths* by Elizabeth Agate for the BTCV is an expensive but wonderfully practical handbook on how to maintain paths.

W. G. Hoskins, and L. D. Stamp, *The common lands of England and Wales* (Collins, 1963), although out of date on some matters gives good background information; the Open Spaces Society's *The Land of Commons and Village Greens*, as well as their magazine *Open Space* gives legislation and cases.

Bailey, J.C., *Parish Councils and Footpaths*, Cumbria Association of Local Councils, 1981.
Godwin, F. and Toulson, S., *The Drovers' Roads of Wales*, 1977.
Hill, H., *Freedom to Roam*, 1980.
Taplin, K., *The English Path*, 1979.
Taylor, C., *Roads and Tracks of Britain*, 1979.

5

Trees and Woodlands

I never had noticed it until
'Twas gone, – the narrow copse
Where now the woodman lops
The last of the willows with his bill

It was not more than a hedge overgrown.
One meadow's breadth away
I passed it day by day.
Now the soil is bare as a bone . . .

Edward Thomas, 'First Known When Lost'

Ancient woodlands are the richest of our wild life habitats, owing to their age and to the continuity of their sympathetic management. More species of birds are associated with woodlands than with any other habitat type and nearly half of the British butterflies and moths are found there. Ancient woodlands are also rich in plants: about 240 species, including about 20 different ferns, are directly associated with woodlands and of these 76 are entirely confined to them.

Ancient woodlands are those woodlands which are known to have existed in the Middle Ages and where there has been a continuous history of woodland cover to the present day. Some of these woods are the descendants of the primaeval woodlands which covered Britain after the last Ice Age.

Many ancient woodlands have been managed since medieval times by a system of 'coppice with standards': the standards – trees such as oak, beech and ash – were left to grow to maturity whilst the understorey such as sweet chestnut, hornbeam, lime, and hazel were coppiced on a

10–20-year rotation. Coppicing simply involves cutting the trees close to the ground. The branches (poles) then grow vigorously and straight from the base (coppice stool) providing wood for fencing, hurdles, fuel, etc. This system is of great benefit to wild life as it allows a mosaic of light and shade to fall on the woodland floor, encouraging a great diversity of woodland plants to grow. Furthermore, it doesn't involve the kind of massive landscape change and destruction which clear felling does and the soil structure under the wood remains virtually undisturbed.

Ancient woodlands can be identified by the plants and trees which grow in them and by the system of woodland management. Some plants will only survive in ancient woodlands as they require the stability afforded by the continuity of suitable woodland and are unable to colonise newly created woods. These 'indicator' species vary from county to county, but may include herb paris, wood anemone, and lily of the valley. Clues to ancient woodlands may also be obtained from old maps and comparing the 1st edition OS maps (1800s) with subsequent editions. Names such as 'new' and 'plantation' on the 2nd edition maps often imply that the woods have been clear felled and replanted, or planted on green field sites (secondary woods). Since the formation of the Forestry Commission in 1919 many old woods have been clear felled and replaced by conifers.

Many kinds of trees are native to Britain. Others, such as the horse chestnut, plane and sycamore, have been introduced in the last few hundred years. Our old established residents – elm, birch, hawthorn, and especially oak and willow – support many insects which provide food for birds and other animals. Introduced trees support fewer insects because British wild life has had less time to adapt to the conditions they provide.

Why protect them?

Individual trees and woods of all ages and sizes can be very important in the local landscape. And yet we seem to value them less and less. Almost half of our deciduous woodlands have been destroyed since 1947. With them have gone their associated wild life, history, mystery and beauty. Their own intricacies, assemblages of trees, shrubs, flowering plants, insects and animals can never be recreated. An old oak tree can support nearly 300 different insects species and over 300 lichens – it will take many long years before a newly planted oak can attract the same astonishing diversity. (See *Woodlands*, BTCV, for the number of lichens and insects associated with common trees and shrubs in Britain.)

Arguments for the conservation of ancient woodland can be based upon landscape and amenity value, historical and cultural interest as well as wild life value: 'not only are they ancient monuments whose value to historians and village community consciousness is arguably as great as that of the older buildings in the parish, but, where traditional management continues or can be revived, they are living demonstrations of conservation in the broader sense of a stable long-lasting relationship between man and nature' (Peterken, 1982). But a wood or tree does not need to be ancient to be beautiful or interesting and good to have in your back garden. The many pleasures of playing and walking among trees of all ages are well known to us all.

How can we look after them?

Tree Preservation Orders
TPOs are designed to stop people from wilfully damaging or cutting valued trees in town or country. They are the responsibility the district council (and can be made very quickly if necessary). The district council keep a register of all TPOs which is available for public inspection. An order may cover any single tree or groups of trees, hedgerow trees or woodlands of amenity value (but not hedges, bushes or shrubs). If you want a tree (or trees) to be

protected, write to your district council tree officer outlining your reasons for wishing the tree to be protected and enclosing a map showing the tree with map reference numbers. Because compensation may be payable to the tree owner, the procedure is complicated, few councils will embark upon TPO's unless there is a threat. If immediate help is needed, telephone the tree officers of the county or district and impress upon them the urgency of the problem – contact your parish, district or county councillor.

Even when a TPO has been placed upon one or more trees you cannot relax – there is no requirement to manage the trees. Farmers and developers often work too close to trees, accidentally or otherwise damaging them. Trees that are dead, dying or dangerous need no permission to fell. Determined landholders have been known to damage trees before the order comes into effect.

What do you do if someone is attempting to cut down a valued (protected) tree? *Be careful* – chainsaws, bulldozers and tempers are dangerous.

1. Play for time, distract the workers (inform them of the TPO and that they are about to break the law).

2. It takes only 1–10 minutes to cut down the uproot a mature tree – do not leave the site.

3. Get someone to: (i) contact the tree officer at the district council; if necessary, contact the police; (ii) Take photos; (iii) Get witnesses; (iv) Ring the Press.

4. Ring the tree: In the last resort gather together some friends and physically surround the tree so it cannot be cut down.

The Campaign for Cowpasture Lane

Cowpasture Lane is a medieval green lane connecting the villages of Mellis and Thornham Magna in Suffolk. It is part of a much longer medieval droving road. The lane is between 30 and 90 feet wide, flanked on both sides by boundary ditches, hedgerows and trees, which have spread from coppice down both sides, so the effect in summer is of walking along a green tunnel.

In late 1980, a 400-yard stretch of Cowpasture Lane came under threat when a local farmer bought the land to one side of it, claimed ownership of the lane itself and announced his intention of filling in the boundary ditch, uprooting the hedges and trees, and ploughing up the lane as part of a larger cereal field. His main incentive was the fact that by doing so he would gain one-and-a-half acres of arable land worth, if sold at the current market rate, about £3,000.

I approached the farmer, a neighbour, and discussed it with him, pointing out the great antiquity of the lane, its status as a footpath of great natural beauty, its value as a wild life habitat in an area of spreading wheat prairies, and its importance as a link, for both humans and other creatures, between two important features of the local landscape – Thornham Woods and Mellis Common (the largest in Suffolk, 174 acres).

He replied frankly that he disliked trees and hedgerows, which he regarded as obstacles for his machinery and harbourers of wild life, which he saw as a threat to his livelihood. He also pointed out how uneconomical it was for him to leave 1½ acres uncultivated.

So when, in January 1981, the farmer began cutting down some of the hedgerow trees in the lane to 3 ft stumps – often an ominous sign that they are to be levered out and uprooted by a digger – I decided to apply to the Mid-Suffolk District Council for a Tree Preservation Order (TPO) on the lane as an area of woodland under threat.

I wrote to the Chief Planning Officer of the Mid-Suffolk District Council pointing out that the lane was under threat, and urging that a TPO be placed on the lane, including both hedgerows, their trees, and a copse at the southern end, as an area of woodland.

In my letter, I pointed out the great age of the lane (at least 700 years), and the natural evidence of that antiquity – thirteen different tree species growing there, its width indicating use as a droving road, and the typically curving medieval field boundaries to either side. I also pointed out its importance as a wild life habitat, mentioning particularly the presence of nightingales in the lane. Finally I made the point that the whole lane is a public footpath – that is to say, the whole width of it from ditch to ditch – and that to grow crops on any of it would constitute an obstruction to the public highway (an offence in law).

I also wrote to a distinguished Suffolk historian and President of the Suffolk Institute of Archaeology and History to draw his attention to the threat to the lane. He in turn wrote an authoritative and persuasive letter to the Council expressing his concern and confirming the considerable archaeological and historical importance of the lane as a feature of the Suffolk medieval landscape.

Mid-Suffolk Council employs a Landscape Officer, who then visited the lane to inspect it and report on its merits as an area of woodland. He recommended a tree preservation order, which was put down for discussion at the next meeting of the Council's Planning and Amenities Committee on 6 February 1981.

The Committee has 26 members, all district councillors, whose names and telephone numbers I obtained from my own local district councillor. I talked to him about the case for preserving the lane, which he came and saw, and I then telephoned all 26 members of the planning committee to discuss the issue with them a few days before the crucial meeting. This was vital, because I was able to highlight and clarify what was for them simply Item 16 on a crowded agenda. I simply made the case as briefly as possible, answered their questions and asked if they would support the TPO at the meeting.

It is, of course, the job of a local councillor to be available for discussions of this kind with constituents, and no one should ever feel shy of approaching them. (You can be quite sure, by the way, that the opposition won't hang back in this regard.)

On Friday, 6 February, the Council Committee decided to put a TPO on Cowpasture Lane, and this was briefly reported in the *Eastern Daily Press* next morning. Evidently it did not escape the attention of the farmer.

On Sunday the 8th, the village awoke to a dawn chorus of chain saws as the farmer and two others went from one end of the lane to the other, cutting down as many trees as time would allow in the one day they knew they had before the TPO (a legal document hurriedly drawn up by the Council's solicitors on the Monday morning) would be served on them. By the end of Sunday, they had cut down every tree and the whole of the hedge along one side of the lane, and most of an oak-maple-blackthorn-hazel copse at one end.

By the time the Council's Landscape Officer arrived around mid-day on the Monday to serve the order on the farmer, the Lane was a tangle not only of felled trees, but of reporters, photographers and TV cameras falling over themselves and the trees to tell the world.

Powerless to prevent the cutting of the trees (short of chaining myself to them) until the TPO had been served, I had spent much of Sunday and Monday telephoning press, television and radio contacts both locally and nationally, as well as informing the Friends of the Earth Wildlife Campaigner, who also spread the word.

By the end of the week, the story had not only appeared on the front page of *The Times*, in the *Daily Express*, on Anglia TV's 'About Anglia' (a full feature filmed in the lane), and in the *Eastern Daily Press* and *East Anglian Times*, but, most importantly, it was the headline story on the front page of the local newspaper, with an editorial deploring the farmer's action.

'Woodland Order is too late' was the *Times* headline, but this was not altogether true. For one thing, the hedgerow and trees down one side of the lane still remained. Far more significant, though, was the fact that even though many of the trees felled were up to 30 feet tall, they were *coppice* trees, and would have been coppiced like this countless times since the Middle Ages as part of the traditional management of the hedge.

And a tree preservation order applies to the rootstock and stumps of trees, even when they have been felled, provided they are capable of regeneration. The precedent for this ruling by the Secretary of State for the Environment was the case of Sladdon Wood in the Alkham Valley near Dover in 1978. As a result of the exertions of its new owner, trying to beat a TPO just as in this case, it became known as the Horizontal Wood. But the order was upheld by the inspector at the inquiry, who accepted the Nature Conservancy Council's argument that a tree remains a tree unless it is uprooted or killed, that the wood would 'return to a woodland appearance', and that 'The reasonable degree of public benefit which must be established before a Tree Preservation Order can be confirmed can be future benefit'.

After all this drama, things began to move even faster. The farmer appealed to the Council against the TPO, enlisting the support of the Mellis Parish Council, most of whom apparently felt that private property is the owner's to do what he likes with, even if the public have a right of way over it, and chose to ignore its value as a wild life habitat or as an important archaeological feature of their parish landscape.

The farmer now retained a large and influential local firm of land and estate agents to represent him in his dealings with the Council.

The appeal hearing was set by the Council for 4 June, and having failed in my attempt to persuade the Mellis Parish Council to withdraw its objection to the TPO, I set about sounding out local opinion on the matter by visiting every house in the village with a petition supporting the TPO and calling for the preservation of the lane in its entirely.

Most of the villagers were amazed to hear that their parish council was objecting to the TPO, and 92 of them signed the petition. Within a couple of weeks 302 local people had signed the petition, which duly went off to the Council Planning Officer. Many others were moved to writer letters to the Council – a most important part of any campaign like this, and more influential than a petition. (Many councillors take the view that you can get people to sign almost anything, but sitting down and writing a letter indicates genuine feeling.)

People expressed strong interest, and strong feelings on the issue, and several of those who signed were themselves farmers or worked on the land.

Besides organising the petition, I contacted the Open Spaces Society, and the Ramblers' Association, both of whom wrote to the Council underlining the importance of saving Cowpasture Lane as public access to the countryside. Friends of the Earth also wrote, pointing out the value of the lane as the kind of undisturbed wild life habitat that is becoming all too rare in the Suffolk prairies. And as another important appeal to authority, I spoke to the Nature Conservancy Council, whose local field officer came over to Mellis and inspected the lane, then wrote a report on its value as a wild life habitat to the Council.

Finally, I visited the County Record Office and, with the help of one of the county archivists, researched the history of the lane, providing ample evidence from the parish records of its long use as a public highway to the Council Committee.

Thus, when the Committee met on 4 June, they had before them an impressive variety of representations in favour of the lane's preservation – not only letters and a petition from local people, but also authoritative, carefully reasoned letters from bodies representing large numbers of people, both in Suffolk and nationally.

Again, a few day's before the meeting, I had telephoned all the committee members, all of whom listened with interest to the case for confirming the TPO. Important, too, was the presence in the public gallery at the meeting of a large contingent of local people, keen to see the TPO confirmed.

For the opposition, the local estate agents had sent all 26 members of the committee a glossy file presenting the case against the TPO.

The issue was eloquently debated, and the vote was 17 to 4 in favour of confirming the TPO on the lane, with 4 abstentions.

The result was again widely reported in the press (including *The Times*), and the local paper carried a leader on the subject entitled 'A Wise Decision'.

Now, two years later, the coppiced trees are six feet tall, and Cowpasture Lane is again a green delight.

(Roger Deakin, 1983)

However, the story does not end here. The farmer has made an appeal to the DOE against some of the conditions imposed in the tree preservation order, and the outcome is still being decided . . .

Felling licences

Any major tree felling needs the permission of the Forestry Commission. However, according to their pamphlet *Control of Tree Felling* (1983), an owner or tenant may fell up to 30 cubic metres (about ten big oak treees) of timber every three months without a felling licence provided that not more than 5.5 cubic metres are sold. Nor do you need a licence to fell:

trees in gardens, orchards, in churchyards or in a public open space;

dead or dangerous trees or trees which are interfering with permitted development or work by statutory undertakers;

if all the trees are below 8 centimetres in diameter, measured 1.3 metres from the ground;

coppice or underwood below 15 cm. in diameter;

thinnings below 10 cm. in diameter;

the felling of trees approved in Forestry Commission Dedication or Forestry Grant Schemes.

In most other circumstances a felling licence is needed. Applications have to be made to the nearest Conservancy office. The Forestry Commission can insist that trees are replanted if a felling application is granted. District councils are consulted by the Forestry Commission about felling licence applications in areas of amenity value. The general public are not consulted, so it is important to keep in touch with the tree officer of the district council. Fines amounting to £500 or twice the value of the trees (whichever is the higher) can be given for unlawful felling.

Trees in conservation areas
Conservation areas in this case refer to built-up areas, streets prized for their architectural or historic worth. Trees cannot be felled in a conservation area without prior permission from the district council. Always ask questions when a tree is being cut.

Vigilance and survey
Find out about the woods in your parish/locality. Are any of them designated as SSSIs, NNRs, or LNRs, or do they have TPOs on them?

Make a map of the woods and trees of interest in your Parish. Send copies to the tree officer of the district and county councils and make it available to interested people

The village oak — an important landmark for this Yorkshire village

in the locality (especially the owners of the woods and trees and the parish councillors) perhaps via a local newsletter or newspaper.

Include the woods and trees of interest on your parish maps (see pages 267-9).

Be alert for chainsaws, roadside log piles and new vistas.

Make sure that people in the locality know what to do if a protected tree or wood is being cut down.

Crockenhill Tree Survey

An appeal for volunteers, who did not necessarily need expert knowledge, established the interest of eight local people. An experienced naturalist advised the group and led an initial meeting, to learn and to standardise techniques. Thereafter, working groups of two or three proved convenient, with one for the paperwork and the others to measure and comment. Equipment included maps, survey sheets, metre rules, tape measures, tree identification books and a letter of authority provided by the Parish Council.

Trees are recorded and mapped using different letters to signify single trees, groups, lines, woods and hedgerows and a note was made of their height, spread, girth and interesting features. Each was allocated a status, from (A) healthy or of particular historic/landscape importance to (D) dead, dying and dangerous.

Survey data was compiled with information from old documents and maps into a comprehensive report which is not only fascinating historically, but also provides a basis for further tree conservation in Crockenhill. One recent development has been the preparation of a tree trail.

(From *Oast to Coast* (Journal of the Kent Rural Community Council), Summer 1983)

Heyshott, Tree Survey

In 1974 a landscape architect assisted the Heyshott Parish Clerk in making a survey of every tree in the parish. 'We listed them as individual trees and groups of trees, and in the case of woodlands indicated the general character of the wood. Trees were given a number and these were entered on a 25 inch Ordnance Survey map and listed on a key to the map. We graded the trees as mature, young mature and young, and noted if the mature were over mature or stag-headed and in poor condition.

Trees were then assessed for their contribution to wild life, and to visual effect as seen from village centres, from roads, from major foot or bridle paths and minor paths and we gave them marks, "0" no comment, "1" makes a contribution, "2" makes an important contribution, "3" makes a very important contribution. On this result we listed those we felt should be the subject of a tree preservation order if ever threatened.' Copies were sent to the County and District Planning Officers.

(K.M.E. Murray, Clerk to Heyshott Parish Council, West Sussex)

Purchase

One way of preventing the destruction of deciduous woodland is by purchase.

The Tree Council and the Woodland Trust both advocate the idea of parish or community woods. They have been encouraged by the existence and success of the community-owned woods which abound on the Continent. In the communally-owned woods in Switzerland, clear felling has been prohibited for more than 100 years. These woods bring profit as well as pleasure. The Tree Council suggests that existing derelict woods or waste ground suitable for tree planting should be purchased by local authorities and voluntary groups; alternatively local woodland trusts could be formed to maintain and manage the woodland in its ownership for public benefit, profit and enjoyment. For further information send for *Tree Planting and Community Woodland* from the Tree Council.

The Woodland Trust buys woods which are under threat. It owns 91 woods and all except 5 are open to the public. Its first Community Woodland Project is at Pepper Wood, near Bromsgrove. The project was initiated by the Monument Trust which has funded a Community Woodland Officer for three years. 'Since the project began in 1981 more than 50 volunteers as well as school and youth groups have been involved. . . . The aim is to show that a community can take on the responsibility for managing its local woodland. If the project is successful, the results will be used to encourage other communities and woodland owners to set up similar schemes – thus encouraging the retention and sound management of our remaining broadleaved woodland.'

The Royal Society for the Protection of Birds has initiated a Woodland Bird Survival Campaign the aim of which is to raise £1m for the purchase and management of ancient deciduous woodland.

But it is most encouraging to see that individuals and parishes are buying woods and managing them for their wild life interest and for the community.

Hardings Wood

'It is believed there may be as many as 50,000 woods under 20 acres in England and Wales. They once played a valuable and varied role in village life, providing timber, firewood, nuts, grazing as well as a place for meetings or celebrations. They are also amongst our richest wildlife sites.

Now the majority are dark and derelict. If they are used at all it is usually as little more than game coverts. The chance of many surviving into the next century is very small unless new uses and meanings can be found for them.'

This is Richard Mabey's introduction to a news sheet about Hardings Wood, a 15-acre ancient wood which he bought in 1981. His aim is to 'revive Hardings Wood as a *Parish wood*, and to see if it is still possible to manage a site simultaneously for wood production, wildlife and human enjoyment'. In the long term he hopes that the village will become involved in decisions about the wood's management and future.

West Wood and Cricket Field Meadow, Hildenborough, are adjacent areas 'linking' the large housing estate at the lower end of the village to the 'old' village at the top of the hill where the church, shops and village hall are. Although previously privately owned, as far back as people can remember it has been used by the public for walking and children playing. The open grass areas is part of an old cricket field.

For many years the Parish Council tried to purchase the land to ensure continuance of this area as a public open space. At last a few years ago, with the help of a grant from the Countryside Commission, all except a small area at the top was obtained, compromising about 8 acres in all.

The Hildenborough Conservation Group, which manages the area with the Parish Council, have sought information and advice from the British Trust for Conservation Volunteers and the Kent Trust for Nature Conservation to assist in making management decisions. A newsletter is produced at intervals and circulated to members to inform them on progress of work, to highlights points of seasonal wildlife interest and to publicise working-party days. The Group has arranged regular working parties to try to encourage anyone interested to join activities such as pond raking, bramble digging, ditch digging, path building, etc. Guides and Scouts have contributed valuable effort to the work. The pond clearing has featured prominently in our efforts and will eventually provide a very important wildlife habitat and area of great natural history interest. Work in this particular area has earned us a grant from Shell to help buy tools. The Group also arrange some indoor meetings of talks and films.

(Lynne Flower, Hildenborough, Kent, 1984)

Management

You do not have to own a wood in order to look after it: you can offer to manage a wood owned by an individual or institution – simply for the pleasure of doing so, or in return for firewood.

A Parish Firewood Syndicate: Rattery

At weekends through this winter, the road beside a four-acre wood in our South Devon parish of Rattery has been lined with cars and tractors, as villagers gather to cut and cart away firewood.

The Rattery Firewood Syndicate has a simple idea – as simple as the age-old cutting of peat from the common bog – namely that the fuel needs, of a village be met from the fuel resources of the parish. Householders want to save costs on fuel. Wood fires and wood-burning stoves provide one answer. Where should the wood come from? Why, from the local woods, many of them unmanaged and needing attention. All you need is a mechanism through which villagers can make a sensible deal with the owners of the woods.

The idea was put first to the parish council. They were about to write to all households in the parish seeking information for the District Council's local plan: they added a note asking who would be interested in a parish firewood scheme. Seven householders contacted me, and we agreed to set up a syndicate, with membership open to any householder in the parish of Rattery. The syndicate's stated purpose is 'to co-operate in the extraction of firewood, for use by members of the syndicate and others, from woodlands in or near the parish of Rattery, in a manner consistent with sound woodland management'.

Our first project is in the four-acre wood owned by Dartington Hall Trust, where there was standing timber which the Trust was preparing to sell. The timber merchant offered the same price either to fell the trees and clear everything including firewood, or to take the stems for timber and leave the lop-and-top and rubbish trees for us to clear. The latter was arranged, and seven householders jointly took the firewood rights from the Trust, on the understanding that we cleared the wood by the end of February, ready for replanting. No rent is charged, but we have paid £20 deposit for each household (to cover the Trust's costs should we fail to clear the wood), and have taken out a joint insurance policy, covering all risks.

Apart from a break during the bleak mid-winter, we have been hard at it since. Of the original seven households, one dropped out, but two more have joinèd. The eight partners include two farmers (very useful, with their tractors, link-boxes and trailers), a farmworker, a teacher, a social worker, a town planner, a gardening expert, and a student teacher. We divided the wood, ravaged by the timber merchant, into eight strips, and each has tackled his own, with help from family and friends.

The buzz of power-saws, the smoke of fires burning the brushwood, the loads of logs disappearing into the village on trailers and link-boxes have become a familiar part of our weekends. By the end of February, we will each have brought in about 20 tons of firewood for next winter's burning; and will be beginning to negotiate firewood rights from the owner of another wood. The long-term aim is to bring all the woodlands in the parish into sound management, with firewood as a proper renewable crop.

(Michael Dower, Devon, February 1983)

As a sequel to this first winter's scheme, the Syndicate sought to negotiate a ten-year coppicing lease on a large, neglected deciduous woodland in the parish, but has not yet been able to do so. Michael Dower has now left the parish to live in the nearby town of Totnes, and further initiative rests with other members of the Syndicate.

Woodland owners who need help with the management of their woods can ask the BTCV to work for them or ask the county naturalists' trust the county council's countryside team or local amenity group for help. Alternatively they can join the Woodland Trust Licensing Scheme. This was introduced to help owners and tenants of land to create new woodland when for one reason or another they cannot themselves undertake the work of planting and maintenance. The licence lasts for 25 years. The Woodland Trust plants native trees on the owner's land and maintains them for 25 years, after which they become the property of the owner. The area planted must be protected against stock and the landholder is expected to contribute to the cost of fencing.

Access

Public footpaths run through many woods. Where they do not, few landholders allow the public access. With the sale of Forestry Commission Woods (under the Forestry Act 1981) where access had been permitted, there is much concern that the new owners will prevent the public from entering the woods.

Arlington Bluebell Walk and Farm Trail

Beatons Wood, an old deciduous wood of 23 acres, always has been a picture during the bluebell flowering season, and in 1973 my wife thought that by allowing parents and friends of our local Primary School to see it one weekend we could help to raise some money towards a School Swimming Pool Fund. It was advertised locally and attracted several people who then asked if it could remain open for the following weekend as they would like to bring friends to see for themselves this beautiful carpet of blue.

There was encouragement from many visitors to open it the following year, but it did make us wonder how we could cope with an apparently increasing number of the public. We were fortunate that the East Sussex County Council were promoting Farm Open Days and had an officer specifically appointed to this project. It was suggested that if we added the words 'and Farm Trail' to 'The Bluebell Walk' title it provided the necessary qualification for their involvement. Their help was paramount in formulating plans in how we hoped it could develop, as from the start we not only wanted to raise money but also to give information and knowledge to our visitors so that this could enhance their enjoyment of what they could see.

My family having farmed in Arlington since 1920 and always been involved with the community made it natural that whatever was to be planned for 'The Bluebell Walk and Farm Trail' should be a group decision. We started a committee jointly with our neighbour from Primrose Farm, as being able to extend the choice of walks on to his farm added to the interest. The Headmaster of our Primary School was a very enthusiastic person, a retired bank manager acted as treasurer, a school parent who was an estate agent looked after publicity, the Church Warden took over the rota duties of who should help where, with two ladies responsible for refreshments and the East Sussex County Council representative.

We felt that all money raised should be for the village needs or organisations allied to the village or of help to the residents. It was a good idea as it reduces who can be considered for financial help as we get many requests for donations from far afield.

We have always charged a very nominal sum for entrance, this year £1.00 adults and 20p for children; purposely the children's entrance is kept low as we want children from an early age to gain an appreciation of the countryside. We have up to now been able to distribute over £26,000 and have had over 78,000 visitors.

Our committee now includes a person responsible for staging an annual exhibition in our barn of local affairs and countryside information; a person to advise on conservation and be responsible for the informative notes around the Walk; and we now have an auditor. The Bluebell Walk is firmly established in the calendar of this community. It has received wide publicity and continues to attract regular visitors every year who do write some lovely comments in the visitors' books.

John McCutchan, East Sussex, 1984)

By letting visitors walk through his wood and farm trail, John McCutchan and Arlington Parish Council have raised over £26,000 for local charities. Boulsbury Wood (SSSI) on the Dorset/Hampshire border is costing the taxpayer £20,000 a year to maintain with no rights of public access – the private landholder receives this payment in order not to 'improve' the land. Perhaps there is a lesson to be learned here.

Tree planting

Because of the continued felling of deciduous woods, and through Dutch Elm Disease, we are still losing many more trees than we plant. Only 8 per cent of Britain's land surface is wooded (we have fewer trees than any other country in Europe except Ireland) and 20 million elms have been lost through Dutch Elm Disease. Young saplings are no substitute for lost mature trees in visual or habitat terms.

Care should be taken not to plant trees in areas in which wild flowers which dislike shade are already flourishing. Plant native trees and those which occur naturally in your locality – they support more wild life and 'belong' in the landscape (see page 56) Advice on tree planting and on the availability of grants abounds. Most county councils produce their own leaflets, which also give information on tree planting and grants aid.

In *A Guide to Habitat Creation* Chris Baines and Jane Smart have suggested that more deciduous woodlands should be planted, as opposed to the planting of single trees. The *Guide* describes how it is possible 'to create a wildlife community within 20–30 years which looks, smells, feels and sounds like real woodland'.

Grants

The Tree Council will give 50 per cent of a planting scheme. Ten parish councils have been given funds by the Tree Council to plant trees in the last three years. It also provides leaflets on *Tree Planting and Maintenance* and many others, including a poster illustration 45 trees.

The Countryside Commission gives grants to county councils for tree planting schemes and in many cases the county council in turn makes grants to individual landholders and local organisations. Schemes vary from county to county. For details contact the tree officer of the county council. In Devon, owners, occupiers and tenants of rural land can be supplied with up to 25 trees by the county council free of cost. A parish council or other public body may receive unlimited numbers of trees, provided the scheme is approved. West Sussex County Council gives grants of up to 50 per cent to farmers and landholders to plant trees along hedgerows and field boundaries, around farm buildings and on areas of waste land. Along with the Coastal and District Council and Sussex Men of the Trees they run a 'Trees for Tomorrow' scheme whereby every pound raised by individuals will be doubled by the campaign organisers, up to a maximum of £100,000.

The Forestry Commission administers a Forestry Grant Scheme, the main aim of which is timber production. This includes grants for broadleaved trees and native pinewoods in Scotland. Write to them for details.

The Monument Trust gives grants for tree planting – for trees in public places, for a public benefit. Planting must be done professionally or supervised and maintenance in the early years must be guaranteed. Every effort must be made to obtain statutory or voluntary help to augment the value of its grants. Apply to the Monument Trust, 13 New Row, St Martin's Lane, London WC2N 4LF.

Many groups and parishes are planting trees. It is a relatively easy exercise, but a tremendously rewarding one. Unfortunately many people (councils can be the worst culprits) forget that trees need after-care – staking, and watering in dry spells. So many trees are neglected after they are planted. People living nearby should be encouraged to look after the trees themselves, rather than letting them die.

Great and Little Broughton Parish Council Stokesley Flood Relief Scheme Tree Planting

Broughton Beck and Ellerbeck were attractive natural streams, with well-wooded banks before the Stokesley Flood Relief Scheme. The scheme involved widening the stream and cutting down nearly all the bankside trees. The parish council are attempting to return the area to a more natural woodland landscape. A scheme has been prepared by the parish council to plant 5,000 small trees, such as willows, alders, and poplars, and to open parts of the area to the public. The trees will be provided by the Northumbrian Water Authority and the Countryside Commission, the parish council providing the voluntary labour.

'The Tree People' started planting trees in the vicinity of Midsomer Norton, Somerset, in 1978, largely because they wanted to compensate for the loss of so many elm trees in the locality. In four seasons the group (about 6-8 people) has planted and maintained over 1,600 broadleaved trees in playing fields, roadside verges, telephone exchanges, cemeteries, factory grounds, river banks, farmland, a disused railway line and sewage treatment stations. They also have a tree nursery. The group does its own fund-raising and each year gives a book on trees to all local school libraries.

Little Horwood, Milton Keynes

The Village Enclosure Act of 1777 gave the village a pit to remove gravel for the repair of the roads. In due course the newly constituted highways authority took this over. This changed several times, until by the beginning of this century the pit had long been exhausted of gravel and the village put in a claim that the actual land was theirs. Only after the pit had been filled with rubbish, and again changed hands under reorganisation of 1974, was their claim recognised. The pit, plus an adjoining part of the tip, again became village property.

Immediately argument raged on what to do with it. One body wanted to let it for grass keeping, one wanted to sell it for building land, and the third, mainly composed of the ones who finally got it back for the village, wanted to make it into a nature reserve.

Fortunately, after a lot of infighting, this last resolution was passed and this year the old pit was planted with approximately 1,000 native trees and shrubs. The layout includes glades, paths and a pond, although it requires a great deal of imagination to see more than a rubbish-filled field and a forest of bamboo canes holding small trees.

The reserve is managed by a small committee appointed by the elected Parish Council. The population of Little Horwood is about 400 (including children).

(Ted Bull, 1982)

Tree nurseries

An exciting way to increase the amount of tree cover in your locality is to collect seed and grow the trees yourselves. It is a way of ensuring the continuity of local varieties and is of

Pollarded Willows on a Gloucestershire village green

particular interest to children, who naturally love to grow things. Why not create a *Parish Tree Nursery*. Find a suitable piece of land (shaded, with accessible water supply) which belongs to the Parish or the district council, or a corner of land which the local farmer can be persuaded to loan. It will probably need to be fenced against stock and/or rabbits.

Alternatively, schools can be encouraged to grow trees in their school grounds. According to the BTCV, only a small area is needed – an area of 10 square metres will be able to produce up to 100 trees each year.

The BTCV as a part of their 'Conservation Project Pack' include a very good booklet on 'Tree Nurseries'. Milton Keynes Development Corporation have published a very interesting and useful book, *Creative Conservation*, which includes the collection and storage of native trees and shrubs to form a wild life area.

Trees remain very small in the first few years of their growth: acorns, conkers, hazel nuts can easily be grown in your backyard in well watered/well drained pots – miniature deciduous forests for later transplantation.

Bledington, Gloucestershire

Following the 1976 drought and accelerated death of elms suffering from the Dutch Elm Disease, the council decided to undertake a 10-year tree planting programme with the support of farmers and members of the community. As over 100 elms had to be replaced in the Parish, it was decided to plan for a minimum of 150 plantings of local types of tree in the next 10 years – bearing in mind the capacity of the community to maintain the trees. Tree nurseries were established in the gardens of cooperators and within almost 5 years all trees required for the campaign were being produced locally. Funds were also raised locally. By 1983 over 230 trees had been established successfully on farms, along roads and on land owned by the council.

(A. P. S. Forbes)

Town trees

Many trees are planted in towns and villages by local councils. They may not be the responsibility of the inhabitants of the street, but individuals can certainly help to look after them – indeed, it is in their interest to do so. So many trees (especially young ones) die through lack of watering in dry summers – a bucket of water a day could save young tree's life.

Keep an eye on the trees in your street. Ensure that they are watered in dry spells and that any broken branches, stakes or tree ties are reported to the council tree officer.

The Town Trees Trust grows trees in inner city areas on plots of land that are not being used. If you know of a derelict site which you think might be suitable for use (even if it is temporary) as a tree nursery, contact them at: 11 Gainsborough Gardens, London NW3.

Statutory agencies

The Forestry Commission, formed in 1919, is in charge of the Government's forestry policy. It plants forests and is responsible for giving advice and grants and administering felling licences. In 1968 it was given the additional duty of providing recreational areas in its woods.

Under the Town and Country Planning Act no formal permission is needed for the conversion of felled or derelict woodland to farming unless the land is subject to conditions of a felling licence. Where a timber crop exists, a licence to fell trees may be necessary and it is advisable to seek the advice of the Forestry Commission.

The Forestry Commission consult the local planning authority on the amenity aspects of any licence application to clear woodland and the appropriate Agricultural Department if conversion to farmland is requested, and take into account their views in deciding whether to grant a felling licence to fell the trees, or to grant a felling licence only on condition that the owner replants with trees. Most licences involving clear felling are 'conditional'.

Where it is desired to afforest farmland and an owner wishes to obtain grant aid from the Forestry Commission under any of its schemes, the Commission consults the appropriate Agricultural Department about the proposed change of land use. The Commission has agreed procedures for consultation with local authorities on the environmental aspects of proposals for planting bareland that has not previously been woodland.

(From Managing Small Woodlands, Forestry Commission booklet 46, 1978.)

As from 1 December 1983 it has been possible for landholders to afforest up to 25 acres of land or 50 acres of rough grazing without consulting the Forestry Commission unless the land has been grant aided within 2 years or is part of an agricultural development plan.

It seems extraordinary that an activity such as afforestation which has such an impact on the landscape should not be subject to scrutiny by people living in the locality. Hampshire County Council, to quote just one local authority, is unhappy with the Forestry Commission's consultation procedures.

The Forestry Commission has Regional Advisory Committees to advise the Commissioners on the effect of their activities on the countryside and on the land uses. Their terms of reference require them to be used 'to ensure the continued good relationship with all other regional bodies directly interested in the use of land, rural protection, nature conservation and the welfare of the countryside'. In Hampshire there is little evidence of the use of these Committees for this purpose.

(Hampshire's Countryside Heritage – Draft Policy, 1983.)

Perhaps this is not surprising since the regional advisory committees 'represent the interests of owners of woodlands and timber merchants respectively and organisations concerned with the study and promotion of forestry'. (Forestry Act 1967, S. 38(3).) However, these committees should also be concerned about public opinion. Find out who sits on the regional advisory committee in your area, and ask them who they consult when large afforestation schemes are proposed.

A consultative paper Broadleaves in Britain issued by the Forestry Commission in June 1984 shows a belated but encouraging concern for our deciduous woodlands. It says that 'there is . . . good reason to expect that the broadleaved resource can be maintained at about its present extent and we believe that this could realistically be the aim of national policy', and further that 'a proportion of the ancient broadleaved woodlands should be managed in the interests of nature conservation'.

However, the Forestry Commission is having to sell many of its smaller woodlands and there is no guarantee that the new private owners will look after the woods or allow public access through them – even though this may have been permitted when the woods belonged to the Forestry Commission. Encourage your parish council to purchase small Forestry Commission woodlands which are for sale. If they can't, alert the county naturalists' trust, the Woodland Trust and the county council tree officer or your local FOE or CPRE group. To avoid future problems, ensure that you make it known to the tree officer at the district council of the value you, your society or the parish council places on the woods in your locality.

References and further reading

Legislation relating to TPO: Town and Country Planning Act 1971, sections 59-62, 102, 103, 174, 175.

Town and Country Amenities Act 1974, sections 8-11 (re trees in conservation areas and offences relating to trees). Local Government Planning and Land Act 1980, schedule 15 (enables TPOs 'to take effect as soon as they are confirmed by the local authority and will no longer be required to be confirmed by central government' (*Heritage Outlook*, March/April 1981).

The Town and Country Planning Act 1971 as amended by the 1974 and 1980. Acts can be obtained from HMSO.

Other legislation: Forestry Acts 1967 and 1981.

Bryn Green's *Countryside Conservation* , 1981, is an excellent general source of information and includes a section on the management of woodlands, wetlands, grasslands, etc.

The best introduction to the history and value of the woodlands is:
Rackham, O., *Trees and Woodland in the British Landscape*, 1976.

Others include:
Mabey, R., 'Woodlands and Forestry' in *The Common Ground*, 1980.
Peterken, G.F., 'Woodland Conservation in Britain' in A. Warren and
    F. B. Goldsmith (eds), *Conservation in Perspective*, 1983.

Surveys and identification
CPRE, *Making a Tree Survey*, 1973.
Mitchell, A., *A Field Guide to the Trees of Britain and Northern Europe*, 1974.
The Tree Council, *The National Tree Survey 1975*
    An Evaluation Method for Amenity Trees.

Advice, grants and management
Hertfordshire Assoc. of Local Councils 'Tree Planting and after-care'
    'Coppicing Woods'
    'Scrub Clearance'
    all from *Landscape Action in Hertfordshire*, 1981.
Countryside Commission, NCC, *et al.*, Managing Small Woodlands
    Dutch Elm Disease – Dealing with the Aftermath
    'The Planting and after-care of Trees and Shrubs' all from the
    Countryside Conservation Handbook available from the NCC
Peterken, G.F., *Woodland Conservation and Management*, 1982.
The Tree Council, *Tree Planting & Community Woodland*, 1978.
    Tree Planting & Maintenance, n.d.
Forestry Commission, *Managing Small Woodlands*, Booklet 46, 1978.
Avon County Council, *Neglected Woodlands – a guide to restoration for farmers   and landowners*.

BTCV, *Woodlands – A Practical Conservation Handbook*, 1982.

Grants and advice on tree planting
Forestry Commission, *Native Pinewood Grants*, 1981.
   Control of Tree Felling, 1983.
   Advice for Woodland Owners, 1979.
   Forestry Grant Scheme, 1982.
CC, NCC, *et al.*, 'Guide to Grant Aid Advice and other Assistance for Farmers and Landowners in England and Wales' from *Countryside Conservation Handbook*.
Countryside Commission, *Grants for Amenity Tree Planting and Management*, 1978.,
   Local Authority Tree Planting Programmes in the Countryside, 1977.

Policy
Hampshire County Council, *Woodland Conservation Strategy* (County Planning Dept, The Castle, Winchester, Hants), 1981.
Grove, R., *The Future for Forestry* British Association of Nature Conservationists (BANC), 1983.
FOE, *A Tax on Nature – The Scandal of Forestry Commission Sell-Offs*, 1984.
Forestry Commission, *Broadleaves in Britain – a consultative paper*, 1984, £3.00.
   Scientific Aspects of Forestry. Select Committee on Science and Technology, Vol. I Report. Session 1979-80. 2nd Report. HMSO, 1980. Minutes of Evidence taken before the H.O.L. Select Committee on Science and Technology'. Sub-Committee 1, Forestry. NCC. HMSO, 1980.
TPOs
DOE, *Tree Preservation – a guide to procedure*, 1978.

Creating new woodlands
Baines, C. and Smart, J., *A Guide to Habitat Creation*, 1984 (available from Ecology Section, G.L.C., County Hall, London SW1).
Yoxon, M. *et al.*, *Ecological Studies in Milton Keynes – Creative Conservation*, Part 1, Milton Keynes Development Corporation, 1977 (available from Bradwell Abbey Field Centre, Abbey Road, Bradwell, Milton Keynes MKI 39AP.)
Liebscher, K.A.R., 'Tree Nurseries', BTCV, 1979, from: *Conservation Project Pack – A Guide to Practical Work for School & Youth Groups*.

6

Meadows, Downland, Heath and Moor

What are they and why should we protect them?

Britain is well know for the variety of its landscape. Meadow, downland, heath and moor form part of the pattern of regional and local diversity. For this reason alone they merit care and protection.

OLD MEADOWS

I used to stand by the mower and follow the scythe sweeping down thousands of the broad-flowered daisies, the knotted knapweeds, the blue scabious, the yellow rattles, sweeping so close and true that nothing escaped: and yet, although I had seen so many hundreds of each, although I had lifted armfuls day after day, still they were fresh. They never lost their newness, and even now each time I gather a wild flower it feels a new thing. . .

Richard Jefferies, *Pageant of Summer*

Hay meadows were once as common as fields of barley and wheat are today. They provided winter feed for stock and the working horses which were a vital part of the rural scene before tractors became common. (There were over a million working horses in Great Britain at the turn of the century.) The cattle were allowed in the meadows for an 'early bite' and taken off in spring to allow the grass to grow long. The hay was then cut and removed in June or July and the cattle were put in again to eat the 'aftermath'.

Because of the changes in farming practice, hay meadows have become obselete, although recent research has found that they are very productive without requiring large inputs of artificial fertilisers. The Nature Conservancy Council estimated in 1983 that only 3 per cent of the unfertilised hay meadows have been left completely undamaged.

Old meadows are very good for wild life, particularly wild flowers and insects. Their richness is dependent on a regular, long-term, simple system of management: a cut once a year, a low level of grazing, and *no* artificial fertilisers. The cutting and the absence of fertilisers prevent the vigorous plants from taking over. Many plants thrive under adverse conditions such as poor or shallow soils or under wet or dry conditions. When farmers change things by using fertilisers or herbicides or by draining the land, these plants lose their advantage and are quickly smothered by a few vigorous species which thrive under less harsh conditions. Similarly when annual grazing is stopped the diversity of plants is reduced as fewer plants, shrubs and eventually trees take over. Although there is still a lot of grassland left in Britain, particularly in the South-West, Wales and Scotland, its quality is poor botanically. Most of the fields have been ploughed, drained, reseeded and fertilised and they usually contain only a few species, Italian rye grass being the most common.

Old meadows are at their best in spring and early summer and can be recognised by the large number of plants they contain. Some fields may have as many as 30, which may include flowers such as lady's smock; ragged robbin, yellow rattle, meadow sweet, cowslip, early purple orchid, field scabious and ox-eye daisy. Butterflies and moths abound – large skipper, marbled white, marsh fritillary, common blue, small copper and meadow brown – as well as grasshoppers and bees. Birds include lapwing, redshank, snipe, yellow wagtail, green woodpecker and fieldfare. Old meadows have often survived on steep slopes and wet ground because they are inaccessible to tractors.

CHALK DOWNLANDS

Up on the downs the red-eyed kestrels hover,
Eyeing the grass.
The field-mouse flits like a shadow into cover
As their shadows pass. . . .

John Masefield, 'Up on the Downs'

The rolling chalk downlands of southern and eastern England are particularly rich in flowers and butterflies. The plants thrive in the shallow, well-drained soil – as many as 40 species of plants have been recorded in one square metre. These include a number of orchids – fragrant and pyramidal early purple, twayblade – thyme, rockrose, harebell, eyebright, salad burnett, ladies bedstraw, germander speedwell, birds-foot trefoil, kidney and horseshoe vetch. Regular grazing is necessary for the plants to flourish. Unfortunately, as much as 80 per cent of the downs has been converted to arable, fertilised or reseeded or has reverted to scrub. But it is encouraging to find that a number of parishes have bought or leased acres of downland and are managing them to conserve their wild life.

LOWLAND HEATH

I love to see the old heath's withered brake
Mingle its crimpled leaves with furze and ling,
While the old heron from the lonely lake
Starts slow and flaps his melancholy wing . . .

John Clare, 'Emmonsail's Heath in Winter'

Heaths are areas of treeless land covered in evergreen shrubs such as gorse and heather and usually occur on poor, acidic, sandy or gravel soils. In the past they have been kept free of tree encroachment by the grazing of domestic animals and rabbits and by burning by commoners. Nowadays tree and scrub clearance is usually done by human volunteers.

Lowland heaths are important because they support a large variety of butterflies, moths, dragonflies and spiders as well as a number of animals and plants which are on the edge of their range in Britain – the smooth snake, natterjack toad, sand lizard, and Dartford warbler. They are one of our fastest disappearing habitats, falling prey to afforestation, improvement for agriculture, housing and industrial development, and sand, gravel, oil and china clay extraction, as well as being used for military training and golf courses or simply left to revert to woodland. Nearly half of the Dorset heaths have disappeared since 1960 and much the same thing has happened in other areas of heathland, including the Surrey, Suffolk, Hampshire, Devon and Cornish heaths.

MOORLAND

High waving heather, 'neath stormy blasts bending,
Midnight and moonlight and bright shining stars;
Darkness and glory rejoicingly blending,
Earth rising to heaven and heaven descending,
Man's spirit away from its drear dungeon sending.
Bursting the fetters and breaking the bars.

Emily Brontë

Our upland landscapes, once dominated by woodland, are now covered by heather, grassland and bog. Extensive sheep farming and management for grouse shooting help maintain the open moor. Birds of prey, red deer, red grouse, curlew, golden plover and mountain hares need extensive tracts of land. Rocky outcrops, stone walls, and up above the tree line arctic alpine plants add to the interest of the high ground. The exhilaration of space, height and wildness adds to the beauty of the landscape. Many are worried by the aesthetic and wild life consequences of the projected spread of coniferous forest, the ploughing of marginal land, the march of electricity pylons, the plans for

The Moors near 'Wuthering Heights'

reservoirs and recreational developments. Much moorland is not accessible even to local people and visitors respond to 'Beware of adders' and 'No Trespassing' signs which ensure that the grouse are not disturbed.

How can we look after them?

Check with the county naturalists' trust, Nature Conservancy Council and county council to see if meadow, downland, heath or moor has been designated as an SSSI, or is in a landscape protection area. Check with the landholder and local planning authority to ensure that there will be no change of use or management which will destroy it. Explore the possibility of the parish council leasing or buying some of the land. Wouldn't it be wonderful for parishes to have their own meadows or heaths where children could play and wild life enthusiasts could just sit and paint to look at what is around them? See if the parish or other council can arrange access (if there isn't any) for the local people.

Purchase, lease, management
Rilla Mill Meadow, Cornwall
Tucked into a valley bottom in eastern Cornwall, the little village of Rilla Mill has for generations enjoyed the use of the water meadows which run beside the River Lynher. As the river flows through the centre of the village, so the meadows have been ideally situated as a playground for the children and a place of relaxation for their parents.

Times change. Recently, the village lost access first to one, then to another of the water meadows as housing developments took place and agricultural practices changed. Finally only one of the four meadows remained – an area of barely two acres. For Rilla Mill, the time had come to take action.

A group of local residents came together to see what they could do to save it for the village. At the end of 1982 they approached the owner, who generously agreed to sell the land to the village at its agricultural value. Faced with this challenge the local people jumped to it and in six months had raised more than £2,000 towards the purchase price of £3,000. By the end of the summer of 1983 the field had passed to the village, for their enjoyment in perpetuity. Ideas have blossomed for future uses for this beautiful stretch of land, but as one resident put it: 'We like it just the way it is.' For Rilla Mill, that is the way it is likely to stay.

(Oliver Baines, Rural Officer, Cornwall Community Council, 1984)

Heyshott Downland: The Downs Conservation Scheme
In 1975 the Society of Sussex Downsmen were leased two areas totally 54 acres on the Downs by the local estate for fifty years. One of the areas, 44.5 acres, is part of an SSSI. It is managed by a committee representative of the Society of Sussex Downsmen, the Parish of Heyshott and other interested bodies such as the Sussex Trust for Nature Conservation, and there are scientists as advisors.

'Scrub was spreading because there are now no sheep in the village and they are no longer taken up and down daily through this area to reach grazing on the top of the downs (now all arable). Our method is to start from areas where there is still good downland turf and to work outwards, removing anything which is or will grow into scrub – young ash, hawthorn, privet, dogwood, beech, oak, birch, rose, etc. There is plenty of all this vegetation in the areas where they have taken over so completely that we do not disturb them. We stop where there is more scrub than grass. Where the area has reverted to woodland we do some coppicing and try to renew the decaying beech with some of the young trees we remove from the turf areas. Cutting down is not enough – the bush grows again and is more difficult to remove. We pull out the smaller plants by hand, and dig out the larger ones with a trowel or a mattock, used gently to prevent erosion. Occasionally we have to remove a large tree and have to use some kind of poison to kill the root, but lately we have avoided use of herbicides entirely. When the area has been hand cleared and rubbish has been burnt the Flymo takes over. We try to get every area which has been cleared mown once, ideally twice, a year – but the work has to be done when flowers are not out, late autumn to early spring. We have a clearance party for volunteers once a month, local societies put these dates in their programmes and with the aid of grants from the Nature Conservancy Council we have employed the British Trust for Conservation Volunteers for two weeks a year, winter and early spring. The Nature Conservancy Council is now entering into an agreement whereby we will receive an annual grant of £300 for the next ten years.

We found the voluntary help available was insufficient. We were losing ground and it was impossible to maintain the areas cleared unless they could be mown. We were extremely fortunate in securing a young man as a part-time warden. He was a qualified forester working on the West Dean estate and a very keen conservationist. He worked for us as self-employed and the Downsmen paid him his petrol and his time. He gave us rather less than a day a week and did all the moving. The Flymo, by the way, was recommended by the Institute of Terrestial Ecology as the next best thing to sheep. It cuts the grass so fine it does not need raking up, and so it does not enrich the soil and so change the nature of the habitat. The Warden also drew up the management plan, which has been a great advantage in negotiations for grants from the Conservancy and convinces them that we know what we are doing! Incidentally in 1976 it was an encouragement that we were, to our surprise, awarded the County Council winning award for voluntary conservation projects – ours was described as 'ambitious'. It seemed at that time frankly mad as we toiled away hand-weeding minute areas of our 40 acres. Today it is wonderful to see the big areas of turf and the meadows of flowers. In March 1984 our first warden obtained a full-time post as warden of the Royden Woods Nature Reserve, but he leaves his successor here with a well-established management policy.

From the first we enlisted the cooperation of the village, addressing the parish council to explain what and why we were clearing and we have had no criticism and indeed much appreciation (even from the game keeper).'

(K. M. E. Murray, Clerk to Heyshott Parish Council, Sussex, 1984)

Influencing planning proposals
Flat land provides an attractive proposition for development. Flood meadows are often identified by

developers and planners as areas of seemingly low landscape value with scope for easy and cheap preparation of land for housing and industrial buildings. However, even if an area has been designated for development in a structure or local plan, all is not lost.

Ancells Farm Meadows: A local Friends of the Earth Campaign

The 158 acres of Ancells Farm in North-East Hampshire is identified in the Structure Plan for housing and industrial development. It consists mostly of wet fields of poor quality used for grazing, broken up by small copses. However, on the eastern side are 15 acres of unimproved meadows.

They have been identified as of potential ecological value, but had not been surveyed or designated. When the local council, Hart District, began drawing up their Development Brief for the farm, the Nature Conservancy Council carried out a hasty survey, in late summer 1982. Although incomplete, it identified over 70 species of plants including 10 nationally scarce species (but no great rarities) and a rich insect fauna. The meadows also provided an ideal habitat for certain birds and for small rodents. Adjacent oak woodlands added to the interest.

The NCC immediately notified the council that the meadow was of potential SSSI standard and should not be developed. The oak woodland, which is about 100 years old, was also worthy of preservation.

However, the council continued to refer to the area as of low ecological value while acknowledging it was more valuable than the rest of the farm. When the Development Brief was published in November 1982, the oakwood was to be cleared for open space and the meadows were covered in houses and crossed by a main road.

At this stage the NCC informed Friends of the Earth of the situation and asked if we would consider making an objection, because negotiations with the council were getting nowhere.

To be honest, for a week I did nothing. Ancells Farm was too firmly established in local planning programmes. If the NCC with all their expertise couldn't change it . . .

But the letter could not be ignored. As a first step I studied a copy of the development brief for the site, followed up by a site visit to relate the planning jargon and maps to reality. It was a wild, windswept November afternoon, yet the meadows had a beauty all of their own. Here was more than just a field: it was a natural community, special and *alive*.

Information was gathered prior to sending an objection. The site visit helped, the NCC gave some details in their letter and a local botanist provided a full flora list. FOE wrote a formal objection to the council, opposing any development on or near the ecologically sensitive area and asking that the road be re-routed.

Letters count. A standard letter giving the main details, a contact for further advice and the address to which objections should be sent was circulated to all FOE members in Hart District and to all potentially sympathetic contacts, such as the Ecology Party, local natural history societies and animal rights groups, urging them to write in as well.

One of our county councillors was also a FOE member. He was given full details and agreed to raise the matter at county level. This led to both Hart Council being ask to justify why it was going against county conservation policies by proposing to develop an ecological area and a formal objection from the County as statutory consultees.

Ancells Farm was already a major local controversy because of its size. The local press were notified of the FOE objection, which led to stories in two papers on the ecological angle. The benefits of contacts with local societies with related interests next bore fruit. The Fleet Pond Society (which manages this local nature reserve SSSI) were holding an autumn social evening. A chat with the chairman beforehand ensured an announcement to a captive audience of 100. The Society also duplicated copies of our letter to hand out to members. A FOE member was present to answer questions. As a result, more letters were sent to the council.

The people who ultimately make decisions are councillors. They are advised by council officers, but equally they will take note of the view of *informed* members of the public. A bonus of the Fleet Pond evening was that two councillors were in the audience and a little concerned that FOE were getting involved.

One was a member of the planning committee. She invited FOE to contact her to discuss the matter further. It turned out that the council advisors had played down the value of the meadows. She was convinced by the FOE argument and gave some useful advice on what to do next and who to contact. It also transpired that no member of the planning committee had actually visited Ancells Farm!

A briefing was prepared for all members of the planning committee, *well before* they were due to discuss Ancells Farm. Councillors receive many pieces of paper, not all of which will get read if time is short. Our contact advised that the briefing should be with them two weeks before the meeting. Copies were also sent to the planning department to supplement the FOE objection and to the press, thus ensuring more publicity.

The briefing described the meadows, explained why it is of value and, *most important*, suggested alternative options which would protect the meadows while meeting the requirements of the development brief.

Avoid jargon; keep the biology basic; be practical and realistic in what you ask.

The briefing involved redrawing the council's proposals for Ancells Farm to relocate over 100 dwellings elsewhere on the site and re-routing the road. This is not just a case of drawing a line away from the meadow: main roads have firmly established limits on curvature and must not, for instance, pass the school which is to be included in the development. There are similar restrictions on all developments – check them out before writing your alternatives.

When the briefing was sent to councillors, FOE offered to take them on a site visit to explain in more detail about the meadow and why we believed it should be made a nature reserve. Two accepted and were suitably impressed, despite its being a frosty January morning. Ancells Farm in winter is very bleak and very, very wet.

Meanwhile, the planning department were being somewhat taken aback by the number of objections they were receiving. The third most common reason for objection and 20 per cent of the total received concerned destruction of the meadows. Hart Council asked the NCC for a meeting and the tide began to turn.

In early January 1983, a planning policy meeting was advised, 'We do not want to deliberately destroy this area and should at least protect the Grade 1 site'. The FOE report was specifically referred to. A sub-committee was formed to sort out all the Ancells Farm problems, including how the meadows might be preserved. It is also good policy to attend all council meetings. It shows interest and strengthens links with councillors. The press were not able to attend them all, so FOE were also able to report back to them and tip them off to potential stories. Reporters are very grateful for this type of help and will often do favours in return as a result (like phoning councils under the pretence of a news story which is in fact an unofficial enquiry for FOE. It's amazing what can come out!)

It was a lot of work, but worth every minute. The final development brief states that the meadow will be designated a nature reserve, a buffer zone will be planted all around it, the road is re-routed, a management agreement will be drawn up with the Hampshire Naturalist's Trust and the oak woodland will be retained as an entity with only minimal clearance.

A less valuable unimproved meadow will be lost, but on the whole Ancells Farm is a resounding victory for conservation. The reward has been to see its many flowers and insects unfold through the spring and know that this special place will live through seasons yet to come. You can enjoy that same feeling.

(Chris Hall, Surrey/Hants Border FOE)

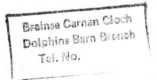

Creating new 'old' meadows and downland

Village greens and other open spaces don't have to look neat and tidy like municipal parks with short, trim mown grass. They could be a blaze of colour and teeming with birds, insects and small mammals during the summer months. The Botanic Gardens, Cambridge, have successfully allowed large areas of grass to revert to meadowland. If necessary, closely mown 'rides' can be made through the long grass to provide paths.

Instead of buying the normal grass seed mixture for open spaces, new 'conservation mixtures' have been devised by various seed merchants which contain a wide variety of wild flowers and grasses with low growth rates which do not swamp/smother and flowers. Different seed mixtures are available for different types of soil. For example, mixtures for chalk and limestone soil might contain quaking grass, clustered bellflower, harebell, horseshoe vetch and wild thyme; whereas yarrow, yellow rattle and meadow barley might be included in mixtures for clay soils. If you have any doubt about what kinds of wild flowers would grow well in your locality, write to Derek Wells, NCC, Peterborough (enclosing a s.a.e.). He will send you free of charge a sheet suggesting suitable seed mixtures and a list of firms which can supply the seeds. 'Watch' also has a special briefing sheet and the GLC have published *A Guide to Habitat Creation* by Chris Baines and Jane Smart (1984) which is essential reading for anyone interested in the subject. It is much easier to sow the seed in new areas – places which have been dug/disturbed – rather than in already established grassland. Individual plants such as primroses and cowslips can be planted in gaps in established grass, but this is a rather laborious process. An excellent booklet available from the NCC called *Creating attractive grasslands using native plant species* provides all the information you will need. It describes what seed to collect, how it can be gathered, cleared, stored, sowed and managed.

Parish seed banks

One of the fears about buying wild flower seed from seed merchants is that the seed could come from a foreign country and 'contain strains of species which may be unlike our native forms or are not adapted to our local conditions' (NCC). It is much better to collect seed from locally growing plants which you know thrive in the area and to know that you are perpetuating local strains.

Wild flower seeds should never be sown indiscriminately around the countryside. It is not only a great waste because few seeds will germinate or succeed against established plants but if they do they might upset whatever delicate balance exists.

On the positive side, sowing locally collected seeds either in seed boxes, specially prepared seed beds for transplantation or in their permanent position, can be an enjoyable and very rewarding exercise.

Drab school playing fields, industrial sites, golf courses, churchyards, parks and gardens can be transformed either by sowing seed or introducing plants, or by simply encouraging the wild flowers around to colonise these areas by creating the right conditions for them.

See what conditions your selected plants grow in in the wild and imitate them where possible.

Locally collected seed, or plants grown from them, could be sold in aid of parish funds. But *remember*: under the Wildlife and Countryside Act 1981 it is illegal to uproot *any* wild plant (including ferns, mosses and lichens, but not fungi) without the permission of the owner or occupier of the land. The Act also prohibits the collection of seed from protected species. Furthermore, the seeds of other endangered, threatened or locally uncommon plants should *not* be collected. Send for *Wild life, the Law and You* from the Nature Conservancy Council for the list of protected plants.

References and further reading

A good general introduction to grasslands is provided by David Bellamy's book, *Grassland Walks*, RSNC and Country Life, 1983.

Meadows
Baines, C. and Smart, J., *A guide to Habitat Creation*, GLC, 1984.
CC, NCC, *et al.*, '*Conserving Old Grassland*', Leaflet 4
in: *Countryside Conservation Handbook*, 1979.
Watch mini-meadows Watch, 22 The Green, Nettleham, Lincoln, 1983.
Well, T., Bell, S. and Frost, A., *Creating attractive grasslands using native plant species* Nature Conservancy Council, 1981.

Downland
CC, NCC, *et al.*, 'Conserving Old Grassland', Leaflet 4
in: *Countryside Conservation Handbook*, 1979.
Kemsing Parish Council, *A Guide to Kemsing Down Nature Reserve* Clerk's Office, St Edith Hall, Kemsing, Sevenoaks, Kent.

Heathland and moorland
Countryside Commission, *A Better Future for the Uplands* 1984.
(Publications Department 19/23 Albert Road, Manchester M19 2EQ.)
Gimingham, C. H., *Ecology of Heathlands*, 1972.
Haskins, L. E. and Nicholson, A., *A report on the Conservation of Dorset Heathlands*, 1978-9.
MacEwen, A. and M., *National Parks: Conservation or Cosmetics?* 1982.

7

Rivers, Marshes and Ponds

What would the world be, once bereft
Of wet and wildness? Let them be left,
O let them be left, wildness and wet;
Long live the weeds and the wilderness yet.

Gerard Manley Hopkins, 'Invershaid'

What are they and why should they be conserved?

Marshes, bogs, mires, fens and floodland are often called wetlands – vital for a great range of bird life, amphibians, insects and plants. The enormous amount of land drainage which has been occurring since the draining of the Fens in the seventeenth century has greatly reduced the number of our wetland habitats. Our lakes and rivers are under tremendous pressure from recreation, pollution, land drainage and river improvements. Twenty-eight species of wetland plants are threatened with extinction and many aquatic plants are now rare. The disappearance of reed beds has lead to a decline in numbers of marsh harriers and bitterns and many other birds such as the snipe which depend on marshy ground in which to feed.

Many marshes and estuaries are internationally important for migrating wildfowl, and locally small ponds and streams may also have great value. A number of creatures depend on open water, streams, canals and ponds for at least a part of their lives – particularly the amphibians, the common toad, natterjack toad, common frog, great crested, palmate and smooth newts and the dragonflies. They all need water in which to lay their eggs and spend the larval stages of their life cycle. All these species (especially the natterjack toad and great crested newts, even the common frog) are becoming less common, mainly because of the destruction of their breeding grounds.

Until recently water authorities have paid little heed to wild life and landscape as they went about their tasks of land drainage, flood prevention, water abstraction and sewage disposal. The 1981 Wildlife and Countryside Act has strengthened the law in relation to the work of water authorities. It requires that water authorities and other bodies involved with land drainage (including internal drainage boards) (a) shall, so far as may be consistent with the purposes of this Act and the Land Drainage Act 1976, so exercise their functions with respect to the proposals as to further the conservation and enhancement of natural beauty and the conservation of flora, fauna and geological and physiographical features of special interest; and (b) shall take into account any effect which the proposals would have on the beauty of, or amenity in, any rural or urban areas or on any such flora, fauna, features, buildings or objects.

Because of these clauses in the Act, a small farmer in Cambridgeshire persuaded the Anglian Water Authority to reinstate a local pond which had dried out twelve years earlier as a result of the Authority's land drainage schemes which had lowered the water table. Eleven years of agitation by the farmer had previously yielded no response.

The Water Authority (Land Drainage Division) carries out two kinds of works:

(i) Capital schemes which attract agricultural grants and usually large-scale river dredging and bank clearance schemes which are designed to prevent flooding or to enable a farmer to drain his land so that he can make better use of it by growing cereals instead of grass or by enabling his stock to use the grass for longer periods throughout the year.

(ii) Maintenance schemes which involve routine dredging, weed cutting and tree cutting. Much of this work is unnecessary and over-zealous and many beautiful meandering rivers and streams have been turned into featureless channels which are inhospitable for wild life. Many flood prevention schemes would be unnecessary if developers didn't insist on building houses on the flood plains of rivers and many water meadows would still do the job of flood control. The ratepayer has to pay the cost of these expensive schemes – not the developers. Moreover, flood prevention and land drainage schemes affect the whole watercourse, not just the section of the river which is being worked on.

There is a good chance that the ponds we see on village greens and in fields are very old. Settlements were either built around ponds or were created by the people living in the settlements. Ponds provided water for humans for animals and later for traction engines. They were created incidentally as a result of peat, marl or clay digging and on purpose to provide water for stock (such as dew ponds), for fish, to grow willows, and to extinguish local fires.

There are also the ponds over which there is no doubt about their 'naturalness' – the spring-fed and flood-plain ponds.

Many ponds have outgrown their practical usefulness. Stock are provided with water by means of piped water to field troughs and houses have their own piped water supplies. As a result, ponds have only in a few places received the kind of management they need to remain good wild life habitats. When left to themselves ponds tend to clog up – this is a natural process. Reeds and rushes and trees such as willow and alder encroach further and further into the water until it becomes marshy and eventually dry. (If ponds are managed well all these stages of development can be maintained – they all form habitats for different species.) Decaying leaves starve the pond-dwelling plants and animals of oxygen, and fertilisers and other farmyard run-offs accelerate this process. Spring-fed and flood-plain ponds have suffered from abstraction, field drainage works and river management schemes. Many ponds have been filled in or used as dumping grounds.

Between 1760 and 1820 our 3,000 miles of canals were dug in England, with hundreds of ponds and leats to help them gather and feed water to the waterways. In the Midlands and other areas this often brought surface water to places which had little before, and with the water came the plants, fish, birds and animals – a new linear ecology had been created.

Over time this has enriched the natural history of some areas. Canals, journeying as they do through town, village and country, have become valued for wild life, recreation and amenity.

As transport moved to rail and then to the road the spread of dereliction along the canals met with responses ranging from rubbish filling by local authorities to increasing voluntary activity in canal restoration. The locks, bridges, buildings and engineering artefacts have attracted the industrial archaeologists, the water, towpaths and hedgerows have attracted anglers, walkers and boaters and nature conservationists.

How can we look after them?

Apart from getting to know the area, by doing surveys of rivers, canals, wetlands and the wild life they sustain, there are various things you can do which are specific to wetland conservation.

Find from the Water Authority Land Drainage Engineer what drainage of flood relief schemes have been carried out, ask what is proposed. Read the Nature Conservancy Council's booklet *Nature Conservation and River Engineering* (see page 106) first so you will have an idea of the kinds of questions to ask and so you know what they *should* be doing.

Contact the county and district councillors who have

been appointed members of the regional water authority (see pp. 104-5). Ensure that they tell you what is going on and that they know your views.

Find out if internal drainage boards operate in your locality. If so, ask the district council land drainage section who the members are. Ask them what policies they have for wild life conservation.

Get to know the local water bailiff (employed by the water authority), the divisional land drainage engineer and the maintenance workers. They all already know so much. While some of the drainage engineers are becoming sympathetic, many problems can be caused by the actual work teams who carry out bank clearance etc. – direct contact will help.

Is the river polluted? If so, where does the pollution come from – sewage, farm run-off, industry, fish farms? (see pp. 170-73).

If you fish or boat, do not leave lead shot/nylon line/ polythene bags or any rubbish. Don't disturb birds/wild life.

Find out about the fishing rights. Are they leased? If so to whom? Is boating and canoeing permitted?

Search out areas which may be in danger because of neglect or change of use and attempt their protection.

Howden Marsh: An Ecological Amenity Area

The area known locally as Howden Marsh is 5 hectares of common land owned by the Borough Council and leased by Howden Parish Council.

Before local government reorganisation, the rural district council whose land it then was decided to make the area available for the use of the people of Howden, and left some money for this purpose. In days gone by the Marsh had been flooded in winter-time, and pasture in summer, as well as a local play area; but modern drainage and changes in agriculture had changed the nature of the place. Gradually it had become little more than a rubbish dump.

In 1975 Howden Parish Council decided to turn the Marsh into an ecological amenity area with a water area to take the surplus water, islands and rough walking. Trees suitable to the soil have gradually been planted and now there are healthy plantations of poplars, alders, willows; and in higher places rowans, hazels, birches and oaks. After initial disturbance plant life has established itself and there are well over 100 different species of land and aquatic plants. There is no shortage of bird life which, apart from common species, includes warblers, buntings, blackcaps, grebes and kingfishers.

Local children have quickly responded to the use of the water for fishing and there is a good variety of coarse fish, and of course the excitement of tadpoles – frogs and toads. Help has been given in a practical way by local Rotarians, Round Tablers, members of the Duke of Edinburgh Award Scheme and school children.

To supplement the small amount of parish money available finance has come from the Countryside Commission, Humberside County Council, and the Monument Trust. Hull University and Hull College of Higher Education have given help and advice. The next step is to provide an all-weather walk-way as some of the land is swampy in winter and also increasing use of the walks is tending to cause erosion. Another problem is growth of invasive reeds in the water area and a scheme of reed clearance is being planned by the BTCV.

Howden Marsh does serve a need for informal recreation so lacking in a countryside which is intensively farmed, and is freely available for all local people.

(Charlotte Hursey, Rural Officer, Community Council of Humberside, 1984)

Management

Canals   Care is needed in restoration and management to ensure compatible conservation for recreation and wild life. The British Waterways Board is the government body with the responsibility for canals, but some are owned by the National Trust or by local trusts. The Inland Waterways Association 'campaigns for the restoration, retention and development of inland waterways and their fullest commercial and recreational use'. The subsidiary Waterway Recovery Group owns equipment vans and machinery and offers advice and organises voluntary effort in canal restoration.

Ponds   There are a few simple ways in which you can manage a pond to benefit amphibians, insects such as dragonflies and the animals (such as hedgehogs and birds) which use it as a watering hole. There is a complication: if

Many oases like this Derbyshire dewpond are in disrepair

you are interested in encouraging frogs and toads, great crested and palmate newts will eat the tadpoles of frogs and toads (as will goldfish and dragonfly nymphs). However, smooth newts, frogs and toads will live harmoniously together.

The pond should have the following:

good surrounding vegetation, but which doesn't shade the pond; e.g. tall grass on the south side and taller shrubs (gorse/bramble) on the north side, to give cover and act as a shelter belt against north or prevailing winds;

shallow, sloping edges (no sharp, vertical sides), some being marshy;

pond weed (for cover and oxygenation);

no goldfish (they eat tadpoles) or other predatory fish such as trout, perch or pike. Resident ducks and moorhens will also reduce the chances of tadpole/newt survival;

If you are collecting frog/toad spawn for your pond, only

take a small clump or part of one. It is important to leave most of the spawn behind.

Ponds should be cleared as seldom as possible. Never clean out an entire pond in one year. If it has to be done, clear it in stages. 'Little and often' is the best form of management. A five-year rotation plan of clearance is ideal.

Thanks to the formation of the 'Save the Village Pond' Campaign organised by the British Waterfowl Association and sponsored by the Ford Motor Company in 1974, there are many examples of parishes and local groups restoring ponds. The following examples give a range of the different methods employed and situations encountered.

Village Pond, Urchfont, Wilts
This is an interesting example because when the parish council discussed holding an event near to the pond it found it didn't know who the owner was. The clerk therefore set about finding out by submitting a formal enquiry to the Land Registry Office, who replied that it was not registered as being owned by anyone. The parish council decided it would like to take 'possession of the land in the interest of the inhabitants'. So the parish council then put up notices on the village notice board, in local newspapers to tell people of the parish council's intentions and to winkle out the owner – if one existed. If no positive proof of ownership by anyone else is produced within twelve years then the council will become legally owners of the pond. Meanwhile the council can formally and legally effectively control the pond as if it was already in their ownership.

For further information the Association of Local Councils has issued a Legal Topic Paper No. 7 entitled *Acquisition of Ownerless Land*.

Penkridge Natural History Society, Staffordshire
'The Swamp', as the local kids called it, lies between two housing estates and was full of rubbish. The area is owned by the district council and the surrounding grass had been scythed rather too tidily for the needs of wild life. The society after talking to the local inhabitants decided to clear out the rubbish and to manage part of the open space around the pond as a nature reserve and part as a general play area.

The district council provided a skip for the rubbish and three days were spent cleaning up the area. The society surveyed the pond and its surrounds for its wild life interest and subsequently drew up a management plan which was presented to the council for endorsement/ approval.

Some wild flowers were moved from a proposed rubbish tip and planted around the pond and some trees were planted to screen off the railway line. Local schools have been involved in various projects including monitoring, erecting nest boxes and making a small butterfly garden. The project won the Staffordshire Village Ventures Award and the money received was put towards the construction of two notice boards which explain the value of the areas.

Galleywood Paddock, Countryside Properties

Countryside Properties, an Essex building firm, has attempted wherever possible in developing small areas for new housing to maintain, enhance or create ponds and water courses. At Galleywood, Chelmsford a pond with its small islands and trees has been minimally and carefully landscaped to enhance not only the housing area but also the local ecology. Many developers would have culverted any stream and filled in any pond.

Galleywood Paddock: old pond incorporated into new housing development

Statutory agencies

Water authorities

There are 10 multi-functional regional water authorities in England and Wales and 9 river purification boards in Scotland (which are not responsible for sewage treatment, unlike the water authorities) and 3 all purpose regional and island councils. Each water authority is separated into divisions. Find out the address and telephone number of the division you are in from the main office of the regional water authority.

Water authorities are responsible for 'statutory main rivers' – the major watercourses from which they abstract water and to which they return treated sewage. (The RWA will hold maps of the main rivers.) The smaller rivers and streams and field drains and ditches are taken care of by internal drainage boards (IDBs). Since the early 1970s, about a quarter of a million acres have been drained annually in England and Wales.

Internal drainage boards

The 214 internal drainage boards are virtually autonomous units and have been described as private clubs for farmers with the power to levy rates.

'They have drainage rights over 8 per cent of the land area of England and Wales and are eligible for 50 per cent government grants for new drainage schemes. . . . Every one in an Internal Drainage Board district, farmer or city-dweller, pays rates to the board, but farmers, who benefit most from land drainage, often pay the lowest rates.' (Caufield, New Scientist, 3/9/81.)

Their policies are strongly focused on increasing agricultural productivity of land within their district and they are not noted for supporting wild life and conservation issues.

Ways of approaching water authorities and IDBs

Water authority schemes   *Since October 1983, when the 1983 Water Act came into force, the regional water authorities have been relieved of the requirement of having to admit the public and press to their main meetings. They are required, however, to establish a consumer consultative committee for each of their divisions, which will include representatives of local authorities and consumers. These meetings will be held in public. A Code of Practice has been drawn up by the chairman of the regional water authorities to ensure the provision of information to the press and public. Each RWA will also have a regional recreation and conservation committee, the compositions of which are still being determined.*

However, to its credit, the Welsh Water Authority has chosen to keep its committee and main board meetings open to the public and press, and the 'Anglian, North West, South West, Thames and Yorkshire Water Authorities are keeping at least some of their committees open to the public' (Frankel, 1984).

The public relations department of your regional water authority will be able to tell you how the consumer consultative committees and recreation and conservation consultative committee operate, the dates of the meetings and the names of the local authority representatives and other members. As Frankel points out in Secrets No. 1, 'although outside bodies will nominate committee members, all appointments are made by the water authorities who also control the budget and supply the secretariat'. So this new procedure can only be regarded as a retrograde step as far as public accountability is concerned.

Internal drainage boards   *IDBs are not publicly accountable even though they can receive 50 per cent grants from MAFF and raise (through the water authority) precepts from the county council – but they may respond to public opinion. Contact the chairman of the regional land drainage committee if there are problems in your area. His name can be found via the regional water authority or by asking the information office at the county council. He will probably pass you on to the land drainage committee in which the problem lies.*

References and further reading

The main Acts of Parliament are the Water Act 1973, the Land Drainage Act 1976, and the Water Act 1983.

General

In 1984 the RSPB/RSNC published *A Rivers and Wildlife Handbook: a guide to practices which further the conservation of wildlife on rivers.* It is a detailed source book for land drainage engineers but also useful reading for anyone wishing to influence their water authority. It is available from the RSPB at £12.50 plus £1.60 postage and packaging.

In 1980 the Water Space Amenity Commission produced the Conservation and Land Drainage Guidelines which recognised the Water Authorities' part in helping to conserve our wetland heritage and outlines the ways in which land drainage engineers should be operating. (Available from WSAC, 1 Queen Anne's Gate, London SW1H 9BT. Price £5.00). Further information is contained in the Nature Conservancy Council's booklet *Nature Conservation and River Engineering* which shows how land drainage engineers can imaginatively combine the job of land drainage and wild life conservation. (Price £3.00.) This booklet should be read if you are at all interested in rivers and wildlife conservation.

British Trust for Conservation Volunteers, *Waterways & Wetlands*, 1976, tells everything you could wish to know on the practical side.
Bellamy, D. *Discovering the Countryside – Waterside Walks* Country Life, 1983 draws you into the natural history and Richard North's *Wild Britain, The Century Book of Marshes, Fens and Broads*, 1983, describes the threats to our dwindling wetlands, and argues the case for conserving them.
Frankel, M. *Secrets No. 1*, 1984 Campaign for Freedom of Information, 1984

Ponds
Bowen, U., *How to make a small pond* Berks, Bucks & Oxon Naturalists Trust.
CC, NCC, *et al.*, 'Farm Ponds', Leaflet 5 in: *Countryside Conservation Handbook*, 1980.
Dyson, J., *Save the Village Pond* BWA/Ford Conservation Handbook. Available from BTCV.
NCC *Farm Ponds and Ditches* Conservation Guides Series, 1979.
Newbold, C., Purseglove, J. and Holmes, N., *Nature Conservation and River Engineering*, 1983.
Water Space Amenity Commission, *Conservation and Land Drainage Guidelines* 1980 (WSAC, 1 Queen Anne's Gate, London SW1H 9BT)

Water policy
Parker, D. J. and Penning-Rowsell, E. C., *Water Planning in Britain* 1980.
Pearce, F., *Watershed – the water crisis in Britain*, 1982.

Canals
British Waterways Board, *Waterways Environment Handbook* 1972.
Gagg, J., *The Observer Book of Canals*.
Hopkins, T. and Brassley, P., *Wildlife of Rivers and Canals*, 1982.

Habitat creation
Baines, C. and Smart, J., *A Guide to Habitat Creation* 1984.

8
Hedges and Verges

HEDGEROWS

It occurred to me that one of the things I had missed most when I was abroad was the ordinary English hedge, which we take for granted, yet . . . it is a theme which runs repetitive throughout the English countryside. The tall unkept hedge of Gander Lane was made of hazel mixed with hawthorn, but it had elm, sloe, bramble, elder, and spindle tree on it too; half a dozen shrubs composed it, yet it was homogenous; it was a typical English hedge. In the spring the place was a great favourite of nightingales, which love hazel, of glow-worms, which like mossy hedgeroots, and of lovers, who take pleasure in quiet lanes.

John Moore, from *'Portrait of Elmbury'*

Why conserve them?

Many of our hedgerows, especially those forming parish boundaries, date from Saxon times and earlier. Some were planted during the two main periods of enclosure between 1460 and 1600, and 1740 and 1830. Most hedges originated before 1700 in the counties bordering Wales and the sea. In the Midlands, where there was a strong open-field tradition, most of the hedges date from 1750–1830. All buildings built before 1700 are given protection; many of our hedges are much more than 300 years old and for this reason alone should be conserved.

Dr Max Hooper has devised a simple method to determine the age of a hedgerow. The method is not fool-proof and should be used as a guide, to be backed up by historical maps and documents. Count the number of trees and woody shrubs in a thirty-yard section of hedge. As a general rule, the number of shrubs increases by one species for every 100 years. Three different woody plants in the section would suggest a 300-year-old hedge, 10 woody plants 1,000 years old and so on. Some recent hedges have been planted with a diversity of species, so beware!

Some hedgerows were not planted but are remnants, descendants of the original forest cover, which have been kept and managed as boundary hedges, the surrounding woodland having been cleared for agriculture. These woodlands relic hedges contain a large number of different plants including shrubs such as spindle, field maple, hazel and dogwood which do not readily colonise newly planted hedges. Research by Dr Hooper suggests that it is not until a hedge is 400 years old (i.e. it has four species in it) that field maple begins to come into it; and for the spindle, a hedge has to be 600 years old before the conditions are suitable for it. Hedgerows of more recent origin are generally of hawthorn alone.

Woodland relic hedges can also be identified by the kinds of flowering plants which grow in them. The presence of bluebells, wood anemone, dog's mercury and yellow archangel are a good indication that the hedgerow is an old one as plants such as these take a long time to spread to new areas. (*Hedges* by Pollard, Hooper and Moore is strongly recommended for further reading.)

The English elm used to be a common hedgerow tree and was often planted for such purposes. As it reproduces by suckering it spreads rapidly. Unfortunately Dutch Elm Disease has wiped out the majority of them – in southern England at any rate. The most common hedgerow trees are now oak and ash, but there are regional variations, sycamore being relatively abundant in Wales and beech and sycamore in Scotland.

Hedges form one of our most important nature reserves and highways along which species can spread and move, but their usefulness to wild life depends on their quality.

Hedges containing a large number of shrubs and plants will provide food for a greater number of animals. Hedges with thick bases will give more shelter and nesting sites and hedgerows with mature trees growing from them will increase the number of breeding birds quite considerably because of the insects and shelter they provide.

The lowland English landscape in particular owes much of its character and domestic intimacy to the patchwork created by hedgerows, but changes in farming practice have removed the need for hedges as barriers and shelter for farm animals in many areas. Hedgerow destruction began in earnest after the Second World War and reached its peak in the 1960s. Nearly a quarter of our hedges have been destroyed since 1945 – amounting to over 140,000 miles.

Hedgerows are usually removed to enable farm machinery to manouevre more easily. In small fields of 5 acres much of the tractor man's time is spent in turning, and in predominantly arable areas such as East Anglia there are no livestock to enclose. But even in the dairy farms of the South-West they are being removed as well. In Cornwall between 1963 and 1976 more hedges were lost than in the previous 75 years.

Machine cutting year after year encourages upward growth, the hedge thins out at the base, and sheep and small stock find it easy to force a way through. Pig netting and old bedsteads fill the gaps for a few years until eventually the hedge disappears altogether. All that was needed was a hedge-laying exercise every 10–20 years and less drastic slashing in between. The cost of hedge laying can be great – but so is the cost of fencing.

It is unreasonable to expect a farmer to retain *all* his hedges, especially those which are not boundary hedges or which do not run along public roads or public footpaths. But great effort should be made to persuade farmers to retain and manage the hedges which are important to the locality, for landscape and for wild life.

Ways of conserving hedgerows

TPOs

Hedgerow trees (if of amenity value – that is, if they are a landscape feature and can be seen from roads/public footpaths, etc.) can be covered by a TPO. But the hedge itself (the shrubs) cannot be covered. Local planning authorities can make an order 'immediately effective provisionally for up to 6 months, or until it is decided whether it should be confirmed, whichever is the earlier' (*Tree Preservation – a guide to Procedure* DOE). However, 'immediately' is often too late.

If you see hedgerow trees being ripped out: (i) ring the district council tree officer as soon as possible and ask for a TPO to be placed on the trees at risk; (ii) if a TPO is already in force, ask the tree officer to come to the site immediately; (iii) if the hedge has no trees in it there is little which can be done, except by explaining politely to the landholder/ contractor that the hedge is of importance to the locality, for whatever reason, the asking him to think again or at least to stop work and allow some people to talk to him first. (See Cow Pasture Lane pp. 58-62 for detailed example.)

Hedgerow management

Good management is the best way of ensuring a hedge's survival. Farmers find hedge trimming an arduous task and they often complain that they can't find the time to keep their hedges tidy and that this is one reason why they should be grubbed out.

There is no reason why some old hedges, especially the parish/county boundary hedges which are of importance to the locality, should not be managed by local volunteers – provided the landholder/tenant is in agreement.

Laying hedges is a fine art and there are all kinds of local/ regional variations. For descriptions and methods of hedge laying see the excellent BTCV handbook, *Hedging*. (BTCV and Countryside Ranger courses provide the basic skills.)

Gloucestershire: newly laid hedge

You may get agreement for a particular length of hedge to be laid as part of a local competition – ploughing societies have done this for many years.

Hedgerow sapling tagging
For many years farmers have not allowed so many trees to grow up out of the hedges. In 1974 it was estimated that hedgerow trees were disappearing at a rate of 2 per cent a year. Apart from being a very important part of the scene, they are necessary to wild life and provide shelter and shading for stock, as well as timber for the farmer.

Hedgerow sapling tags are available from the Tree Council or the tree officer of your county council. The idea is to place tags around healthy, straight-stemmed trees such as oak, ash or field maple – or trees which are prevalent in the locality – so that the hedge trimmer sees them and can avoid cutting them. Collaboration must naturally be sought from the landholder/tenant. This is a task which the parish council or local school could well undertake. Saplings from well-established old root systems can grow more quickly – this is a very good way of restocking the landscape.

Know your parish boundary hedges and walls
Trace the boundary of your parish (with permission from the landholders). The hedgerows, hedgebanks and walls which run along the boundary are likely to be very old. They are living historical documents and should be conserved wherever possible. Their age can be estimated by the Hooper method described on page 109-10 and by looking at the tithe map in the county record office and early OS maps. Make records of the hedges, noting their position (are they bound by ditches on both sides?) and length, list the tree and shrub species, ground plants, etc. Note the condition of the hedge: disappearing (odd trees and ditch left); continuous but spindly, in need of laying; recently laid; or thick and well managed.

A slightly more ambitious project is to make a *parish hedgerow survey*, mapping the internal hedges of the parish as well. Make sure that no one has already made one – check with your CPRE branch and naturalists' Trust first. (See CPRE leaflet, *Hedges – Historical Surveys*.)

Parish hedgerow seed nursery
Collect the seeds from the hedgerow shrubs and trees in your parish such as field maple, holly, hawthorn, elderberry, hazel, dogwood, rowan, spindle, guelder rose and dog rose and sow them in seed boxes or a specially prepared seed bed. (For information on how to collect etc. see *Creative Conservation-Ecological Studies in Milton Keynes*.)

You will need to be patient because many of the hips, haws and berries are slow to germinate and need to be kept in the ground or undisturbed for 2–3 seasons. When the plants are old enough to be transplanted you can discuss with the parish council how they can be best used – either to fill in the gaps of an existing decaying hedge or to plant new ones. Many farmers would welcome a gift of shrubs and trees.

WALLS AND EARTHBANKS

Why conserve them?

Our ancestors were building dry stone walls for protection and control of animals in prehistory but the main stone-walling periods seem to have been during the Dark Ages, between the fourteenth and eighteenth centuries and during the Enclosures (particularly between 1780–1820) which demanded rapid extension of stone walls. Built of sandstone, limestone, granite or slate, walls and earthbanks are, like hedgerows, significant landscape features. They are useful where farming still involves animals, where inclement weather is common and as boundaries. Their construction and the patterns they make are historical records and their age, bulk (1¾ tons of stone per yard) and length (48,000 miles in the pre-1974 West Riding of Yorkshire) are testimony to hard labour and great skill.

Walls and earthbanks provide well-drained habitats (often differing immensely on north and south sides, east and west sides in exposed areas) for all kinds of plants, particularly lichens, mosses and ferns. Insects, spiders, snails, snakes and lizards love them, birds nest in them, smaller mammals inhabit them, domesticated animals and ramblers shelter by them. Like hedges they are good safe highways for movement. Their presence in the landscape gives a strength of regional character and often expresses locally the details of the underlying rock.

While derelict walls still make good habitats, the danger of them disappearing is increased. Farmers may not value their walls if they no longer have stock. Their upkeep can be costly, but their removal may cost even more unless the stone is desirable to someone and accessible enough for easy removal. Some of the walls of Yorkshire are being 'quarried' for rockery stone.

Ways of conserving them

As well as the parish boundary survey (and with the landholder's permission) make a study of all the walls in the parish – this may be a lifetime's work! – map them on an OS map, locate different styles of construction. Do wild life and landscape surveys. Note those lengths which most need maintenance, ask the owners if they intend to repair them or if they would be happy to see voluntary workers do so. Sketch and photograph stiles, through-holes and other features.

Never climb walls and dissuade others from doing so. Be vigilant for stone rustlers ('let's just take a couple of rocks for the garden . . . '). The Dry Stone Walling Association has branches in many counties, from Cumbria to Devon, and regional branches in Scotland. It would like to see the continued growth of groups, apprenticeships, competitions and demonstrations. The Derbyshire branch gives walling demonstrations at the annual Bakewell show, and attempts to win local authority walling work when new by-passes etc. are being built. There is much encouragement for amateur involvement and progression towards professionalism through courses and activities. Much practical advice on maintenance and construction, ideas and information is to be found in the BTCV book *Dry Stone Walling*.

RURAL ROADSIDE VERGES

Why conserve them?

Many roadside verges are very important for wild flowers, birds, insects and small mammals. In fact they are thought, by some botanists, to be the richest single habitat for wild plant species in the country covering the spectrum of our soils. They cover a large area – there are over 56,000 miles of classified non-principal roads and almost 100,000 unclassified roads in England and Wales; these with the major roads have over 500,000 acres of roadside verges (including hedges, ditches and scrub).

Even those areas were at risk in the late 1950s/60s. The 'meticulously tidy engineers and surveyors mowed or sprayed every shaggy strip of nature that ran alongside their tar macadamed highways' (Roy Hattersley, *Guardian*, 4/6/83). Luckily many councils can no longer afford to manage them so intensively. Our roadside verges are once again assuming the colour and exuberance that they displayed decades ago.

Most countryside roads are extremely old: ancient trade routes, Roman roads, drovers' roads, tracks around and between settlements dating from the Anglo-Saxon spread of villages, or roads made during the Enclosures. In any event, the type of treatment they received will have been broadly uniform. If there was grass they were grazed by animals and/or cut for hay once or twice a year – until the invention of the motor car, which changed everything.

The range of plants you can expect to find in a rural roadside verge is enormous – as many as 700 different kinds of flowering plants. Many of their names describe their habitat: jack-by-the-hedge, 'waybread' (an old name for the greater plantain), and traveller's joy which reminds us that our forbears enjoyed the wayside plants as much as we do.

The maintenance of verges is the responsibility of the district surveyor in the highways department, and he must ensure adequate visibility at bends and junctions by regular cutting. Less frequent cutting is detrimental to the smaller, less vigorous plants and management regimes have been devised to overcome this. Different areas need different systems but many wider verges would thrive with a three-tier system: a strip 3–5 wide near to the road cut regularly; a wider belt cut in mid-summer and early autumn; the vegetation fringing the hedge cut only in early autumn.

A number of county naturalists' trusts have agreed procedures with district surveyors about the management of specified sections of secondary and minor roads. In some instances, marker posts have been placed to identify verges of particular conservation interest.

How to help your verges

Contact the conservation officer of your county naturalists' trust and find out what they have done/are doing. Ask if they are doing surveys; if they have management agreements with the district surveyor.

Conduct a survey of the plants, insects, animals and birds which you see in the verges in your parish/locality at different times of the year.

Ask the county council maintenance/works division of the highways department *not* to use chemical pesticide or herbicide sprays. Use conservation, cost and visual attraction arguments.

Tell the naturalists' trust of any verges which you think deserve special (sensitive) forms of management.

Encourage people to take photographs or to paint local hedgerows.

List the local names of the wayside flowers.

Ask older people what they used to see in the hedgerows.

References and further reading

Hedges
The most exciting and comprehensive book is *Hedges* by E. Pollard, M. O. Hooper, and N. W. Moore, in the Collins New Naturalist Series, 1974.
British Trust for Conservation Volunteers *Hedging: A Practical Conservation Handbook* 1975.
CC, NCC, *et al.*, 'Hedge Management' 1980, in: *Countryside Conservation Handbook*.
CPRE, *Hedges – Historical Surveys*, 1973.

Hoskins, W. G., *Fieldwork in Local History*, 1967/1982.
MAFF, *Planting Farm Hedges* leaflet 763, reprinted 1982.
Managing Farm Hedges leaflet 762, reprinted 1982.
Standing Conference for Local History, *Hedges and Local History* National Council for Voluntary Organisations, 1971.
Sturrock, F. G. and Cathie, J., *Farm Modernisation and the Countryside* Department of Land Economy, University of Cambridge, Occasional Paper No. 12, 1980.
Yoxon, M. *et al.*, *Creative Conservation (Part 1) Ecological Studies in Milton Keynes* Milton Keynes Development Corporation, 1977.

Walls and earthbanks
BTCV, *Dry Stone Walling – A Practical Conservation Handbook* 1978.
Hoskins, W. G., *Fieldwork in Local History* 1967 and 1982.
Muir, R., *Shell Guide to Reading the Landscape*, 1981.

Rural roadside verges
Briggs, M., *The Guinness Book of Wild Flowers*, 1980.
Lousley, J. E. 'The Influence of Transport on a Changing Flora" in: F. Perring (ed.), *The Flora of a Changing Britain* 1974.
Way, J. M. (ed.), *Road Verges – their function and Management* Symposium Proceedings N.C. 1969 (Available from the Institute of Terrestrial Ecology, Monks Wood Experimental Station, Abbots Ripton, Huntingdon.)

9

Wild Corners

They won't let railways alone, those yellow flowers.
They're that remorseless joy of dereliction
darkest banks exhale like vivid breath
as bricks divide to let them root between.
How every falling place concocts their smile,
taking what's left and making a song of it.

Anne Stevenson, 'Ragwort'

Many opportunities for keeping or bringing wild life close to us exist – in our own gardens, along old railway lines, in recreation grounds, churchyards or overgrown quarries. But through neglect, over-tidiness or lack of thought we often fail to take advantage of the possibilities for simple conservation or even habitat creation.

CHURCHYARDS

Why conserve them?

Country churchyards hold many fascinations – local and family histories, monuments and gravestones, old trees and lychgates – and with the intensification of agriculture churchyards are becoming even more important oases for wild life. Victorian cemeteries and churchyards in towns and cities make excellent places for wild life as well.

Churchyards are particularly rich in plants. Many have developed over hundreds of years and house very old trees and hedgerows and complex associations of plants. Suffolk Naturalists' Trust identified more than 300 different varieties of wild flowers and flowering grasses in one Suffolk churchyard.

Norfolk, Suffolk and Warwickshire Women's Institute branches have already done extensive work, surveying monuments, graves and natural history in churchyards. For further information contact the National Federation of Women's Institutes. The Botanical Society of the British Isles is also organising scientific plant surveys of Churchyards. Contact BSBI, c/o Botany Dept, Natural History Museum, Cornwall Road, London SW7, for details.

Churchyards provide considerable areas of 'rock face' and gravestones assume an important role in areas where natural rock exposures are few in number. Churchyards are fascinating to people who study mosses and lichens since gravestones can be accurately dated, giving clues to the growth rates of lichens, and changing levels of pollution can be measured (many lichens being sensitive to dirty air). There may be more than a dozen types of lichen on one gravestone, and even in the dry churchyards of East Anglia 30-40 different species of lichens can be found on the gravestones.

Churchyards can be havens for creatures such as bats, voles, shrews, foxes, hedgehogs, rabbits, lizards, slow worms and snails and birds such as goldcrests, coaltits, blackbirds, thrushes, fieldfares and redwings who benefit from the evergreen trees. (Thrushes are not usually short of 'anvils' for snail-bashing!)

How to look after churchyards

Find out what management plan exists from the vicar/ rector. If the management is over-zealous and tidy or non-existent, try to get support to draw up your own management plan. Get a team together if none exists and carry out the work yourselves.

Colin Ranson, Nature Conservancy Council, East Anglia, has drawn up some proposals for churchyard management. Briefly they are:

only the essential paths need to be cleared;

the long grass needs only be cut twice a year – once in mid June and once in autumn. The cut should be 3 in. above ground level and the cut grass should be raked off in June, but left as a protective covering in the autumn;

If cowslips, primroses or bulbs grow in the grass they should not be disturbed until mid-July to allow them to set their seeds.

Churchyard, Clewer, Berkshire

The Rev. Denis Shaw has combined local history with wild life conservation in churchyard by providing a network of cleared paths to graves of special interest referred to in a printed guide. The remainder was kept as a preserved 'wilderness' where patches of wild violets, everlasting pea, several vetches, wild poppies, chicory and foxgloves, among other plants, were introduced. The Church Lodge, attached to the Lynchgate, was also preserved by being converted into a Museum of local history and income was derived from admission charges and the sale of catalogues. (Kenneth Allsop Memorial Prize Essay, *Sunday Times*, 1982.)

Put up bird nest boxes, and build hedgehog houses, make sure that owls and bats have easy access to the belfry.

Plant native trees and shrubs which provide food for birds and butterflies; including the traditional evergreens yew and holly.

Make sure any hedges are managed well. They could be very old.

Carry out surveys on the lines of the Norfolk/Suffolk WI surveys. (Be sure not to damage any of the headstones in an attempt to read the inscriptions. Do not pull off ivy from the stones or remove the lichen.)

If there is room, put in a small pond., Even 2' x 4' plastic moulded one would be better than nothing. Churchyard with ponds and lots of long grass provide wonderful habitats for frogs, toads and newts.

Ask for a ban on the use of pesticides and herbicides.

Plan a small exhibition showing and explaining your work in the church or church hall.

YOUR GARDEN

Why encourage wild life?

Although some animals and plants have very specific requirements and are unable to adapt to new conditions, many others are more adaptable and will readily move to areas where the right conditions prevail. So much of the countryside these days has been ruined for wild life – drained, levelled, sprayed with herbicides and pesticides and fertilised – that we can at least offer refuges in our 1,500,000 acres of gardens. Here are a few ideas needing less effort than your current gardening habits (including a great justification for nettles).

Guiding principles

Tidiness is not a virtue in gardens. We are obsessed with it. Ordered chaos is far preferable for wild life. Leave a part of the garden wild.

Avoid using poisons – pesticides, herbicides and fungicides. Many animals need insects to eat – try encouraging those which will eat aphids, slugs, snails etc. rather than obliterating everything that moves.

Grow the food plants for the creatures you wish to encourage – thistles for goldfinches; cotoneaster etc. for blackbirds, thrushes, redwings and fieldfares – and so on. Allow the birds to eat a percentage of the fruit.

The following garden plants provide nectar for butterflies and bees: (for a longer list see *Butterflies – an introduction to their conservation* from Butterfly Year 1981-2).

polyanthus	catmint	alyssum
phlox	aubretia	hyssop
wallflower	buddleia	thrift
verbena	honesty	echium
sweet rocket	cornflower	valerian
heliotrope	mignonette	aster

sweet william	golden rod	lavender
michaelmas daisy	sedum spectabile	

Useful wildflowers include: primrose, dandelion, bramble, clover, teasel, vetches, scabious and pussy willow. Nettles are one of the most useful plants to grow for butterflies. They are the food plants for the caterpillar of the peacock, small tortoiseshell, red admiral, and comma. Grasses are important for the meadow brown, gatekeeper and speckled wood.

Provide artificial homes: bird boxes – including swift boxes under the eaves of buildings – hedgehog houses, and bat boxes, damp rock and log piles for frogs, and a bird table for regular feeding from November to end of March before the young birds hatch.

Plant native trees – they support a larger number of insects than foreign ones. Field maple, birch and rowan are among the trees which are suitable for small gardens. Plant native ivy for winter bird roosts and nesting.

Put in a pond. This will greatly increase the variety of wild life to your garden and provide sanctuaries for frogs, toads and newts (see pages101-2). It need only be 3 feet square, but the larger the better.

Sow native flowers and grasses (tall, medium and low growing), either from seed collected in the neighbourhood or from one of the many seed merchants who now sell wild flower mixes.

You will be amazed at how quickly birds and other animals will come to your garden if you provide food and create the right environment for them. There is no greater joy than seeing migratory and hibernating species return to your garden in spring – the frogs and toads returning to your pond to spawn, the spotted flycatcher coming back to its old nest site, the hedgehog awakening from his winter hibernation to forage once again around your (her) garden, and the first brimstone of spring.

If it reappears, watch 'Blue tits and bumblebees – the making of a wildlife garden', a BBC TV documentary by Chris Baines.

POCKET PARKS

Northamptonshire, a county with little land which is not busily farmed, is advocating the creation of 'pocket parks'. Through the Leisure and Library Services Department of the County Council advice, information and encouragement are available to parish councils or village groups to help create 'a pocket of countryside where young and old could explore and enjoy the pleasures of our landscape and wild life. What about the old quarry or railway embankment; that last remnant of meadow by the stream that has no owner, or the orchard that the owner can no longer afford to maintain? Such an area could be landscaped and managed to provide simple facilities – a play area, a picnic site, an outdoor classroom, a habitat for wild life or an area to relax and enjoy the fresh air.'

A number of parishes have established their own equivalent of pocket parks. For example, Shalfleet in the Isle of Wight 'created, with Manpower Services help, a pleasant village amenity out of an overgrown acre. Now all can enjoy the beautifully planted area for play and relaxation.' (*Rural Viewpoint*, June 1983.)

WASTELAND

Many overgrown plots or areas of 'wasteland' may look unwelcoming, but can be marvellous habitats for wild life. Before taming a piece of wasteland, ask local naturalists to make a survey of the area for its wild life value and draw up management plans accordingly. If a piece of land looks derelict it tends to attract litter.

Eastmoor Copse, Haxey, Humberside, which belongs to the village and is administered by the Haxey Townsman 'was becoming a dumping ground for rubbish, so the parish council, at the request of the Townsman, undertook the work of clearing the site and made it a project for tree planting and obtained a grant from the county council for this. Various native trees have been planted here, e.g. oak, ash, beech and shrubs, and with the parish council's assistance this copse is being kept in good condition and it is hoped when these trees come to maturity the Eastmoor Copse will be a place of beauty and will continue to be conserved by generations to follow.' (Mrs M. Peers, Clerk to Haxey Parish Council)

RECREATION AREAS

Playing fields of all kinds require a good deal of maintenance, it would often be very beneficial to the local wild life and the groundsmen to leave small unkept corners. Nettles behind the pavilion, brambles out of reach of the footballs, and so on.

Belmont Parish in Durham owns 28 acres of rough pasture used for all kinds of recreational purposes. In one part of a small south-facing valley an area has been planted with native species – nettles, violets, jack-by-the-hedge, cuckoo flower – and some cultivated plants – honesty and buddleia. An area of a quarter of an acre has been simply and inexpensively laid out. It will enable children and adults to enjoy watching caterpillars and butterflies, which have few habitats left in the fields.

References and further reading

General
Baines, C. and Smart, J., *A Guide to Habitat Creation*, 1984.
Wilson, R., *The Backgarden Wildlife Sanctuary Book*, 1981.

Churchyards
Ashbee, R., *Recording Norfolk's Churchyards*, Norfolk Federation of WIs Project, 1980/81.
Barker, G.M.A., *Wildlife Conservation in the case of Churches and Churchyards*, Board for Social Responsibility of the General Synod of the Church of England, 1972. (Church Information Office, Church House, London SW1.)
Ransom, C., *Churchyards*, NCC Eastern Region.
Stapleton, Rev. H. and Burman, P., *The Churchyards Handbook – Advice on their maintenance*, 1976.
Suffolk West Federation of Women's Institutes, 'Notice to all the Churchyard Recorders'.

Gardens, pocket parks, wasteland and recreation grounds
Chinery, M., *The Natural History of the Garden* 1978.
Farrell, C. and Rothschild, M., *The Butterfly Gardener*, 1983.
Goodden, R. and Thomas, J., *Butterflies – an introduction to their Conservation* Published by Butterfly Year 1981-2; c/o The British Butterfly Conservation Society, P.O. Box 2, Compton House, Sherborne, Dorset (leaflet).
Owen, J. *Garden Life*, 1983.
RSPB, *Gardening with Wildlife*.
Soper, T., *Wild Life begins at Home*, 1978. *The New Bird Table Book*, 1975.
Whalley, P., *Butterfly Watching*, 1980.

10

The Conservation of Plants and Animals

. . . To see the World in a grain of sand,
And a Heaven in a wild flower,
Hold Infinity in the palm of your hand,
And Eternity in an hour.
A robin redbreast in a cage
Puts all Heaven in a rage.

William Blake, *Auguries of Innocence*

Legal protection

By far the best way of safeguarding plants and animals is through protection of their habitats but some species once common have become rare because of hunting, chemicals, farming practice as well as diminishing habitats. Protection for these under the law has developed in a piecemeal way over the past fifty years or so. Some creatures are protected as game and some because of persecution, many because of rarity.

Apart from Acts of Parliament, the best general source of information on the law is *Wildlife, the Law and You* published by the Nature Conservancy Council in 1982. For more specific information, the RSPB has a leaflet on 'Wild Birds and the Law'; COENCO has two leaflets, *Wild Plants* and *Reptiles and Amphibians*, which can be obtained free on receipt of a 9" x 6" s.a.e.; if you need interpretation on what the law says, write to: Legislation Section, Nature Conservancy Council, Northminster, Peterborough PE1 1GA.

Under the Wildlife and Countryside Act 1981 (available

from HMSO, most birds (except 13 'pest' species and game birds – for which there is a shooting season), all 15 species of bats, the otter, 3 species of dolphins/porpoises and the red squirrel are specially protected, as are 2 reptiles, 2 amphibians, 1 fish, 4 butterflies, 5 moths, 5 other insects, 2 spiders, 3 snails and 62 wild plants.

Deliberate killing, injuring and taking, and disturbance of a protected animal's breeding site or place of shelter are all illegal (a licence to photograph a protected animal in its place of shelter is needed from the NCC) and it is also prohibited to possess or sell any of these creatures or their parts or products without a licence.

With regard to plants, *it is illegal to pick, uproot, destroy or sell any of the 62 plants; to collect or sell their seed; to uproot any other wild plant* unless you are the owner or occupier of the land, or someone with their permission; and *to plant in the wild some species of plants not native to this country.*

Methods of killing any protected and other animals are specified under the 1981 Act. For example, 'the use of self-locking snares, bows and crossbows, explosives (other than firearms) and live decoys' are prohibited. If a snare (which is allowable under the law) is set it must be inspected at least once a day.

Prohibited methods of killing birds include: gins, pole traps, snare, nets, bird line, electrical scaring devices, and poisons and the use of decoys.

Badgers are protected under the Badgers Act 1973 – as amended by the 1981 Wildlife and Countryside Act – and the hunting of deer and seals is regulated under separate Acts (Conservation of Seals Act 1970, Deer Act 1963, Deer (Scotland) Act 1959).

Responding to specific problems

Badger digging
It is an offence for anyone (including a landholder) to kill a badger without first obtaining a licence from MAFF.

(Killing includes snaring, the use of gin traps, gassing, poisoning and shooting.) You may tend, or kill – if it has no reasonable chance of recovery – an injured badger provided you can prove that you did not intentionally injure the animal yourself.

Despite this legal protection, badger persecution still continues, particularly in the South-West, Wales, Cumbria, the Yorkshire Dales and Cheshire. Badger digging is an illegal sport which usually takes place in the early hours of the morning. It involves putting terriers down a badger sett, digging out the badger, pulling it out of the sett with tongs (pincers) and disabling it in some way so that the dogs have a better chance of killing it.

If you suspect badger digging or baiting is occurring or has occurred:

> make notes on what you have seen – how many people – describe them if possible, the dogs – breed/number, and the equipment – spades, bags etc. Take down the car registration number;
> call the police;
> arrange to meet the police some distance from the sett and show them where to go on foot. Do not attempt to stop badger diggers yourself; they can be violent;
> contact your local badger protection/RSPCA group;
> contact the League Against Cruel Sports. They have offered a reward of up to £2,000 for information leading to a convinction for badger-hunting.

What to look out for:

> groups of men carrying spades and perhaps an iron bar or tongs accompanied by terriers;
> a number of cars parked in or near a field at night or in the early morning;
> a sett which has been dug out.

Be prepared. A Badger digger, if caught, has two standard defences: (i) that one of his dogs went down a badger sett without his knowing it and that he had to dig out the sett to get the dog out; and (ii) he was digging for foxes and was unaware the earth held badgers. (From the Gwent Badger Group Newsletter.)

Get to know where your local badger setts are – but make sure you do not disturb the badgers while doing so. Be especially vigilant in spring when badger digging is most likely to occur – though it does happen all year round.

The Gwent Badger Group have written an excellent booklet on badgers called *Briefly on Badgers*. It contains sections on badger watching, persecution, the law, and badgers and bovine tuberculosis. They have also made a film for the BBC 2 series 'Open Space' called 'Badgers in Gwent' which may be available for hire.

Barn owls

'The barn owl is an emblem of our traditional English farmland, floating in dreamy silence over misty meadows, the white sentinel of rustic fence post and moonlit roof top.' So wrote Colin Shawyer, Barn Owl Project Officer of the Hawk Trust. The Barn Owl project has been initiated because habitat destruction and lack of nesting and roosting sites in old barns, outbuildings and isolated trees have reduced the barn owl population considerably. The Trust provides leaflets on how to construct and site nest boxes for barn owls, and on conservation measures on farmland. It is also organising a national census.

Swans and anglers

Many swan deaths (the RSPCA suggests as many as 3,500 each year) are caused by lead poisoning. The swans ingest the lead weights discarded by anglers, in their search for grit – which helps their digestion. An estimated 250 tons of fishing lead is lost each year. The National Anglers' Council has produced a Code of Practice which emphasises not spilling shot or throwing it away on the bank or in water. Alternatives to lead shot – tungsten putty and stainless

Know the 'waterside code'

steel pin-weights – are already available and should be used instead of lead shot. Contact the RSPCA for details.

Nylon fishing line, if discarded, can also cause injury and death to birds. It should always be taken home.

If you find an ailing swan contact the RSPCA Wildlife Department. (Send for *Lead Poisoning in Swans – Report of the Nature Conservancy Council's Working Group 1981*.) The National Anglers' Council has also produced *The Waterside Code of Behaviour for Freshwater Fishermen* and a *Code of Practice for Handling Fish*.

Birds and the winter
The provision of food and water in winter, especially when the ground is frozen, is the best way to help birds. The erection of nest boxes and the creation of a wild garden with useful food plants will be much appreciated. For advice, write to the RSPB.

Road casualties
Many animals are run over by cars, especially at night, on

country lanes. Road casualties would be reduced if people drove more slowly. Is there a way of creating safer routes for badgers, hedgehogs, toads, deer, horses and sheep? Check with the county surveyor.

The following examples show just what a small number of people can achieve. They need money, but more than anything else they want others to follow their lead.

Toad Crossings

On the A40 east of Cheltenham in spring time travellers giggle at a temporary road sign – it asks drivers to slow down because this is an area where toads cross the road on the way to their breeding ground. Not funny for the toads who for generations have travelled the same way and who are no match for tubeless tyres. People do respond and perhaps it makes them think.

Farmers and other local people remember toads crossing here in their thousands before the build-up of traffic. When the Lewis's began their campaign to save them in 1979, the numbers had dwindled dramatically. Thanks to the dedication of two people and their friends who patrol the area through the night from February to April speeding the toads across the road, the numbers are building up. The Ministry of Transport have

February/March on the A40, Cheltenham

placed the signs but, for safety reasons, they will not reduce the high kerbs which pregnant toads find impossible to climb, neither will they allow collection sheets of polythene which could prevent the toads reaching the road and make the job of those minding their crossing easier. They still die. The Lewis's have now extended their work to care for all manner of animals and birds in difficulties locally. They are willing to advise anyone on toads. Write to: The British Wildlife Rescue Team, Hospital Field Centre, Little Shirtington, Cheltenham, Gloucestershire.

In 1984 as part of the European Campaign for the Water's Edge the British Herpetological Society ran a campaign with volunteers and the local county naturalist trusts to help toads, frogs and newts in their migrations to breed, using special fences which move the amphibians to points where they can be collected and then carried over the road to other obstruction to be released nearer to their breeding ponds.

Hedgehog Ladders

Cattle grids can be death traps to small animals. A campaign begun by Major Coles in Shropshire exhorts all with cattle grids to fit escape ramps – a rough surfaced slope of wood or concrete – to enable hedgehogs and other creatures to climb out of the hole. The society, founded in 1982, has taken off with such rapidity, the membership now extends to many overseas from USA and Australia to Japan – the hedgehog is unknown in these countries! Hedgehogs are very lovable creatures but as Dr Pat Morris points out in Newsletter No. 1 of the British Hedgehog Protection Society, they 'are not major pests, do not carry horrible diseases and are not worth a lot of money, nor are they threatened with imminent extinction. As a result, they come low in the list of priorities for government research grants and they lie outside the scope of many animals protection societies . . . so although everyone thinks of hedgehogs as familiar and well known animals, they are in fact one of the least studied of all British mammals.' The society, its popularity and usefulness in disseminating information about the hedgehog, is a monument to the strength of an idea and the resourcefulness of just one person.

Bats

Because bats have come to rely on houses and barns for roosting sites (their natural roosts – caves and hollow trees –

have largely disappeared) they have been given special protection under the Wildlife and Countryside Act.

'It is now an offence to damage, destroy or obstruct access to any place that a bat uses for shelter or protection or to disturb a bat while it is occupying such a place; and this applies even in houses and outbuildings. The only exception is for bats in the living area of a house.' (NCC, *Focus on Bats – their conservation and the law*.)

If you want to remove bats from your loft or to get the timber treated with wood preservatives in a loft which contains bats, you must consult the Nature Conservancy Council first for advice.

Under the Act it is also illegal for anyone without a licence to intentionally kill, injure, handle or possess a bat or to disturb a bat when it is roosting. Such measures are necessary because bat populations are declining so rapidly. 'The greater horseshoe bat has declined by over 98 per cent in a century and even the common bats have recently declined by about 50 per cent in two years.' (*Focus on Bats*.)

Information on ways in which to encourage bats by providing roosting sites is contained in the excellent NCC leaflet *Focus on Bats – their conservation and the law*, and from the Fauna and Flora Preservation Society.

The conservation of varieties of fruit and vegetables

As few as 30 plant species provide 95 per cent of our food, and few varieties of each are commercially exploited. If any of these varieties are wiped out by disease we are in trouble. Many old varieties are hardier, and more resistant to drought, pests and disease than the modern hybrids.

EEC legislation is reducing our choice of varieties as plant patenting legislation now prevents the sale of unregistered seeds. It is only financially viable for a seedman to register an old variety if he can sell over 5,000 packets a year. Several thousand vegetable varieties have vanished from the seed catalogues in the past twenty years.

Old varieties are generally less popular than new ones because they are often smaller, less colourful, less easy to package and may have blemishes. But most people will readily confess that their flavour is far superior. Their colourful names – such as the Martock Lean, Ragged Jack Kale, Cornish Gillyflower and Norfolk Biffins apples – are a party of our local history and genetic heritage.

Fortunately it is still legal to *exchange* the seeds of old vegetable varieties. The Henry Doubleday Research Association, spearheaded by the veteran campaigner for organically grown produce, Lawrence D. Hills, runs a seed library for its members. Members ('seed guardians') take on the responsibility of growing some seeds and returning a proportion of them to be stored by the Association. Mr Hills is always on the look-out for seeds of little-known varieties; contact him if you think you have some. For information, write to the Henry Doubleday Association, Covent Lane, Bocking, Braintree, Essex.

A number of vegetable sanctuaries – where old varieties are grown – are open to the public. They include Harlow Car Gardens, Harrogate, Yorkshire; Wakehurst Place, Sussex; Quarry Bank Mill, Styal, near Wimslow, Cheshire; Dean's Court, Wimborne, Dorset; and the Bishop's Palace Gardens, Wells, Somerset. Send a s.a.e. to the HDRA for further information – the leaflet, *Vegetable Sanctuaries*, costs 10p.

Apart from the Kew Collection a gene bank has been set up at the National Vegetable Research Station at Wellesbourne, near Stratford-upon-Avon, with funds from Oxfam. It has already collected 4,700 different kinds of seeds.

Although over 6,000 different varieties of apples have been recorded in the UK, only 300 varieties were available commercially in 1977. 'May we hope that everyone who plants trees will draw a map of his orchard with the names of the varieties on it, and nail it to one of the roof beams inside his attic to keep their names for others? The future owners may not even be able to identify the many apples, pears, plums and cherries from the past that still survive today.' This sensible advice was written by Lawrence D. Hills in the introduction to *The Fruit Finder* which lists the more uncommon varieties which are available from nurseries. (The leaflet costs 50p.)

If you cannot identify the fruit trees in your garden, the Royal Horticultural Society at Wisley, Ripley, Surrey, may be able to help. They run a Fruit Identification Department.

Scots Nurseries, Merriott, Somerset, and New Tree Nurseries, Canterbury, Kent, will take grafts of your favourite fruit trees, should you want more of them. The purchase of an apple or pear tree is an investment for life, so it is wise to make sure you really like the flavour of the fruit from the trees you choose. Some nurseries have fruit tasting days to help you make your choice. Information on the nurseries which participate in the scheme and fruit lasting days is available from the Apple and Pear Development Council, Unicorn House, The Pantiles, Tunbridge Wells, Kent. Tel: 0892 20255.

Ways to help to save old varieties of fruit and vegetables
Find out from the local horticultural or garden society about the varieties of fruit and vegetables which are peculiar to your locality.

Write to the HDRA for information about the Seed Library Scheme and see if you can help. If you do not have the expertise (this can be gained by participating in working weekends on organic farms), or a garden, you can always help by sending a donation to the Association.

Take over or create a *parish allotment or orchard* where people who are interested can tend and grow old local varieties.

Seed exchange: devise a method whereby seeds/cuttings can be exchanged amongst the people of the village. Make sure accurate records are kept.

Write a *village/parish cookery book* using local varieties of fruit/vegetables and local recipes handed down by generations of locals.

Record the memories of old residents about local varieties.

Interest your local horticultural or allotment society.

References and further reading

Main legislation: Wildlife and Countryside Act 1981 (HMSO, £6.35).

Conservation of plants and animals
CoEnCo, *Wild Plants; Reptiles & Amphibians* (leaflets).
Corbet, G. G. and Southern, H. N., *The Handbook of British Mammals*, 1977.
Gwent Badger Group, *Briefly on Badgers* (Gwent Badger Group, Elm Tree, Caer Licyn Lane, Langstone, Newport, Gwent NP6 2JZ.)
Harrison, M. L., *British Mammals*, 1952.
Hawk Trust, *The Construction and Siting of Nest Boxes for Barn Owls; The Barn Owl – Its Conservation on Farmland in Britain; Barn Owl Census of Britain and Ireland (1982–1984)*. (Available from the Hawk Trust, Freepost, Beckenham, Kent.)
National Anglers' Council, *The Waterside Code of Behaviour for Freshwater Fishermen; Code of Practice for Handling Fish* (NAC, 11 Cowgate, Peterborough PE1 1LZ.)
NCC, *Focus on Bats* (leaflet). *Lead Poisoning in Swans – Report of the Nature Conservancy Council's Working Group*, 1981. *Wildlife, the Law and You*, 1982 (free leaflet).
RSPB, *Wild Birds and the Law* (leaflet). Available from the RSPB, The Lodge, Sandy, Bedfordshire.)

Fruit and vegetables
Greenoak, F., *Forgotten Fruit*, 1983.
Hills, L. D., *Save Your Own Seed*, 50p; *Books, Products & Seeds for Organic Gardeners*, 15p; *Vegetable Sanctuaries*, 10p; *The Fruit Finder*, 50p. (All from the Henry Doubleday Assn, Covent Lane, Braintree, Essex.)
Mabey, R., *Food for Free*, 1975.
Mabey, R. and Greenoak, F., *Back to the Roots*, 1983.
Myers, N., *The Sinking Ark*, 1979.

11
Buildings

Houses live and die: there is a time for building
And a time for living and for generation
And a time for the wind to break the loosened pane
And to shake the wainscot where the field-mouse trots
And to shake the tattered arras woven with a silent motto.

T. S. Eliot, 'East Coker'

Why conserve them?

Despite their often substantial appearance, old buildings are very vulnerable – to change wrought simply by age, by weather and air pollution; to change brought about by the demands of modern times – new uses, new neighbours; to changes small, perhaps, but insidious – poor repair work and short-term fashion (like the ubiquitous new 'Georgian' door); and to the problems of increasing maintenance costs and disappearing skills.

Buildings of special historic and architectural importance may be easy to argue for on documentary and aesthetic grounds, but consider too the buildings of local importance, made from local materials by local craftsmen, which contain the minutiae of history of labours and skills and everyday needs of former times. Buildings of even the meanest kind can give delight simply by their appearance, position or association with people or events. Buildings have symbolic values, spiritual connections, political connotations, but usually our first feeling for them is an emotional one. Our culture and heritage are reflected in buildings whether grand or modest.

To conserve and re-use an old building rather than build

anew is to prevent a repeated exploitation of natural resources, and, like a farmer taking care of the soil, is good husbandry.

As with landscape and habitats the responsibility for conservation lies mainly with the owners. Without their goodwill, time and money and the effort of voluntary organisations like the Society for the Protection of Ancient Buildings, the Civic Trust and its affiliated local groups, many more locally prized buildings would have long disappeared. On the grander scale, the National Trust has responsibility for over 200 historic buildings. The expenditure on its properties reached £21.9 million in 1982. The degree of back-up to paper protection which the local authorities can offer for old buildings is limited by their will and their finances. 'Listing' (described below) draws attention to the value placed on a building but does not guarantee long life. Problems arise from (a) the original function of the building becoming outdated and the difficulty of conversion for new uses; (b) the lack of money or interest to carry out repairs or restoration; and (c) the delays in 'listing' caused by the need to resurvey – mainly through lack of manpower and finance.

In 1982 the Civic Trust for Wales and the Prince of Wales Committee surveyed an area comprising the three Glamorgans and Gwent and found that 42 per cent of the buildings considered to be of architectural or historic interest were unlisted. An extensive survey of neglected historic buildings carried out by the Kent Building Preservation Trust in 1980 found that 319 buildings of a listable standard were identified as being in a state of disrepair – only 137 of which were on the Statutory List. (*Crumbling Kent* n.d.).

Even those buildings which have been placed upon the Statutory List are vulnerable – 145 listed buildings were demolished in England in 1982 and a further 1,627 were partially demolished. Of the 523 applications for demolition, 72 were made by local authorities, mainly district councils. In Wiltshire 80 per cent of the applications for demolition of listed buildings between 1975 and 1981 were successful. One of the reasons is money, or the lack of it. Wiltshire (1982) needed over £100,000 to help maintain their 9,000 listed buildings. They received £12,000. In the Glamorgans and Gwent 1 in 20 listed buildings were in a state of disrepair and at least 200 buildings were in danger for this reason. (*A Wasting Asset*, Febuary 1983.)

Conservation of old buildings, however small and 'ordinary', can help in a general sense to up-grade the local environment. Some villages and owners of individual buildings have found that this makes economic sense too. Individual buildings need attention but so also does the general environment – much can be achieved by tidying, painting, revitalising and repairing the railings, gates, lamp posts, paving stones, and other details of the everyday scene.

Conservation should also apply to the wider town and village environment. Much new building is going on in the countryside; in order to retain the character of the settlement while enhancing its functions, much care is needed.

Ways of conserving buildings

Statutory methods: listed buildings

Under the Town and Country Planning Act 1971, the Secretary of State for the Environment has the duty to compile lists of buildings of special architectural or historic interest. The purpose of listing is two-fold: to make local authorities aware of these buildings and to give the buildings some degree of protection. Owners are prevented from making any alterations to a listed building which would affect its character in any way, inside or out, or from demolishing it, without having first gained permission from the district council or the Secretary of State in the case of grade I and II buildings. By 1982 there were

287,744 listed buildings in England alone, 7,549 of which were added during that year. The criteria for selection are:

All buildings built before 1700 which survive in anything like their original condition are listed.

Most buildings of 1700 to 1840 are listed, though selection is necessary.

Between 1840 and 1914 only buildings of definite quality and character are listed, and the selection is designed to include the principal works of the principal architects.

A start has been made on listing selected buildings of high quality of 1914 to 1939.

In choosing buildings, particular attention is paid to:

Special value within certain types, either for architectural or planning reasons or as illustrating social and economic history (for instance, industrial buildings, railway stations, schools, hospitals, theatres, town halls, markets, exchanges, alms-houses, prisons, lock-ups, mills).

Technological innovation or virtuosity (for instance cast iron, prefabrication, or the early use of concrete).

Association with well-known characters or events.

Group value, especially as examples of town planning (for instance, squares, terraces or model villages).

The buildings are classified in grades to show their relative importance as follows:

Grade I. These are buildings of exceptional interest (only about 4 per cent of listed buildings so far are in this grade).

Grade II*. These are particularly important buildings of more than special interest.

Grade II. These are buildings of special interest, which warrant every effort being made to preserve them.

(DOE, *A Guide to the Legislation on the Listing of Historic Buildings in England/Wales.*)

Listed Bridge near Fifehead Neville, Dorset

The definitions are widely drawn and can include tombs, walls, milestones, bridges, and so on. Contact the conservation officer/historic buildings architect in the county or district planning office for local information.

The statutory lists, to which the public have access, are held by the planning department of the relevant county and district council; the National Monuments Record (DOE, Fortress House, 23 Savile Row, London WLX 2HE); the Conservation and Land Division of the Welsh Office (Room G 046, Crown Building, Cathays Park, Cardiff CF1 3NQ); and the Historic Buildings Branch, Scottish Development Department, 25 Drumsheugh Gardens, Edinburgh EH3 7RN.

Using the legislation and Secretary of State for the Environment, local authorities and members of the public can initiate a variety of actions to protect buildings.

Spot listing. Members of the public can bring to the attention of DOE/Welsh Office buildings which are threatened with demolition or unsympathetic alteration. In urgent cases these buildings will be immediately assessed and added to the statutory list if they qualify. Approach the county or district conservation officer for initial advice, stressing the urgency of the problem.

A *building preservation notice* can be issued by the district council. This protects a threatened building which has not yet been listed, for up to six months, while the Secretary of State/Welsh Office decides whether to add it to the statutory list.

Listed building's consent is needed from the district council (or Secretary of State for grades I and II*) for demolition/ alteration/extension/work which would affect the character of a listed building in any way. (Permission also has to be sought for the demolition of *any* building in a conservation area.) Local authorities must not allow demolition or alterations without consulting the relevant amenity societies. The local authority has to advertise any applications and erect site notices. Under the 1980 Planning and Land Act this provision has been extended to cover buildings which affect the setting of a listed building. Comments from the public on listed building consent must be sent to the Secretary of State, who will decide whether the decision should be left to the local authority, or whether he should 'call in' the application for his own decision. If listed building consent is refused, the applicant or local authority can appeal and ask the Secretary of State to hold a local inquiry. If listed building consent is granted, the Royal Commission on Historical Monuments must be given at least one month in which to make a record of the building before it is demolished or altered.

If a local authority considers that a listed building is not being properly preserved, it may serve a *repairs notice* which specifies the work which must be done. If the owner does not comply within two months, the local authority can make a *compulsory purchase order* (with the consent of the Secretary of State).

If a building is unoccupied, the local authority can serve notice on the owner giving seven days' notice of intention to do urgent repairs to secure the building's preservation and recover costs from the owner.

If the owner deliberately neglects a building in order to redevelop it, the local authority may acquire the building at a price which excludes the value of the site for redevelopment.

The local authority may also serve a *dangerous structure notice* if a property is run down. It requires the owner to make it safe or to demolish – after obtaining listed buildings consent.

Owners of listed buildings can, in some cases, get *grants* or *loans* to help them with repair or maintenance.

Owners of listed buildings can serve a *purchase notice* on a local authority (after making attempts to secure alternative uses by seeking planning permission and being refused listed building consent) requiring it to buy the building. (This often inhibits local authorities from issuing repairs notices in case the owners respond by demanding that the council buy the buildings which it cannot afford.) Buildings preservation trusts are now stepping in to back the local authority and may be able to purchase the building themselves if necessary. The Secretaries of State have reserve powers enabling them to serve repair notices on local authorities which fail to preserve listed buildings in their own ownership.

Many of these powers are little used. They need political will, individual effort and money to make them work. Some county and district councils need encouragement. Lobbying councillors and supporting conservation officers to create a political climate of caring at the local level can do much to help those old buildings which are not even listed.

Statutory methods: conservation areas
It is possible under the Town and Country Planning Act 1971 and the Town and Country Amenities Act 1974 to protect whole streets or areas 'of special architectural or historic interest, the character or appearance of which it is desirable to preserve or enhance'. District councils may designate 'conservation areas' and here special attention must be paid to the appearance of the area when planning

Listed Cottage Hazelbury Bryan Dorset

permissions are given. No buildings may be demolished, no trees cut without permission of the local authority or Secretary of State. Anything which might affect the character of the area must be advertised and the public have a right to express their views.

Enhancement schemes can be drawn up by the district council. These and 'Town Schemes' may attract grant aid through the Historic Buildings Council of the DOE for repairs and improvements.

Local groups, with district council approval, may approach the DOE for conservation area grants if they are well organised and can raise funds elsewhere as well.

It is likely that the local authority has appointed a conservation officer/historic buildings officer within the planning department, whose responsibility it will be to coordinate all listed building and conservation area activities. Over 5,000 conservation areas had been designated in England and Wales by April 1983 – 60 per cent of these are in rural areas. Some of them have boundaries drawn wide enough to encompass areas of historic landscape too.

In order to control the smaller elements of buildings which are not listed, especially with conservation areas, the district council may make *Article 4 Directions*. These bring under planning control classes of development normally not needing planning permission – things like changing roof lines (where a dormer window might alter the character of the whole street, for example), shape of windows and so on.

Heckington Station Yard and Mill Conservation Area

Heckington Village Trust struggled for over a year to persuade the district council to designate this conservation area – many meetings and finally a case with the Ombudsman secured the first industrial conservation area in Lincolnshire. 'Heckington Railway Station lies at the centre of a group of 19th-century buildings which together create an environment from the past which has a character worthy of conservation and adaptation to modern requirements. A number of authorities and individuals are involved in the ownership and/or development of the buildings and land. For several years now, the Village Trust has been endeavouring to secure a comprehensive plan which would give coordinated guidance to all proposals for rehabilitation or development so that they eventually came together to ehance the area, rather than detract from it. The buildings in the vicinity of the station include:

the typical decorated barge-board gable-ended 19th-century signal box; the early 19th-century eight-sailed windmill in the ownership of the county council which has been repaired by them and made available for public inspection; the railway tavern and coach house now used for residential purposes; the disused four-storey seed warehouse, the Pearoom, and adjoining storage building; engine and storage sheds previously part of the railway operation; the disused sidings which are now zoned for industrial purposes.

The Village Trust was concerned when it heard that British Rail had sold the railway sidings and buildings thereon, including the station master's house, to the district council, and feared that the procedure being followed by the district council in selling off sections of the land without an overall plan would lead to a deterioration in the environment, as well as an inefficient arrangement from the point of view of the users. British Rail have only retained the former waiting rooms and ticket office on the north platform and the shelter on the southern platform.

When it was learned that British Rail proposed to demolish the station and the shelter on the south side, replacing them with open concrete shelters, the Village Trust approached British Rail to see whether, by a joint effort, it would be possible to repair and maintain the existing buildings, putting some of the accommodation to practical use for village and local purposes. After discussion meetings at the station, agreement was reached that the Village Trust, supported by the South Lincolnshire Archaeological Unit and in cooperation with British Rail, carry out works of repair and conversion so that the larger waiting room and ticket office was available for meetings, offices and museum purposes, whilst the smaller waiting room would be rehabilitated for use by the public.

It was proposed to exhibit railways posters and photographs of railways events in this part of the country on the walls of the new waiting room, and in the meeting room of the Village Trust and Archaeological Unit to arrange for changing exhibitions on local history and archaeology. Future developments, however, are not confined to the physical condition of the buildings, for the basic reason for rehabilitation was to make a pleasant environment for railway passengers and enable the Village Trust and the Archaeological Unit to carry on its work for the people of Heckington and South Lincolnshire. Regular meetings are now being held at the railway station as part of a programme to develop a Heritage Workshop. These take the form of study groups to build up information on local history and archaeology.

The Pearoom now houses craft workshops, with hopes of a heritage centre and museum of South Lincolnshire life. In addition, the eight-sailed windmill will be used to display the interesting implements and elements of milling in the past.'

(The Heckington Village Trust)

Vigilance and survey

Find out from the planning department of your district council which buildings are listed in your locality. Make a note of the buildings and their addresses so you can then look at them yourself. Make a note of the reasons why they have been listed.

Find out from your district and county council how far the process of surveying and relisting is progressing.

If the county council conservation team has not already made a survey of the listed buildings in your area which are neglected and in need of repair, put pressure on them to make one. Keep a constant eye on the listed buildings. If you feel they are in need of attention, contact your local amenity group and decide how to approach the district council.

Contact the voluntary amenity societies which are concerned with the appearance and well-being of the locality – for example, your local civic society (over 1,000 local amenity societies are registered with the Civic Trust), rural community council, WI, buildings preservation trust or CPRE branch. Your local library or citizen's advice bureau will be able to give you names and addresses, or look in the telephone directory. Find out what the society is doing. You can either persuade them to take up your concern or help them with one of their projects. They are in constant touch with local government and will be able to advise you on how, when and where to exert pressure. Learn from them. Read their reports/proceedings.

Find out as much as you can about the history of your locality from the library/county museum, publications by the local history society, etc. Do a building survey (see pp.255-6). The Society for the Protection of Ancient Buildings are asking for volunteers to help with a Domesday survey of barns – no special expertise is needed.

Make your own record of old buildings which you feel are worthy of listing or other protection and discuss this with the amenity society. Encourage the society to maintain a register. Give your final list to the district/county council and ask them to consider it. It will carry more weight if this list comes from an amenity body/residents group than from an individual. Send a copy to the local newspaper if necessary.

Do a village appraisal, ask the district council to designate a conservation area, work out a plan for improvements to the village scene (see pages 149-50).

If a new owner takes over a building you care about, be extra vigilant. If a new housing estate is to be built, encourage the local council to negotiate high standards of design and extra green space, ponds, etc. for the village.

'Crumbling Kent'

Read the local newspaper regularly. Look out for the public notices and columns which show the planning applications. The district council will have to advertise in a local paper if it wishes to permit the demolition of a listed building, new buildings, etc.

Make good use of your parish/district/county councillors. Discuss your concerns with them and send them copies of your research and findings. Make sure they are discussed in the relevant council meetings.

Attend parish council meetings and the planning committee meetings of the district and county councils, and/or read the minutes of their meetings. Make sure you know what is going on.

Make sure the district council uses the powers it possesses to issue a building preservation notice, hold a local inquiry, issue a repairs notice, use its powers of compulsory purchase, serve a dangerous structure notice, make article 4 directions and designate conservation areas etc.

In the last resort, remember to use your MP and the local ombudsman (via your councillor) if you feel that your district or county council is not carrying out its statutory duty (see pages 288-9).

Conversion of old buildings for re-use

In the past decade there has been a phenomenal growth in the formation of buildings preservation trusts which take on the work of renovating buildings of national or local importance. In 1982 there were 60 such trusts and in the last ten years about 200 buildings have been restored by them. They have been able to achieve this by the use of a revolving fund administered by the Architectural Heritage Fund, an independent charity administered by the Civic Trust. The buildings preservation trusts secure a loan from the Architectural Heritage Fund and find the balance of the funds from local sources to purchase a building which is in desperate need of repair. It is hoped that when the building is sold or rented, the profit – after the repayment of the loans – can be put towards the renovation of another building. Most building preservation trusts will only step in as a last resort to undertake work that owners cannot do themselves. Some trusts are independent charities, others are administered by county councils.

Many building preservation trusts keep lists of local craftsmen and set up material banks where irreplaceable materials saved during demolition can be collected, cleaned and restored.

Some trusts are launched specifically to safeguard the future of one property; others move on to other buildings once they have restored their first building. In addition to some county-wide trusts (which can offer financial guarantees to small trusts), regional trusts have also been set up in the North-East and North-West of England on the initiative of the civic trusts in those areas. A new national British Historic Buildings Trust has also been set up to operate in areas where trusts do not exist and to 'take on the really frighteningly large projects that a local Trust cannot possibly have the resources to deal with'.

A celebrated example of renovation is Derby's Railway Cottages which were about to be demolished to make way for a major road scheme. The Derby Civic Society campaigned for the recognition of the social and historical importance of the cottages and for the creation of a conservation area. The Victorian Society, the Society for the Protection of Ancient Buildings and Save Britain's Heritage supported the campaign, and the ability of the Derbyshire Historic Buildings Trust to purchase the buildings and renovate them finally secured their existence. The whole triangle of the 57 terraced cottages has been restored and improved and all have been sold.

'In order to increase and diversify farm incomes and to create alternative employment opportunities in rural areas, the Development Commission has set up a scheme for grant-aiding the conversion of redundant farm buildings for craft or light industrial use.' The scheme, administered by CoSIRA, was originally limited to villages and towns with less than 10,000 population in the Development Commission's Special Investment Areas. In March 1983 the scheme was extended to cover conversion of *any* suitable building for *any* employment creating use – in the Special Investment Areas and now in the new Rural Development Areas.

The Countryside Commission, the British Tourist Authority and regional tourist boards are all active in promoting recreational and farm-based tourism projects, using old barns and other farm buildings. Contact your regional organiser for information.

The rural community councils have also been prominent in supporting local initiatives, especially in promoting surveys of potentially suitable redundant buildings.

All kinds of organisations need premises and often collaboration can be useful in re-using old buildings. County naturalists' trusts have converted a wide variety of old buildings for use as headquarters, interpretative centres etc. – for example, Brough Beech Oast House, by the Kent

Trust; Stables at Fyne Court, by the Somerset Trust; Willsford Mill, by the Avon Trust; Earls Hill Barn, by the Shropshire Trust; Penmuenpool Signal Post, by the North Wales Trust; and Llandyfeisant Church, Castle Woods, by the West Wales Trust.

The Henley Award is organised by the Country Landowners' Association and the Council for the Protection of Rural England (sponsored by Blue Circle Industries). Biennial awards are given in recognition of outstanding work to restore or convert old farm buildings to modern use while preserving the architectural and aesthetic characteristics of the site. (For other awards of grants see pages 291-303).

An encouraging initiatve has been taken by *Wiltshire Small Industries Trust* (based with CoSIRA in Salisbury), which aims to purchase, or take on long lease, redundant buildings which can be converted for light industrial use. These can be let or sold to small firms.

Many modest initiatives have saved barns or walls from destruction or neglect. Burrator Parish Council on the edge of Dartmoor even owns the local pub. This not only preserves its character as the locals would wish but it also makes enough profit for the parish not to need to levy a local rate.

Pennine Heritage and Burnley Borough Council have together produced a scheme for *Queen Street Mill, Harle Syke*. This nineteenth-century cotton weaving mill established as a worker's producer cooperative is to be subdivided in part to form small industrial units; the remainder is to be kept and a new weaving company set up to use the original machinery. The whole mill will be promoted as a visitor centre. It is hoped to create at least 100 new jobs to replace those lost when the mill closed in 1982. *Nutclough Mill in Hebden Bridge* will also be restored and converted for small firms and public facilities by Pennine Heritage, Birchcliffe Centre, Hebden Bridge, W. Yorks.

Prema Project
It is a community arts centre, for the practice and promotion of cultural activities in South West Gloucestershire.

'Prema' is a Sanskrit word, connoting selflessness and the impulse of human beings to give what they can and share what they have.

The physical conversion of the Chapel was largely carried out with local and voluntary labour. The building work was done by a team of young people from Shire Training workshops. This organisation, with which Prema retains a fruitful connection, was established as a means of helping the young unemployed to acquire marketable skills and work experience: it forms part of the Youth Opportunities Programme, funded by the Manpower Services Commission.

There was also invaluable assistance by a party of volunteers from Leyhill Open Prison.

The ground floor of the Chapel now comprises four workshops/ studios for working artists, and includes a fully-equipped pottery (with kilns), and an etching and engraving workshop with printing presses. It is on this floor that most of Prema's day-to-day activities are carried on, and where regular classes are provided for adults and children in drawing, painting, etching, engraving and claywork. Special weekly classes are also held for unemployed young people.

The centre also provides week and week-end courses conducted by visiting artists and craftsmen in specialist subjects, such as film animation and puppet-making. For a period in 1981 a professional musical instrument maker worked at the Chapel, introducing others to his techniques.

The upper floor occupies the whole roof-space of the old Chapel, with a fine set of roof-timbers in a rare and remarkable configuration, and large windows on all sides which command a view over the village and surroundings. Here there is to be a regular programme of exhibitions, theatre, music, films, poetry-readings and other events, involving the participation of professional artists both local and from further afield. The main part of the upper rooms is available for hire.

(Prema Project, 1983)

New housing estates and the villages

Many villages have been spoiled by housing estates constructed by speculative builders. Often the houses are of unsuitable design overwhelming the villages's historical character. On the other hand, villages where all development is forbidden cannot meet the needs of their young people and eventually become museums, beautiful but dead.

An incident in Rutland illustrates what can be done by

concerted popular action to bend a developer's actions in the direction of the village's own interest.

South Luffenham is a fine limestone village in rolling agricultural country. It had, however, lost many of its amenities over two decades. The railway station had closed, so had the school. One pub had been converted into a house. The church no longer had a resident vicar.

In 1972 a local farmer obtained outline planning permission to build twenty houses on a ten-acre field in the heart of the village. He sold the field to a speculative developer. With the proceeds he rebuilt his livestock yard and so added to the prosperity of one of the three farms round which the economy of the village is organised.

The developer allowed the field to lie unused throughout the depression of the mid-seventies. It was not until 1977 that he applied for detailed planning permission – to erect not twenty but *sixty* dwellings on the field. By this time local government boundaries had been reorganised and the new planning authority was less subservient to developers' and farmers' interests. The South Luffenham parish council was also now more vigilant. There was an outcry against the proposal.

South Luffenham was scheduled within the county plan as a village for 'limited infill' only. It was felt that the developer's scheme was going to change the village drastically for the worse. The firm, it was suggested, had already made considerable profit out of Rutland and

New village green in South Luffenham, Rutland

spoiled several villages in the process. On the other hand, it was not only the business interests in the village (local shopkeepers and publicans) who saw advantage in having additional housing. No one wanted the village to become moribund.

Intense negotiations ensued between the planning authority (Rutland District Council), the parish council and the developer. Public meetings were called in the village. The local district councillor suggested that permission be given for a smaller number of dwellings but that, in exchange, the village should get something from the deal.

There existed a rule of thumb specifying a certain amount of open space within and between new housing. On other estates where such space had been provided by the developer the newcomers buying houses on the estate had tended to see it as something for their own exclusive use, not for the village and its children. South Leffenham Parish Council decided to make the minimum condition for their acquiescence in a development scheme by this builder the gift of some of his land to the village. The villagers as a whole should be able to decide on its use. They set as their goal an acre and a half at the end of the field nearest the centre of the village, a plot containing some fine sycamore trees. It would become a village green and playground.

The struggle became more acute when it was found that the builder had delayed so long in his intended development that planning permission had meanwhile lapsed. He re-applied. The district council turned down the scheme entirely. The builder set in motion an appeal to the Secretary of State and threatened legal action. He made it know that, if he won, he would not agree even to the promised village green. It would be sixty houses and no compromise.

Some members of the parish council were now frankly sorry for the builder, whose prime building site, through a mere technicality, had reverted to cheap grazing pasture. Others, however, feared that if development rights were to be altogether denied now, it would be only a matter of time before a more sympathetic council gave the go-ahead. It would be difficult meanwhile to hold together the militant resolve of the village.

A compromise was therefore reached. The builder got permission for thirty-six houses on the outer part of the field. The village acquired the inner end as public open space. It is perhaps the only amenity that it has gained, among the many that it has lost, in this century.

(Cynthia Cockburn, 1983)

More recently Bishops Caundle Parish Council in Dorset negotiated the modification of a new housing development incorporating all sorts of environmental features including a village green.

Pewsey Parish Council, Wiltshire, anticipating the need for green space, had put aside money from the rate precept into a capital fund. With the help of this and a generous legacy they have purchased three areas of land, two small and one of about seven acres. The County Structure Plan included the possibility of 300 new houses being built in the years up to 1991. The green spaces – some with woodland walks and seats, some to be left as streams, wetland and nature reserve – will provide old and new residents with amenities all can share. Even the developers are attempting to enhance the village atmosphere with a recently built group of 100 houses which includes new hedges and ditches in the gardens.

In other villages the story is less optimistic.'I would like to stress that conservation is a sore point with the older inhabitants of W****. We have seen . . . beautiful trees uprooted, likewise the cricket field which was the focal point of the village has been forfeited for another housing estate.'

Help and advice can be sought from the district and county planning offices. The county planning departments have compiled the 'National Register of Conservation Craft Skills in the Building Industry', which lists local firms, The Crafts Council coordinates the register and may help if there is no one in your local area with necessary expertise (see p. 187- Crafts). The Conservation Source Book produced in 1979 lists craft organisations and societies.

Contact the Civic Trust – ask for its publications list – and affiliated societies, and consider subscribing to its bi-monthly magazine *Heritage Outlook* which is full of useful information and examples.

The Society for the Protection of Ancient Buildings (founded by William Morris in 1877) was the first body to concern itself with the repair and protection of Britain's architectural heritage and today the Society performs an important role as a leading expert on aspects of the maintenance and preservation of old buildings. 'No project is too small for our attention . . . ' SPAB will advise on problems affecting old buildings, investigate cases of threatened buildings, advise on designation of conservation areas, organise lectures and run courses on repair; it also maintains an index of threatened buildings available for purchase and produces a range of publications. It is promoting a Domesday Survey of barns at the parish level. Contact it for survey forms and leaflets on agricultural and new uses of barns, grants for barn conservation and conversion. Volunteers for parish barn surveys are urgently needed.

There are many smaller societies which have been successfully campaigning for decades for the protection of buildings, villages and towns: The Vernacular Architecture Group and many independent archaeologists are heavily involved in surveying and classifying domestic buildings.

For sources of finance see Chapter 17 and the addresses in, Chapter 18 – particularly DOE, Development Commission, Architectural Heritage Fund, Historic Buildings Grants, local authorities, and the Ecology Building Society.

Statutory agencies

For The Historic Buildings and Monuments Commission and the D.O.E., see pages 18 and 21.

References and further reading

Main Acts:
Town and Country Planning Act 1971
Town and Country Amenities Act 1974 (Conservation Areas)
Local Government Planning and Land Act 1980

ADAS, *Converting Old Farm Buildings* Booklet 2407, 1982.
The Architectural Heritage Fund Annual Reports.
British Tourist Authority,*Britain's Historic Buildings: A Policy for their future use*,£3.00
Buchanan, T., *Photographing historic buildings for the record* , H.M.S.O.
Civic Trust, *Pride of Place – How to improve your surroundings* 1974, £2.00.
Clifton-Taylor, A., *The Pattern of English Buildings*, 1972.
Current Archaeology – journal.
Derbyshire Historic Building Trust, *A List of Historic Buildings thought to be*

empty, neglected or in need of repair in the County of Derbyshire, April 1983.

Design Council and RPTI, *Streets Ahead*, 1975, £6.50.

DOE (& Welsh Office), *A Guide to the Legislation on the listing of Historic Buildings in England/Wales* (leaflet).

Development Commission/CoSIRA, *New Life for Old Buildings* (leaflet).

De Zouch-Hall, R. (ed.), *Bibliography of the Vernacular Architecture Group*, 1972.

English Tourist Board, *English Heritage Monitor 1983*.

Essex County Council, *Conservation in Essex No. 4. Historic Buildings* 50p; *The Essex Countryside – Historic Barns*, 1983, £2.00.

Hampshire Buildings Preservation Trust Ltd Annual Report 1981, 1982.

Harvey, N., *A History of Farm Buildings in England and Wales*, Vernacular Architecture/Buildings Society, 1970.

Kamm, J., *Saving Old Farm Buildings – Hampshire's Heritage*, Hampshire County Council Planning Department.

The Kent Building Preservation Trust, *Crumbling Kent* £1.30.

Mercer, E., *English Vernacular Houses*, HMSO, 1975.

Michelmore, D.J.H., *Bibliography of the Vernacular Architecture Group*, 2nd edition, 1976.

MAFF, *New Uses for Surplus Farm Buildings*, Leaflet 805, 1982.

Percival, A., *Understanding Our Surroundings – A manual of urban interpretation*, Civic Trust, 1979.

The Prince of Wales Committee and The Civic Trust for Wales, *A Wasting Asset*, 1983, £2.50.

Scottish Development Department (Historic Buildings Branch), *Scotland's Listed Buildings – a guide to their protection*.

SPAB. leaflets on barns – grants, agricultural uses, new uses, plus survey forms (free).

See also the county volumes by N.Pevsner for descriptions of buildings valued by architects.

12
Farming and Pollution

We spray the fields and scatter
  The poison on the ground
So that no wicked wild flowers
  Upon our farm be found.

John Betjeman, 'Harvest Hymn'

Most farmers are conscientious and sensitive to the needs and feelings of the community. The long hours, dedication and endurance of the small farmer, in particular, are greatly admired by most people and we are not wishing to undervalue the work they do or contribute to their workload. But there are always those who are in the business for short-term gain or who are prepared to take short cuts and who do not take into consideration the effects of their work on the community at large. We are often cajoled by the National Farmers' Union (NFU) and others about the bad behaviour of visitors to farms as if the farming community alone is capable of sensitive behaviour. Those of us who have endured the smells of slurry or 'bad' silage, thick mud coating sections of road, farm machinery and fertiliser bags dumped at field corners, smoke from straw-burning blotting out the sun and ruining the washing, polluted rivers and streams, know that farmers could sometimes take more care.

Farming practice dominates the countryside, so while bad neighbourliness and pollution are just as likely to emanate from small industries, quarrying and even households, the extensiveness of agriculture and the number of poisons in everyday use must be acknowledged.

We hope the following will give a set of procedures to help cope with agricultural pollution in various forms.

Remember that pollution occurs by mistake as well as from bad management, so be prepared to give the farmer the benefit of the doubt in the first instance – he may be just as upset as you are.

Be tolerant, but not over-indulgent – don't complain at the first horrid smell. However, the careless pollution of rivers and unnecessary destruction of wild life by pesticides is unforgivable and should in no way be tolerated. Julian Huxley has said that because of pesticides 'we are losing half the subject matter of English poetry'.

The amount of information available to farmers on pollution control and wild life conservation is enormous. The Ministry of Agriculture, Fisheries and Food (MAFF), the Agricultural Development and Advisory Service (ADAS), the National Farmers' Union (NFU), the Country Landowners' Association (CLA), the Farming and Wildlife Advisory Group (FWAG), the Nature Conservancy Council (NCC) and the Countryside Commission all produce leaflets and codes of practice. So there is little excuse for ignorance nowadays.

Planning controls and agriculture

In general terms agricultural land is exempt from planning controls. It was omitted from the 1947 Town and Country Planning Act because it was thought farmers should be left alone to feed us and planning should only apply to urban activities. These notions have been encouraged by farmers and MAFF ever since.

A general policy regarding agricultural land will be contained in the county's structure plan and in the district council's local plans. However, planning permission is required for agricultural land if there is a proposed change of use and the land service of ADAS must be consulted on applications for development for non-agricultural purposes of 10 acres or more. In other words, a farmer may rip out a 1,000-year-old hedge or cut down an ancient wood and grow barley without planning permission, but he will need it if he plans to build houses or accommodate caravans, or cut a white horse on his chalk down.

There are some differences of interpretation about whether intensive livestock units are covered by planning controls or not. Much depends on whether the feedstuff is produced by the farm on which the intensive unit stands or if it is imported from elsewhere. If the farm does not produce 'the bulk' of the foodstuff itself then it should be subject to the planning system. There are proposals to bring certain intensive livestock units under planning control if they are close to residential properties.

There is further exemption from planning controls for farm buildings under 40 feet (12 metres) in height covering an area of less than 465 square metres (5,000 square feet), provided they are 25 metres from a trunk or classified road. New buildings within existing units are also exempt, provided the existing building is two years old or more or is separated from the new one by a distance of 90 metres (100 yards) or more.

Limited controls include the use of Landscape Areas Special Development Orders in three national parks to regulate the design and appearance of farm buildings. Listed farm buildings are subject to the same listed building controls as non-agricultural buildings, and farm houses and workers' cottages are subject to normal planning controls.

If you have any worries about the siting, design or size of a proposed agricultural building after discussions with the farmer and you cannot come to an amicable agreement you can try approaching the following:

parish council (if the farmer is chairman or influential on this or other councils then your chances via this route are thin);
the local ADAS office;
county planning officers;

district council;
local CPRE branch or civic amenity society;
in national parks, the national park authority.

Water pollution

Farm slurry

Great changes in livestock farming have taken place in Britain during the last twenty years. Nowadays there are many more intensive livestock units and there are many more animals per farm than ever before and as a consequence problems with the disposal of the animals' excreta (slurry) have arisen. About 170 million tonnes of undiluted excreta are produced by farm animals in the UK each year. About a third of this comes from animals kept indoors, the rest from grazing animals. The amount of excreta produced by farm animals in the UK is equivalent to that of 150 million people. Most of this is applied to the land untreated (the cows could have done this themselves) whilst sewage plants are needed for human waste.

Slurry can pollute rivers and streams. Because it contains so much nitrogen and phosphorous some green algae thrive and starve fish and other water life of oxygen. The slurry gets into watercourses either because the lagoons and tanks are defective or over-filled or because the slurry is applied to the land in excessive amounts or when it is waterlogged or frozen.

Between 1977 and 1981 the number of farmers convicted for polluting watercourses rose by 250 per cent (*Times*, 28/4/83).

In 1983 the Wessex Water Authority said that farmers were responsible for fouling a record number of waterways that year. Twelve convictions have been obtained by the Water Authority with a dozen more prosecutions pending. Fines up to £3,000 have been imposed. Some enterprising farmers are now building methane digesters which use the slurry to produce electricity for the farm.

Nitrate levels in water supplies

There is increasing concern about the high levels of nitrates in some water supplies, especially in areas such as East Anglia where arable farming predominates and there is extensive use of nitrogenous fertilisers. Sewage effluent, and the ploughing up of grassland, which causes the release of large quantities of nitrates that are bound up in the soil, are contributory causes. High nitrate levels in water are dangerous to babies and are increasingly suspected of causing cancer.

The following suggestions for action are taken from *Nitrates*, a leaflet prepared by Friends of the Earth:

write to your local water authority and find out the levels of nitrates in your tap water.

If they seem high – around or above 50 milligrams per litre – try to find out where the supply comes from and what causes the high levels of nitrates.

If an inadequate sewage works is the cause, press the water authority to improve sewage treatment provisions. Contact your local councillors about this matter too, and ask them to bring pressure to bear on the water authority.

If you live in a rural area, campaign for planning controls on agriculture to restrict deep ploughing above ground water sources.

Individual farmers are unlikely to want to give up high fertilizer use until more information is available through MAFF and ADAS. Ask your MP to write to the Minister of Agriculture for information and comment on fertilizer use and nitrate pollution in your locality. Support local organic farmers and Land Heritage , a new charity which buys land which will be protected in perpetuity – farmed organically by suitable tenants.

Silage

In recent years there has been a large increase in the

production of silage, and according to Wessex Water Authority the liquor running off from a leaking silage clamp is 200 times stronger than sewage and by far the strongest polluting waste. The NFU has commented that pollution due to silage effluent is probably the single most frequent cause of prosecutions brought by water authorities against farmers. Pollution can be avoided by proper construction and by siting silage clamps well away from watercourses.

Sheep dips
Carelessly disposed-of sheep dips (used against infestations such as sheep scab) can also pollute watercourses as they contain a very toxic pesticide, lindane (gamma HCH). A MAFF code of practice advises farmers how to dispose of the used dip – by using a soil soak-away, or by spreading it on the nearest suitable level area of soil provided there is no chance of its seeping into sewers, ditches or watercourses. The code also advises farmers to consult water authorities on the siting and construction of the dips.

MAFF informs the water authorities of the main dipping times (usually 8–10 weeks from 1 September) and district councils are informed about the location of the sheep farms.

The disposal of pesticide containers and surplus pesticides
Recently thousands of fish in the river Torridge in Devon died because a farmer had buried cans of pesticides – dieldrin and aldrin – by the river. The farmer then sold the land and the new farmer inadvertently dug up and damaged the cans in the process of constructing a new building. These problems arise when records of pesticide disposal are not kept. A MAFF code of practice also specifies that used, empty and cleaned containers should be crushed and buried 18 inches deep, well away from boreholes, watercourses and ponds. As 1½ million 25-litre drums of pesticides are sold to farmers each year, the disposal of these containers poses real problems.

Fighting pollution

The Anglers' Cooperative Association (ACA) does an excellent job in fighting river pollution and in taking the polluters to court: 'The ACA has handled more than 1000 cases of pollution, recovered hundreds of thousands of pounds in damages to enable club and riparian owners to restore their fisheries.' The ACA has an excellent leaflet called *What to do in case of pollution*. It is summarised below.

Under common law every riparian owner or tenant is entitled 'to have the water flowing past his land in its natural state of purity. If there is any infringement of this right, the owner or tenant (with the assistance of the ACA if required) can apply to the courts for an injunction to restrain the polluter. If the offender disobeys the injunction and continues the pollution he is guilty of contempt of court and can be imprisoned. Where riparian owners or tenants have suffered material or financial loss, or loss of enjoyment of their fishing or amenities, damages can be awarded to the riparian owner or tenant. This law applies to rivers, streams, lakes, ponds, canals, and tidal rivers, and to estuaries in some cases.'

The major difficulty is in proving where the pollution comes from, particularly as there are no rights of access to discover the source.

Only riparian owners and people who have a legal lease of the water they fish are entitled to bring an action in the courts. Written statements by eyewitnesses and samples of polluted water or fish are usually required. Try to find the source of pollution (ask permission from the landholders first). Get samples of polluted water (at least 3 litres are needed, preferably in glass bottles) – label and date the containers. Take them quickly to: (i) the public analyst – see in Yellow Pages under Chemists-Analytical; phone him first; (ii) the regional water authority; (iii) the ACA. If there is no polluted water left to collect, gather any dead fish for analysis. Deep freeze them as soon as possible.

Write to the ACA for their leaflet for more detailed information.

Remember that one incident of toxic pollution can kill off a clean river for months or years. Fish can be restored at great expense, but it is more difficult to bring back the otters and kingfishers once they've gone.

If you find a stream which has been polluted (dead fish, bad smells etc.) and the source of the pollution has moved downstream, inform the divisional office of your regional water authority as soon as possible. Contact your district council representative on your local advisory committee. (Find the name from district council offices or from the *District Council Yearbook* which will be in your local library.) Follow up with your parish council to ensure pollution doesn't occur again. Inform the local anglers' association and ACA. Inform the local naturalists' trust so that they can monitor the effects on wild life. Write to your local paper.

Aerial spraying of pesticides

The aerial spraying of fertilisers and pesticides is on the increase. 38 contractors were licensed to operate in 1980 and they sprayed up to 900,000 acres – mainly of wheat, potatoes, barley and peas. Operators are issued aerial application certificates by the Civil Aviation Authority and they can be inspected by them and by an inspector of the Health and Safety Executive Agricultural Inspectorate which is responsible for inspecting and controlling the handling of toxic materials used in agriculture. The following is summarised from the Seventh Report of the Royal Commission on Environmental Pollution (1979).

Before spraying, an operator, is supposed to undertake the following procedure in order to safeguard the public and environment from inadvertent contamination. He should carry out a reconnaissance to determine whether the use is acceptable, taking into account: the safety of persons, farm animals, property, wild life, bees and other creatures. If he intends to spray ¾ mile from a SSSI he *must* contact the Nature Conservancy Council. Advance warning must also be given to the office of the chief constable, and, as far as practicable, the occupiers of land and buildings within 75 feet of the boundary of the area to be treated; any hospital, school or institution within 500 feet of any potential flight paths; and the reporting point of the local bee-keepers' spray warning scheme (where such exist).

Only those pesticides which have been cleared under the Pesticides Safety Precautions Scheme for aerial application may be used.

If you have problems with spray drift from aerial spraying, or the noise from low-flying aircraft is unacceptable, you can take the following steps. (i) Talk to the farmer concerned. Find out the name of the firm which is doing the spraying and the chemicals used. (ii) Make complaints to ADAS, the police, the Civil Aviation Authority, the Health and Safety Executive Agricultural Inspectorate, the district council the parish council and the NFU. (iii) Write to the Civil Aviation Authority and ask them to issue a warning letter to the operator concerned.

Spray drift emanating from spray booms mounted behind tractors can cause as many problems as aerial spraying. The Soil Asociation has produced a useful report: *Pall of Poison – the 'Spray Drift' Problem.*

Farm smells and noise

According to the NFU, the smells emanating from intensive livestock units are one of the main sources of friction between the farming industry and the community.

The worst smells occur when the slurry is stored – they tend to disappear through oxidation soon after the slurry is spread on the land. Pig slurry is more offensive than cattle slurry, yet paradoxically grant aid is more easily obtained for treatment equipment for cattle slurry.

Discuss the problem with the farmer to see if something can be done. If no joy, contact ADAS (its Farm Waste Unit in Reading offers specialist advice), the environmental health officer, and the parish council and district council (environmental services committee).

Correspondence in *The Times* has thrown light on another hazard of living in the contry: the noise of farm machinery, especially the night-time harvesting of oilseed rape and the racket from explosive bird-scarers. It seems that there is little one can do except plead with the farmer concerned, talk to the parish council, district council and environmental health officer, or act through the law of nuisance.

Legal Action can be taken by a private citizen or local authority under the Public Health Act 1936 to seek the abatement of the existing nuisance. A local authority can also take action under the Public Health (Recurring Nuisances) Act 1969.

Local authorities and the environmental health officer will try to settle problems by persuasion and discussion. The public should not be reticent about complaining, for only by doing so will funds be allocated for research into smell alleviation and adequate grants be given to farmers to purchase equipment which reduces smells and noise. Life can be made miserable by persistent noise and foul odours which permeate one's house and clothes.

Strawburning

Much irresponsible strawburning in 1983 led to the call for a tightening of the NFU Code of Practice by some and a complete ban by others.

According to Friends of the Earth, 'every year British arable farmers burn a larger proportion of their straw than any other country in Europe – 6-7 million tonnes with an estimated value of £500 million which could provide all of agriculture's need for heating fuels'. In their report *Strawburning – You'd think farmers had money to burn* they continue: 'Strawburning causes the destruction of trees and hedgerows and kills wild life despite preventative measures taken by farmers. For instance in 1981, 81 hedges were burnt in Bedfordshire alone . . . '

A model by-law was published by the Government in March 1984 which is stricter than the NFU Code of Practice. It restricts strawburning to the hours of daylight on weekdays only, and (i) restricts burning to 25 acres of straw at any one time; (ii) allows a gap of 150 metres between each fire; (iii) creates a 5-metre fire break; (iv) requires that fire-fighting equipment be ready for use, i.e. two men in the field with a supply of water; (v) bans burning within 25 metres of hedges, woods and private housing; (vi) obliges farmers to plough in ash within 36 hours of burning; (vii) requires farmers to inform the fire brigade before beginning to burn.

If councils enforce the by-law, farmers could be fined up to £2,000 for each offence if they breach the Code. For a copy of the model bye-law, write to the Association of District Councils, 25 Buckingham Gate, London SW1E 6LE.

If a neighbouring farmer doesn't consult you before burning and/or if you feel the burning is dangerous or is causing a nuisance, discuss the problem with him. If there is no responses check at your district council offices to see if there are any by-laws controlling strawburning. If your council has not made any, ask if they would consider doing so. Report the incident to the agriculture committee of your district council, the local ADAS office and the Environmental Health Offices and the police. If there is any damage to wild life, trees hedgerows or buildings send for the fire brigade and take photos of what is happening. Send a copy to your local newspaper. Inform your local FOE/ CPRE group. Write to your MP.

It is worth remembering that fires are also caused by accident by picnickers and on purpose by irresponsible people.

Country Codes

In 1982, when the Countryside Commission published a revised version of *The Country Code* directed at visitors to the countryside, Faith Sharp helped *The Countryman* (of Burford, Oxfordshire) to devise a code for farmers or landholders. The two are given below – *The Country Code* and The Farmers' Code.

1 *Enjoy the countryside and respect its life and work.*
 Respect those who come to enjoy the countryside and make them welcome.
2 *Guard against all risk of fire.*
 Guard against damage to trees and hedges by strawburning.
3 *Fasten all gates.*
 Make sure that gates on public paths are in good repair and easily openable.
4 *Keep your dogs under close control.*
 Keep bulls (always a potential danger) out of fields with rights of away.
5 *Keep to public path across farmland.*
 Reinstate public paths across fields immediately after ploughing and never plough headland paths. (It is illegal.)
6 *Use gates and stiles to cross fences, hedges and walls.*
 No barbed wire where paths cross, please.
7 *Leave livestock, crops and machinery alone.*
 Do not remove or twist around path signposts, or put PRIVATE notices where there is a right of way.
8 *Take your litter home.*
 Including old fertiliser bags.
9 *Help to keep all water clean.*
 Do not pollute watercourses, ponds, and lakes with farm sprays or effluents.
10 *Protect wildlife, plants and trees.*
 Do not destroy wildlife by indiscriminate ploughing, hedge clearance, draining, or pond-filling.
11 *Take special care on country roads.*

Avoid damage to verges and the wild life there with heavy farm machinery.

12 *Make no unnecessary noise.*

Don't shout at walkers in your corn. They are probably on the right of way you have planted over.

Statutory agencies

The Ministry of Agriculture Fisheries and Food (MAFF), Whitehall Place, London SW1A 2HH. 'The Government's agricultural policy is administered in England by MAFF which also has animal health responsibilities extending to all Great Britain.' (MAFF, At the Farmer's Service.) The Ministry is also responsible for the payment of grants and subsidies to the farming and horticulture industries and for the control and eradication of animal and plant diseases. Grants are available, mainly under the Agriculture and Horticulture Grant Scheme and the Agriculture and Horticulture Development Scheme.

The Welsh Office Agriculture Department and the Department of Agriculture and Fisheries for Scotland and the Department of Agriculture for Northern Ireland are responsible for agriculture in Wales and Scotland and Northern Ireland respectively.

There are 5 regional and 43 divisional (county) offices in England and 1 head office and 6 divisional offices in Wales.

For information about the work of MAFF, send for At the Farmer's Service from MAFF (Publications), Lion House, Willowburn Estate, Alnwick, Northumberland NE66 2PF.

The Agricultural Development and Advisory Service (ADAS) is the part of MAFF which is in everyday contact with farmers. It has the duty of 'providing scientific, professional and technical advice to the agricultural industry aimed primarily at the improvement of agricultural productivity . . . ADAS was first set up in 1971 and is an amalgam of 5 services, under the direction of a Director General, who is answerable to the Permanent Secretary of MAFF. The total complement is about 5,800.' (Strutt Report.) There are now four services: the State Veterinary Service; the Agricultural Service; the Agricultural Science Service and the

Land and Water Service. 'ADAS is organised for operational purposes on the basis of the Ministry's Regional and Divisional Structure. There are 30 geographical Divisions in England and Wales, grouped together to form 8 Regions reporting to Headquarters.' (Strutt Report.) Most of the Services of ADAS are provided in Wales by MAFF staff acting for the Secretary of State for Wales on an agency basis. In Scotland, the three Scottish Agricultural Colleges provide an advisory service to farmers.

Farming organizations

The National Farmers' Union of England and Wales (NFU), Agriculture House, Knightsbridge, London SW1, was started in 1908. There are 49 county branches and 866 local branches in 344 groups. 600 staff are employed in the counties and 240 in London, giving a total of 840. The membership is in the region of 140,000.

'Each county branch is made up of local branches which elect representatives to their County Executive Committee. These Executive Committees, in turn, elect delegates to the Union's Council in London.' The NFU maintains a permanent office in Brussels – the British Agricultural Bureau. 'Politically and economically, the NFU deals with everything that affects agriculture.' 'The Union now has its own fully-equipped radio station in which courses in radio technique are run for members and staff, and from which material can be supplied to national and regional radio programmes. Similar television facilities have now been installed and are about to come into use.' (From The National Farmers' Union and NFU Structure.)

The Country Landowners' Association (CLA), 16 Belgrave Square, London SW1X 8PQ, 'was founded in 1907 as a membership organisation of owners of agricultural and other rural land in England and Wales. Membership is open to all owners of such land, with no upper or lower acreage limit, and to life tenants. Its 50,000 members comprise mainly agricultural owner occupiers: half the members own less than 100 acres and some 20 per cent own more than 250 acres. But the membership also includes owners of private let estates, institutional landowners and the owners of rural land used for forestry and recreation. The head office is in London and there are 18 Regional Secretaries, 15 in England and 3 in Wales.

The CLA's main objective is to ensure the continuation of private land ownership together with the privileges and responsibilities that entails. Its free specialist advisory service to members is wide ranging and covers such issues as land ownership and tenure, economic, financial and fiscal concerns, land use and development, rural employment, sporting rights, public access to the countryside and conservation of rural resources and amenity. The Association's political strength is well known and long established, being in continuous contact with Ministers and Government Department, Opposition representatives, and national and local organisations on all matters connected with land and its ownership.' (Susan Bell, C.L.A. 1984)

The Farming and Wildlife Advisory Group (FWAG), The Lodge, Sandy, Bedfordshire SG19 2DL. Farmers, naturalists and others have now formed voluntary FWAG associations in many counties. Their main objectives are to seek ways of reconciling modern farming with landscape and wild life conservation and to make their work as widely known as possible. Farmers can approach them for advice on conservation on individual farms. Expert advice, leaflets etc. are available through them. Several FWAGs are now employing full-time staff who work as conservation advice officers. Contact the local ADAS office or county naturalists' trust for the local group's address.

The Society for the Responsible Use of Resources in Agriculture and on the Land (RURAL), Bore Place, Chiddingstone, Edenbridge, Kent TN8 7AR. Rural is a farmer-initiated group which was launched in 1983. 'The aim of the group is to achieve changes towards those systems of farming and land use whch are not only economically but also biologically sustainable in the longer term.' They are particularly concerned with (a) encouraging the conservation of landscape and wild life; (b) reducing wastage by making full use of by-products; (c) reducing dependence on fossil fuels; (d) increasinging productive rural employment.

References and further reading

General books on agriculture and wild life
For a general introduction read *The Theft of the Countryside* by Marion
Shoard, 1980, and *Conservation and Agriculture* by Professor Norman
Moore (Nature Conservancy Council, 1977). Richard Body's *Agriculture:
The Triumph and the Shame* (1982) and *Agriculture, the Countryside and Land
Use* by J. Bowers and P. Cheshire (1983) describe in detail the current
agricultural policies and how they affect the countryside.

Working the land – a new plan for a healthy agriculture by C. Pye-Smith and
R. North (1984) is illustrated by case studies of conservation-conscious
farming and sets out a practical programme for future farming.

Pollution
The most useful source of information on all topics is:
Kornberg, H. (Chair), *Seventh Report – Agriculture and Pollution*, Royal
Commission on Environmental Pollution, Cmnd. 7644, HMSO, 1979,
£6.00.
Advisory Council for Agriculture in England and Wales, *Agriculture and
the Countryside*, The Strutt Report, 1978.
ADAS, *Farming and the Countryside*, Booklet 2384.
The Game Conservancy, *Farm Hazards to Game and Wildlife*, 1981, £1.50.
MAFF, *At the Farmer's Service, 1983/4*, Booklet 2442, 1983.
Moore, N., *Nature Conservation and Agriculture*, NCC, 1977.
Price, B., *Friends of the Earth Guide to Pollution*, 1983, £1.95.

Slurry
MAFF *The uses of sewage sludge on agricultural land* Booklet 2409, 1982;
Slurry handling – useful facts and figures Booklet 2356, 1980; *Profitable
utilisation of livestock manures* Booklet 2081, 1982; *Barrier ditches – farm waste
management* Booklet 2199, 1981.

Nitrates
Price, B., *Nitrates*, Friends of the Earth 1982 (leaflet).
Silage, MAFF booklet 2429 on silage effluent disposal.

Pesticides
ADAS/MAFF, *Aerial Spraying Great Britain 1980*, Survey Report 28,
Reference Book 528, 1982, £2.35.
MAFF *Guidelines for the disposal of unwanted pesticides and containers on
farms and holdings* Booklet 2198, 1980.
Rose, C. (ed.), *Pesticides – the case of an industry out of control*, A Friends of

the Earth report for the Pesticides Action Network (UK), FOE, 1984.
Thorpe, V. and Dudley. N., *Pall of Poison – the 'Spray Drift' Problem*, The
Soil Association, 1984.

Strawburning
Association of District Councils, *Model By-laws for Strawburning* 1984.
Dunwell, M. and Rose, C., *Strawburning . . . you'd think farmers had money
to burn*, Friends of the Earth, 1983.

A gate "harr," with burdock growing near.

An oak gate and staple catch, with great mullein growing near.

13
Celebrating the locality

Glory be to God for dappled things –
For skies of couple-colour as a brinded cow;
For rose-moles all in stipple upon trout that swim;
Fresh-firecoal chestnut-falls; finches' wings;
Landscape plotted and pieced – fold, fallow, and plough;
And all trades, their gear and tackle and trim . . .

Gerard Manley Hopkins, 'Pied Beauty'

Very often we do not appreciate our everyday surroundings until we learn that someone else values them. Paintings, photographs, descriptive writing and poetry can all help us to see familiar things in a new light, and give us the courage to take a pride in what may appear, at first glance, to be a very ordinary place, and in turn to take more care of it.

When we attempt to write about or paint our surroundings ourselves our powers of observation increase enormously; we see shapes, outlines, details, colours which we had never noticed before or make connections we had missed. For this reason alone it is worth the effort – apart from any sense of achievement and enjoyment it may also bring.

In this chapter we offer ideas and examples of some of the things which individuals and groups can do or have done to celebrate their locality through festivals, crafts, poetry, drama, film, photography, painting and music. You may need ideas and practical help – the regional arts association, adult education and arts centres, WEA, extramural departments of polytechnics and universities, resource centres, colleges and schools, poetry, music, drama societies, film, photo and arts clubs have enthusiasts and resources worth exploring. Regional arts associations are running workshops and training courses for community arts. Southern Arts, for example, put on the following in 1984: managing your project, making a festival, fund raising, video in the community, community newspapers, inflatables workshop, community music workshop, community festival workshop. Regional arts associations should also be able to put you in touch with *community arts* groups who will come to you to help initiate all manner of activities, events, workshops.

Fair Exchange Community Arts, founded in 1977, was the first team of its kind in the country. The team has a variety of skills in the media-arts: photography, sound-recordings, ceramics, sculpture, painting and a wide range of printmaking techniques. We aim to help villagers in East Devon, Teignbridge and Mid-Devon to improve their own communities, using the arts in original approaches to find solutions for some rural problems. Working with village organisations and groups, we mount projects which aim to inspire a sense of imaginative special events, celebrations and self-help programmes of all kinds.

Projects can last for as long as it takes for a community to provide the facilities it needs, and normally involves a series of visits by the team, often culminating in a week of residence in the village. The team is fully equipped with a wide range of media-arts materials and its own van. (Jane Tymkow, Fair Exchange, 1984)

Fairs and festivals

Markets and fairs are a long-established tradition in town and country and many have provided an excuse for activities outside those of buying and selling, hiring seasonal labour and exchanging gossip. Many small and large fairs have disappeared, but in some areas they not only persist but have been reborn. The idea of reviving fairs or creating community festivals to rekindle traditions, bring people together and to have a good time is one which has seen a resurgence in the 1970s and 80s. Events of all kinds can be a lively way to explore history, create new traditions and emphasise the individuality of your place.

A single event each year like a communal bonfire night, a frequent round of fairs (like the ones created anew in Norfolk and Suffolk in the early 1970s, Barsham, Rougham, and Bungay), resuscitating medieval traditions and adding very modern celebrations, or more elaborate arts based festivals – all of these offer opportunities for creative expression, hard work and shared fun. You may not wish to organise performers, exhibitions, craft demonstrations, food, costume, processions, side shows, games, music and dance – much enjoyment can be had with the simplest of ideas.

Stowlangtoft Bonfire Night
Bonfires in the autumn must have been a commonplace in the past, not to commemorate Guy Fawkes or any pagan need, but simply to burn the leaves and useless wood affording the chance of a parish get-together.

The problem of ridding the farm of dead elm wood led Mrs Catchpole to the idea of organising a village bonfire party. Stowlangtoft in Suffolk has no shop, no school and up until five years ago had little community activity.

The first bonfire was built on the farm with helpers, and £100 was spent on fireworks. The entrance charge made a profit of £150. Since then Christmas parties, special events, barn dances have led to an embarrassing surplus of money. A village meeting was called and the decision taken to raise yet more money to make a village room where all kinds of activities could bring people together year round.

The annual bonfire in 1983 had 20–30 helpers organising food/bar/music/fire and fireworks (safety being of major importance). 700–800 people came and although £200 was spent on fireworks £450 was made. For two weeks before, fifteen people each day cut, transported and stacked any dead or dangerous trees from around the village and farms. About thirty people turned out to help clear up the following day. The initiative and drive of one person has escalated to enthuse helpers and watchers into joining in community events of various kinds.
(Mrs. C. Catchpole, Stowlangtoft, Suffolk.)

1983 Saddleworth Festival
Saddleworth is a typical Pennine community; two thirds moorland with close interrelationship of moorland and valley; farming and industry;

traditional local recreational pursuits, such as rush carts, brass bands, choirs, amateur dramatics. A place without bingo, cinema or dance hall so that everybody involves themselves in active recreation: Rotary, Round Table, youth clubs, cricket; a place – underneath all that rain and mist and wind – of bustling activity.

If every district took a look at itself it would find more going on that it realised – maybe regular concerts (Saddleworth is particularly rich in music) or literary output, or historical research, feeding an increased awareness of one's heritage. Perhaps every district should be made by law to have a festival every decade, to find out something about itself, to see what it can do, to work together voluntarily on a basis entirely of giving, not taking. I can think of a number of Pennine communities which qualify for a successful festival.

Although Saddleworth started off 25 years ago as a festival of the arts, it is now regarded simply as a festival, with as many outdoor events – cycle races, fell races, fireworks etc. – as indoor. One tries to accommodate as many ideas as possible commensurate with maintaining a good standard. Saddleworth has no grand houses or large listed building of architectural beauty, so those are not essential for attracting events. Nor does it have a large manufacturing company to shelter under for sponsorship. In the last resort it has the one asset needed for a successful festival, the enthusiasm and community spirit of its people which is marvellous to sense. People realise that what they are doing is significant. Eventually, everybody wants to jump on the band-wagon and belong.

For the young there are plenty of outdoor events, firework displays, cycle races, discos; Wolfgang Manz, the prizewinner at the Leeds Piano Competition; Sally Ann Bottomley, the local-born pianist; fell races, the Young Musician of the Year finalists, the Fivepenny Piece, and so on. Expensive items (relatively) will include Janet Baker singing in *The Dream of Gerontius* in the Parish Church, Benjamin Luxon, the Medici Quartet.

Participation will include a family marathon, the churching of the Chairman of the Council when the Dean of Windsor will preach, the Male Voice Choir, the Music Society, local artists' exhibitions, local dramatic societies, Saddleworth at Work exhibition and Saddleworth at Play exhibition – participation is a major item.

The festival has been able to initiate, or to encourage, or to sponsor, music making on record and books of historical interest, and to commission works of music. This time we have commissioned a work for brass band and are helping to bring out a book of early maps of the district, produced by members from the Historical Society. Last time but one we commissioned drawings of local buildings by Geldart. We have also had generous assistance from Wedgwood in producing special commemorative plaques.

(Roger Tanner, Chairman of Festival Committee, from a longer piece
first published in April/May 1983 in *Pennine Magazine*)

Crafts

There are many ways of using crafts to celebrate locality –
from embroidery/tapestry of local maps, local scenes, local
characters and legend to maintaining local variations in
basket work, corn dolly making, spinning, dying and
weaving. The 'outdoor' crafts can do much to perpetuate
regional and local distinctiveness. Preference for local
materials, reliance on local style and interest in local detail
are the routes to maintaining local 'dialects' in building,
thatching, gatemaking, fencing, walling, stone masonry,
sign making, blacksmithing . . . the list goes on. If you have
an interest in practising craft skills, in the absence of being
able to learn crafts alongside farmers/builders/craftsmen, it
is possible to go on training courses. Crafts like hedge-
laying and drystone walling show strong regional and even
local variations and these are sometimes demonstrated at
agricultural shows or in competitions (often run by
ploughing societies).

Information on courses, competitions, etc. can be sought
from the county branch of the National Farmers' Union,
British Trust for Conservation Volunteers, Council for
Small Industries in Rural Areas, and the Dry Stone Walling
Association.

If your interest is in finding someone with craft skills to
give advice or do a job, the 'National Register of
Conservation Craft Skills in the Building Industry' has been
compiled by County Planning Departments in England and
Wales. If they cannot find a local firm with the necessary
expertise, the Crafts Council who coordinate the register
should be contacted. *The Conservation Source Book* (1979)
produced by the Crafts Council lists over 200 organisations
and societies concerned with conservation of buildings and
objects.

The Crafts Council has a conservation section which runs an information service giving details on supply of materials and conservation activities. Technical advice is not available but every effort is made to direct you towards professional advice.

Conservation in craft terms includes prevention of damage to objects, cleaning, consolidation and, if necessary, repair or restoration as well as correct positioning or storage. Conservators can be found in museums, building firms, craft centres, etc.

The increasing interest in craft as work has led to a demand for small, low-cost workshops. Heckington Village Trust combined the desire to save and restore a building and to create a place of work and tourist interest – an ambitious project for a small group.

Heckington Village Trust
Restoration of Pearoom: Creation of Craft/Heritage Centre, Proposed Usages for Restored Building
This project seeks to draw together under one roof, full-time professional craftsmen, skilled amateur craftsmen, archaeological and historical research workers, part of whose work involves investigating the origin of crafts, and provision for serious teaching of the crafts. More casual tourist interest will also be provided for and there will be provision for display and an information and sales outlet.

The opportunity for constant exchange of ideas between professional and serious amateur craftsmen and historical and archaeological research workers will have a vitalising and stimulating effect upon the workers in all these disciplines and at all levels of activity.

The project draws together concepts of such diversity that at first glance it seems to present a disorderly tangle of threads. However, from the experience gained of the scheme already started in a small way in the Station Buildings and in temporary accommodation around the village and county, we have learnt that this association of disciplines is extremely fruitful and an orderly interweaving of ideas, in fact, ensues.

From the initiation of the scheme we have been working with our local Industrial Organiser for CoSIRA and with the Crafts Advisory Officer of our Regional Arts Association: Lincolnshire and Humberside Arts. We have, now, also, the advice and support of the Crafts Advisory Council. (Heckington Village Trust, Lincolnshire)

Wooden and painted signs, metal signs, stone signs – all

could call on the skills of letter-cutters, carvers, artists, blacksmiths, sculptors and masons. In various parts of the country, notably Norfolk, Suffolk and Lincolnshire, local groups and parish councils have commissioned village signs.

Potterhanworth Village Sign
The idea of a village sign was conceived at a meeting of the Festival Committee in the autumn of 1981. Very successful local celebrations had been concluded for the royal wedding and members expressed the wish to provide a permanent reminder of the occasion for the village. The Parish Council welcomed the idea and so it was resolved to obtain a decorative village sign complete with suitable commemorative plaque.

A working party had several long meetings and eventually formulated ideas for design content, shape and size. Main features of the design are that it is completely symbolic and as uncluttered as possible with unnecessary detail. The design depicts some part of the village heritage and its broadly rural, arable aspect.

Mr Graham Stringer of Radcliffe on Trent accepted the commission to carve and paint the sign. Graham was very helpful with suggestions for final design details and colouring. He worked exactly to schedule and the sign really came to life for us when he delivered it in the late summer of 1983.

The village sign is a Parish Council project but it has been financed to a large extent by voluntary funds – funds from the Festival Committee and from its forerunner the Jubilee Committee. A very generous grant was also received from the Lincolnshire and Humberside Arts Association. (Potterhanworth Parish Council and Festival Committee, Lincolnshire, 1983)

Writing

So much of our poetry and literature has been inspired by landscape, place and nature. From John Clare's Northamptonshire changed by enclosure, Thomas Hardy's Dorset, the Yorkshire of the Brontës, Robert Burns's Border country, to D. H. Lawrence's Nottinghamshire and Betjeman's Surbiton – the list of well and lesser known writers is lengthy. Their poems, plays, novels, diaries, letters, essays, and guides have in turn inspired us to look again and cherish more perhaps those places and creatures about which they wrote.

Anything written about your locality should be avidly gathered together, from small quotations to whole novels. Search the local section of the library, explore the old local newspapers and magazines. You can do many things on a personal level or enthuse others to try their hand – perhaps in response to creative writing competitions run by the county council or regional arts association.

Poetry – try gathering a parish poetry book. Send poems to the local newspaper/poetry society. Collect old and new poems about the locality for a parish book (see pp. 270-71).

Diaries and journals – Gilbert White, Kilvert and that Edwardian Lady have shown how fascinating it can be to keep a diary and how illuminating it is for future generations.

Letters – when friends and relatives are away we often lift our prose to keep them in touch with seasons, nature and place. Keep copies and edit them.

Prose – essays, articles for local newspapers, guide books could all take literary/descriptive views of your parish.

Others might be lured into activity if you held poetry or prose readings in the parish hall or pub – local celebrities may respond to invitations (you will be surprised at how little they charge, if anything).

You could arrange essay and poetry writing around certain themes and in gathering the material together may find that a mixture of old and new literature warrants local publication.

In Skinningrove (Cleveland) a group of women ('Women Live') encouraged people in the locality to write poetry, especially about their reactions to unemployment. The response and enthusiasm led them to publish *Village Voices* and *East Cleveland Way*.

South Yorkshire Council supports 'Versewagon', a mobile writing workshop specially created to serve small communities in rural areas, literary and folk festivals, and educational bodies. They hope to reach shy 'attic' writers who have never offered their work for professional criticism and advice. They tour villages and park their 'shop' (motorised caravan) in a central location for a day. They can also offer more formal evening reading, perhaps with the aid of local writers and musicians.

The *Arvon Foundation* holds a variety of interesting weekly courses given by established writers/poets for aspiring and accomplished poets at Totleigh Barton, Sheepwash, Devon EX21 5NS and at Lumb Bank, Heptonstall, Hebden Bridge, West Yorkshire HX7 6DF. On a more modest level *Word and Action* (Dorset) provide instant theatre, poetry events and courses in creative writing, poetry and theatre in the West Country: Word and Action, 23 Beaucroft Lane, Colehill, Wimborne, Dorset BH21 2PE.

Poets and writers are often appointed as writers in residence in schools, libraries, etc. They help and advise writers and prospective writers with their work.

Parish books were often written and privately printed in the nineteenth century by local people about their locality – often about history, social customs and/or natural history, and often by the parish vicar. Gilbert White's *The Natural History of Selborne* and Kilvert's *Diary* are classic examples of such work. *Akenfield* by Ronald Blythe and *Wiltshire Village* by Heather and Robin Tanner are contemporary examples. Ask the county record office if such a work exists for your parish.

Parish books can be produced by individuals or by a number of people from the parish contributing an essay, poems, photographs, drawings and so on. Each parish council could form a group which is responsible for their production and publication. They could be updated at intervals, depending on the enthusiasm of the participants.

Parish books could encourage the searching for local individuality and distinctiveness. They could be descriptive as opposed to historical and could include contemporary musings (modern-day Cobbetts), accounts of conversations with people, and so on. Visual

contributions could include portraits of local features –
trees, buildings, people, animals, front doors, windows,
swallows' nests, stone walls.

The master copy should be kept in a very safe place, but
available for people to see it. If you think of publishing
copies, get competitive quotes from local printers.
Reproduction can be expensive if colour plates are used,
but black and white reproduction can be quite reasonable.

Drama

Drama can help to bring place and local history alive. It is
also a marvellous way to bring people together and to create
community spirit. Many drama groups, village groups, etc.
put on a wide variety of work from straight theatre to
pantomimes. A selection of more specific projects is given
below.

Plays by local people based upon local legend, events,
places and personalities help to bring the locality alive in a
different way. For example, a play by Tim Rose Price called
The Fine Tuning of Ivor Gurney about the life of the poet and
songwriter Ivor Gurney also gave great insights into the
Cotswolds, where he lived; and *The life and writings of John
Moore*, an evening of John Moore's poetry and prose
prepared in his home town of Tewkesbury, revealed much
about the local countryside.

Local schools, guide/scout groups, WIs and drama
groups could write and produce plays about the natural
and built heritage of the area.

Warkworth Medieval Pageants (Northumberland) have been events of
long-standing in Warkworth, but were revived as an idea from a few
local people to mark the Queen's Silver Jubilee. Since then there have
been 2 other pageants plus other productions. In 1983 the pageant was
based on the fortunes of Warkworth Castle and the Percy family from the
11th century to the 17th. 200 villagers were involved, their ages ranging
from 5 to 75. The performances are always sold out and the money raised
is ploughed back into the community.

With a *community play* – every creative skill is needed from researching and writing to performing, costume design and making, organisation, lighting and sound. Directors and professional actors can be hired to help if necessary. Local TV and radio stations may be interested to sponsor and broadcast your work and performance. It is an exciting way of dramatising the life, work and play the history and geography of local people. If only the weather could be relied upon the parish itself could provide the backdrop.

The Colway Theatre Trust has been putting on plays in different towns in West Dorset and East Devonshire since 1979. 'A study is made of the area's history and resources and a play is especially written for the town by a playwright of national standing. Amateur and professional actors are used and the Trust's hope is to work with a whole community, using every available resource – schools, drama societies, local skills and talents – to produce a work of art of the very highest standard.' Up to 500 people may be involved. The Trust is now starting a new series of village plays 'using local rather than established writers'. Their plays have included histories of Sherborne and Lyme Regis. Ann Jellicoe Director

Colway Theatre Trust, Colway Manor, Colway Lane, Lyme Regis, Dorset OT7 3HD.

Common Knowledge Theatre Trust is another company which involves the community and writes plays about and for a particular locality. In 1982 it put on an event in Brecon called 'The Usk Valley Project' involving hundreds of people from Crickhowell to Sennybridge. More events are proposed in the same area. For information contact Joan Mills, 14 The Watton, Brecon, Powys.

Junction 28 Community Arts Project, South Normanton, Derbyshire: 'A Penn'orth o' Duck' was the culmination of Rib Davis 2½ years work with their oral history project; it depicted life in South Normanton between the wars. As a documentary drama the writing involved interviewing, looking into county archives, school log books etc. The *play* involved local writers from the writers' workshop, actors from the Twenty Steps drama group (named after a local landmark), musicians and dancers from local school. The play was hugely successful – having been enjoyed by about 1200 people.

Frost and Fire Theatre (Adam and Kim Strickland) involved themselves with the community in Pendeen, Cornwall, for about a year. Their intentions were to foster participation of all age groups, to offer celebratory theatre of social and seasonal events and festivals, to work on small-scale presentations leading up to a large-scale community event or play, to present original material, to draw on oral tradition using local legend and lore, to work in non-theatre spaces – streets, churches, houses, gardens, wasteland, playgrounds – and to use traditional hand-made props and costumes with local help. Children and adults were involved in many productions like: '*The other way of the world* – Frost and Fire's 22nd production in the Pendeen/St Just area and the fourth major production involving both children and adults . . . This play was written from material collected by Kim over a two-month period. During this time she read many books on the Cornish tin mining industry and talked to local people at Geevor and in their own homes. The action of the play takes place in the middle of the last century. Act 1 is set in Pendeen and Act II in Australia. The first and last scenes are set in the present.'

Sadly, funding to continue the work was not forthcoming, but Frost and Fire returned to Pendeen to produce a community play for Christmas 1983 and hope to do so again.

As well as staging your own productions you can invite *travelling theatre groups* to perform in your village or neighbourhood.

Fair Exchange, Pentabus, Word and Action, I.O.U., Nutmeg Theatre (puppet) Co., and Welfare State

International are just a few of many large and small theatre companies and community theatre groups which will perform indoors and outdoors in unconventional locations. Mikron Theatre will arrive by canal boat, Horse and Bamboo by horse and cart. Ask your regional arts association for a list of community/travelling theatre groups in your area.

Groundwell Farm Arts Workshop (Upper Stratton, Swindon, Wiltshire) is a travelling company which concentrates on children's theatre from an ecological view and performs sketches for all ages on things such as river pollution. For example, *Sprayit or Burnit* is a colourful environmental piece, set at an agricultural demonstration stand, with a dance of the Butterflies and Crop Spraying Aircraft.

Northumberland Theatre Company (1 Oaklands West, Alnwick, Northumberland NE66 2QU) performs in village halls, hotels and community centres. Three recent plays have been commissioned from local writers relating to local heroes and legends. *Reivers* by Peter Dillon is about the Border bandits whose forages for sheep did much to give the Border region its infamous and bloody reputation. *Grace* is Peter Dillon's version of the Grace Darling story that, and *The Laidley Worm of Bamburgh* by Steve Chambers is about one of the local mythical beasts that were supposed to have ravaged the Northumbrian countryside.

Photography

Photographs can be very useful in helping us to look at familiar things in new and different ways. For example, the artist Hamish Fulton uses a single photograph (with captions) to distil his experience of a walk (which could be 100 or more miles long); and David Hockney is now using a collage of photographs to expand upon the single moment which is normally captured by just one photograph.

Many photographers enjoy immersing themselves in particular places. James Ravilious has been documenting life in North Devon in photographs for the past twelve years for the Beaford Archive. His book (written with his wife Robin), *The Heart of the Country*, published by Scolar Press in 1980, provides a wonderfully intimate record of life in a small area.

For three years the Forestry Commission and Northern Arts have funded three photographers to each spend a year in the *Kielder Forest*. The first resident photographer there, Murray Johnston, explained the local resident's reaction to his work: 'The first reaction was that they didn't like the pictures very much at all. They really didn't see much in them but that changes as people looked at them more and more, and then, the main reaction was the people came up to me and said; "I was out walking today and I saw the kind of pictures that you took, I saw the sort of things you were looking at. I'd never really seen that before, I'd never thought of looking at that before." ' (Artists Newsletter, April 1983.)

Pinhole photography is becoming popular in some localities as a way of arousing new interest in the place and involving people in learning the basic ideas about photography. Boxes or biscuit tins with a pinhole in one side can be made and handed out to anyone interested, together with a piece of photographic paper and a cover for the pinhole. The box can be stood in the village, field or roadside, the hole uncovered for a few minutes and the box then returned for immediate development. The results can be wonderful – individual portraits of the locality by anyone at a very low cost.

Exhibitions of pinhole photographs, or old photographs, of favourite places in the parish can be a very good way of provoking memories and ideas.

Many other topics could be used to encourage people to look another way at familiar places; for example, footpaths – linear progressions which tell a story – portraits of trees, buildings, people, animals, birds of the parish. Paul Castin has taken photographs of a walnut tree from the same position throughout the year and has made a composite of the photos into an attractive poster.

Junction 28 Community Art Project entitled *Everybody's Somebody* produced a display of arresting portraits of local people about their everyday business. They capture people at work – coppicing, hedge laying, stone walling, building, cultivating.

Competitions may be used to good effect to choose photographs for parish/village postcards, or to gather exhibition material, or to document a year in the life of the parish.

Slide-tape shows using photographs and sounds of nature, or interviews of how the landscape used to look as a backdrop to photographic exploration, can be very effective. Local WEA evening school, college, etc. may have the facilities needed for making and showing slides and tapes.

See p. 258 for photography as documentary and further examples.

Film and video

Making films and videos is easier than you might think, great fun and very good for involving a group of people. But, it can be expensive and time consuming.

Professional film makers use 16mm film but Super 8mm is much less expensive – indeed a short unedited silent film need cost only about £15. The chances are that you will want to shoot more film and edit it. This takes the time and the money, but it enables you to communicate more clearly and concisely. You may need £100 to do something reasonable, and several thousand to produce a long professional film. Videos have the advantage of instant playback, re-use of tape and playback on TV, but the equipment is expensive and the incompatibility of different makes of tape and equipment is annoying.

The search for equipment to hire or borrow and for help and advice can begin with questions to the Rural Community Council or the Regional Arts Association (Community Arts Section). The Regional Arts Association and the British Film Institute also offer grants. Schools and colleges and film clubs often have video and film equipment, and community arts projects will often help in all aspects of film making.

Tealby Film Society

. . . the film society in Tealby, a very small village (population 514) situated in the Lincolnshire Wolds . . . has been running since 1959 with an average membership of forty. Apart from the usual programming of films which should be, in any film society, only the basis from which other related events can operate, Tealby also enjoys an off-shoot of the society which makes its own films! This is the Tealby Film Co-operative, for which members sell 'shares' to themselves. The money collected has gone towards the financing of a film called 'Happening', which won the Lincolnshire Arts Association Award. The Co-operative has also filmed a documentary about Tealby to be shown at a special evening event of members' films, in order to promote interest in the Society. Another evening show included vintage films of material about Grimsby, the nearest large town to Tealby.

Whereas many film societies display a keen interest in helping the community in various admirable projects, Tealby is actually helping itself by involving the community in the film society, which in some ways is a much harder task. By way of making a film about the village and its inhabitants the film society is benefitting the community as well, through making the society a cultural base for operations. Tealby is a fairly isolated community, but the efforts of the film society have not only brought the best of international cinema to this small village but also put Tealby on the map for Lincolnshire and into some sort of context for the rest of the county; it gives it a positive relationship to the region as a whole. Film-making is seen as a serious activity, complementary to the passivity of sitting down and just watching films. It is an endeavour to involve their members and thereby develop members' critical insight. Amateur film-making is often totally separated from the experience of appreciating professional films, as if not of this earth. It is to Tealby's credit that they are trying to overcome the false barriers between amateur and professional film production.

(From Ian Scott (ed.), *Reels on Wheels: A guide to Rural Community Film Shows*, Dorset Community Council, 1978)

Northumberland Community Arts is a part of the Community Council of Northumberland based in Alnwick. Amongst many other activities they help local people plan and make films.

Over the last four years they have helped people produce Super 8 films about their localities. *A Hundred Years On* was made with the methodist community of Craster during their centenary celebrations. *Into deep water* was made with the Cheviot Defence Action Group about the dangers of dumping nuclear waste into the Cheviot Hills. *A Hiding to Nothing* was made by Amble fishermen about the life on the boats, and the threat to their livelihood posed by the restrictions of the Common Market

Fisheries policy. *Carry on Embleton* is an impression of life and work in the village of Embleton.

In 1983 they were making a film with the Community Council and representatives of local village hall committees, about rural halls – their place in the community, how they run and what they offer.

Showing films can be a very good way of getting people together, alerting them to problems or simply having an enjoyable evening. Dorset Community Council's booklet – *Reels on Wheels* – is a very good guide to rural community film shows and how to run them, and where to find films (from 57 High West Street, Dorchester, Dorset DT1 1UT – 50p including postage).

CoEnCo have produced an Environmental Film Directory 1984 (available from them) which lists hundreds of films (and distributors) covering topics ranging from birds and botany to environmental issues and the built environment. Concord Films Council Ltd is a particularly good source of community and environmental films (201, Felixstowe Road, Ipswich, Suffolk IP3 9BF. 0473-76012).

Film Archives In addition to the National Film Archive, there are four other archives outside London – the North West Film Archive in Manchester, the East Anglian Archive in Norwich, a Scottish Film Archive in Glasgow and the South West Film Archive in Exeter. These regional archives specialise in collecting and preserving film and video which has a particular significance to their regions in cultural and historical terms.

Painting and drawing

Perhaps drawing and painting make us study and observe our surroundings more than any other art form. There is no need to make long journeys to beauty spots to find subjects to draw: Constable wrote that his art was to be found under every hedge and in every lane. Nothing was too ordinary or too small for consideration.

Even the smallest parish offers a bewildering choice of

subject matter. The influence of others may help in selection, perhaps a special theme for the parish book, or parish map (see pp. 270, 267).

For inspiration, go to art galleries and museums to see what others have done. We have a great tradition of landscape painting and there is much we can learn from others. But perhaps the experience of painting is more important than the end product. Ben Nicholson once said, 'Can you imagine the excitement which a line gives you when you draw it across a surface? It is like walking through the country from St. Ives to Zennor.'

Exhibitions are popular. They could be on parish themes, of established artists who have painted locally, or paintings of the same place each year or season observing the changes.

Competitions could be run on many themes, e.g. for a village/parish postcard or designs for a mural, or for the best parish book/sketch book including sketches, paintings, notes, pressed flowers, found objects, photographs. Tony Foster, the Cornish artist who painted the cover of this book, does beautiful watercolours of his experience of a walk, incorporating feathers, flowers or other found things and a map of the route taken.

In Dittisham, South Devon, two cards are for sale in aid of the village hall fund. One was commissioned from a professional artist while the other was painted by a local resident. The cost of printing of both cards was loaned by private sponsorship until the proceeds from the sales covered their costs.

Experiments Local schools and evening classes can help with collage, silk screen, batik, murals.

Brompton Ralph Rural

The newly opened Brompton Ralph Village Hall was converted from a school and cottage to serve a small village on the edge of the Brendon Hills. The decorations are rather special.

Along sixteen feet of the main hall wall there is a pictorial map of the village, painted in acrylics by a team of artists. Two years' evening class

Mural in new housing, N.E. London

work has been led by Mrs Gillian King, from Holcombe Rogus. "You can see each painter's different characteristics within the mural," explained Gillian. "Some enthusiastic and expansive, others concentrating on fine detail." One of those details is Willet Tower, painted as it can be seen from the window next to the mural wall, but most impressive are the village buildings faithfully recorded by Mrs Patten, Mrs Conway, Mrs Elliott, Mr Pointer and their friends.

'This is a slow disciplined process, quite different from the youth club's instant mural done in a weekend,' said Gillian, introducing the hall caretaker, Mrs Parsons, parish councillor and churchwarden, but until she tried a brush on this wall never before an artist. Her attractive wildlife and flower paintings appear at the base of the mural to prove her hidden talent.

The artists, intense concentration showing on their faces, allowed me to ask their views while they worked – 'We want it to be as authentic as possible'; 'It has certainly extended us artistically'; 'I now look at the village with open eyes'; 'We really have Gillian to thank, for her vision of what we could create.'

Gillian King, who teaches calligraphy as well as painting, said she has enjoyed working in Brompton Ralph so much that she would like to take the idea with her to another hall.

(The Community Council of Somerset)

Music

Music in its many and varied forms offers the opportunity to explore, express and appreciate feelings about places which cannot be said or evoked in words. Landscapes and seascapes have been a great inspiration to many composers. Gustav Holst's *Egdon Heath*, Frederick Delius's *Brigg Fair*, Benjamin Britten's 'Four Sea Interludes' from *Peter Grimes*, *The Sea* by Frank Bridge, Vaughan Williams's *Sea Symphony*, *Black Pentecost* by Peter Maxwell Davies, *Hergest Ridge* by Mike Oldfield and *Penny Lane* by the Beatles are just a few examples.

Birds have been another notable source of inspiration: demonstrated by Ralph Vaughan Williams's 'The Lark Ascending', and Delius's 'On hearing the first cuckoo in spring'. In 'Catalogue d'oiseaux' and 'The Wood Thrush' from *From the Canyons to the Stars* Olivier Messiaen tries to convey 'the melodies, rhythms and timbres of many different bird songs'. In 'Catalogue . . . ' 'the representation of bird songs are as accurate as he can make them, and the colours of the sky, plumage and environment are rendered by harmonies which, for him at least, summon the appropriate visual impression . . . ' (Paul Griffiths, *Modern Music*).

But as Christopher Small says in his excellent book *Music – Society – Education*, 'art is more than the production of beautiful, even expressive, objects (including sound-objects such as symphonies and concertos) for others to contemplate and admire, but is essentially a *process*, by which we explore our inner and outer environments and learn to live in them'.

Attempting to write music is a valuable experience in itself. Performing it with others is an added bonus – the communality of music making is an experience to be envied – from bell ringing (which is almost a part of the landscape), and folk music to brass bands and chamber music. Our heritage of folk music, dance and song has been passed to us through the oral tradition, changing with the performers and with time and rich in references to history, to place, to work and to events. Many strong regional and local strands to the traditions are still perpetuated and in areas of Wales, the North-East and other regions, are a living part of local culture.

Schools, music societies and local music festivals may be persuaded to commission pieces about local landscape to be performed at the school or festival. Amateur musicians may be encouraged by competition, the prize being the public performance of the music.

Yanomamo is an example of an exciting collaboration between school teachers, school children and the World Wildlife Fund who commissioned the work. This moving musical was performed in 1983 by the musicians and choir (aged 11–14) of St Augustine's RC High School, Billington, Blackburn, and written by teachers Peter Rose and Ann Conlon. It is all about the Yanomamo, a tribe and their forest in the Amazon basin which is being overtaken by the twentieth century. The performances, which were given to packed houses in London, Blackburn, Manchester and Edinburgh, were of a very high standard, illustating well what can be achieved with a relatively small budget, lots of enthusiasm and hard work.

Village concerts: all kinds of music may involve all kinds of people.

Village musicals can tempt people into joining in as Jan Verrill discovered in *Long Newton (Co. Durham)*. 'Of course, it wasn't easy persuading villagers to come along and "have a go". My first script for the village was a revue which included quite an amount of music. I quickly learned how to overcome one of the most common excuses for not taking part. "I'd love to really, but I can't sing" was soon countermanded by my "that's easy – just open your mouth and look as though you are". We now have a cast of some thirty villagers and only two of these admit to being able to sing! Nevertheless, these thirty people have been a smash hit with the community who turn out in force to see their local celebrities tread the community centre boards.'

Jan Verrill, *The Village*, Vol. 32, No. 3, Autumn/Winter 1977)

Old folk songs, ballads, brass band music, local pop music can be collected and recorded on tape. New music can be written in all styles by music societies, evening class groups, individuals, schools – to celebrate places, people, animals, rivers, etc.

Regional arts associations, or local education athorities, may sponsor a composer in the community or school. Lincolnshire/Humberside Arts in the Community Project aims to 'provide opportunities for school children, students, adults and amateur performing groups to work with the composer on a variety of projects and hence to increase the accessibility of new music by involving a number of sections of the community in its practice and appreciation'. Workshops will be organised with choral societies, orchestras, brass bands, WEA classes, amateur performing groups etc.

Blandford Music Week April 1984 initiated by South West Arts offered the chance for children, amateur players and singers and all the people of the town to involve themselves with the Bournemouth Sinforietta. Chamber music concerts were interspersed with members of orchestra playing in ones and twos in shops and factories throughout the town. Workshops led up to a final concert involving amateurs and professionals together under the guidance of Richard McNichol and a new rock musical, *Bird brain*, was performed by and for the people of Brandford and its villages.

References and further reading

Second Nature (ed. R. Mabey, S. Clifford and A. King, 1984), an anthology of essays and pictures about the land by people from the arts, explores the philosophical links between nature, landscape, place and the arts.

The magazines/newsletters produced by the Regional Arts Associations will give you an insight into activities in your area. The following directories should be perused in the library: Arts Council of Great Britain, *Community Arts Projects in England*; S. Barbour and K. Manton, *Directory of Arts Centres*, Arts Council of Great Britain, 1981; H. Waddell and R. Layzell, *The Artists Directory – A Handbook to the Contemporary British Art World*, 1962; *Writers and Artists Yearbook*.

The Community Festivals Handbook by John Hoyland and others, CPF 1983 (from the Community Projects Foundation, 60 Highbury Grove, London N5 2AG) gives valuable practical advice on why run a festival, who to organise it, involving local people, holding public meetings, working with a committee, planning the festival, raising money, drawing up the programme, publicity, legal and administrative aspects, site management, catering, health and hygiene and clearing up.

Build another Barsham – a guide to fairmaking by Sandra Bell, 1976, covers organisation, the site, ground work, loos, water, clearing up, spectacles and showmen, fireworks, games, theatre, dance, music, craft, food and drink, car parks, money, publicity and insurance (available from the Waveney Clarion, 38 Reeve St, Lowestoft; Suffolk).

The *Crafts Council Conservation Sourcebook* lists and describes useful organisations and societies, and the National Register of Craft Skills in the Building Industry should be available from your county planning department. *Creative Landscape of The British Isles – writers, painters and composers and their inspirations* by Bernard Price, 1983, about 'the spirit of place and its impact on writers, painters and composers', is well-worth reading.

Writing
Drabble, M., *A Writer's Britain*, 1979.
Grigson, G., *Poems and Places*, 1980.
Thomas, E., *A Literary Pilgrim in England*, 1980.

Parish books
Blythe, R., *Akenfield – Portrait of an English Village*, 1969.
Buckinghamshire Federation of Women's Institutes, *A Pattern of Hundreds*, 1975.
Jennings, P., *The Living Village*, 1969.
Kilvert, F., *Kilvert's Diaries*.
Tanner, H. and R., *Wiltshire Village*, 1939/1978.
White, G., *The Natural History of Selborne*.

Drama
Itzin, C. (ed.), *British Alternative Theatre Directory – A Complete Guide to Fringe and Touring Companies, Venues, Children's Theatre, Playwrights, Directors, Designers*, 1982.

Photography
BBC Grapevine, *Photography*, 1982.
Community Action, *Photography in Action*, Community Action No. 40, 1978.
Johnston, M., *Two Kielder Residents*, Artists Newsletter, April 1983.
Ravilious, J. and R., *The Heart of the Country*, 1980.

Film and video
Community Action No. 59, Nov/Dec 1982, for action notes.
Scott, I. (ed.), *Reels on Wheels: A guide to Rural Community Film Shows,* Dorset Community Council, 1978.

Painting and drawing
Clark, K., *Landscape into Art*, 1949.
Rosenthal, M., *British Landscape Painting*, 1982.

Music
Burke, J., *Musical Landscapes*, 1983.
English Folk Dance and Song Society, *Folk Directory* (2 Regents Park Rd, London NW1 7AY, £3.00 incl. postage).
Griffiths, P., *Modern Music*, 1978.
Small, C., *Music – Society – Education*, 1977.

14
Organising local action

I thought it would last my time –
The sense that, beyond the town,
There would always be fields and farms,
Where the village louts could climb
Such trees as were not cut down . . .

Philip Larkin, 'Going, Going'

People sometimes argue that those who are interested in the conservation of buildings and nature are against progress – that they don't want new housing or industry in their village or the landscape to be touched. People are innovative and conservative; we welcome change and yet at the same time we hate it. But most of us will accept or even welcome it provided it isn't intrusive, it does not occur too rapidly and we can see good reasons for it.

Many new housing developments in rural areas are being sensitively planned and are incorporating environmental features such as village greens or retaining existing ones such as ponds. Other villages are fighting the prospect of new housing on their only piece of open space. The system of grant aid to agriculture is encouraging the destruction of woods, meadows and wetlands – and this is occurring at a time when stockpiles of some foodstuffs in the EEC are reaching embarrassing proportions. Yet more land is being brought into cultivation, destroying valuable areas for wild life in the process. Through ignorance or lack of care historic features in the landscape are being eroded by farming practice, road extensions, etc. Old buildings are being allowed to stand empty and deteriorate, while people search for houses and work spaces.

The action guide below is intended to complement the preceding chapters by offering practical advice on:

1. How to be vigilant: personal territory, choosing your subject, monitoring, listing essential information, being aware of the activities of statutory undertakers.

2. How to gain influence: knowing your patch, checklists of contacts, knowing the right procedure, individual or group action, forming a group, projects to undertake, producing a newsletter/paper, how to influence your local councils, voluntary cooperation with landholders, consultations, parish maps, open days.

3. How to mount pressure when cooperation fails: gathering the facts, approaching the media, press releases, making use of your local radio station, demonstrations, direct action.

4. The history of a successful campaign: Donyatt Cutting – FOE Somerset.

5. An active local society: the range of activities one group can initiate – Yalding and Nettlestead Protection Society.

How to be vigilant

Vigilance is a way of life: it is a continuous process and an attitude of mind. It is not something which can be done today and forgotten tomorrow, because new problems are always arising. People are always wanting to alter buildings and land. Some of these changes are desirable and beneficial and are to be welcomed. Some are harmful and insensitive and should be questioned or opposed. It is dangerous to think that you have ever won a case – especially if it involves preventing a development. Developers are well known for biding their time and for relentlessly chivvying away at the planning authorities until they give way. For example, they have been forty planning applications and over twenty appeals in twenty-five years for one site in the parish of Hampton-in-Arden, near Solihull.

Personal territory

It could easily become a full-time job to find out what is going on in your parish or locality, so it is advisable to partition the parish (into separate areas) and to find people to take responsibility for different parts of it. People have different conceptions of their 'personal territory' – for some it may mean a small area around their home, while for others it could include their route to work or school a few parishes away. It is important not to be too ambitious, and to take responsibility only for an area which you feel comfortable with. If you take on too much it will become a burden and a chore, not something which is done instinctively.

Choosing your subject

People may be more interested in a particular aspect of their parish: one person may be interested in natural history while another will prefer to look at archaeological remains or old buildings. Similarly, some people find field work or practical outdoor tasks enjoyable and would hate to do research or other desk-bound jobs. So in order to cover more ground, individuals or small working groups could take responsibility for different interests.

It is important that they all come together regularly so that an overview can be made. Subject groups can easily become immersed in their work, introverted and insular. They may even vie with others groups for funds and publicity, forgetting their original purpose – the well-being of *all* their surroundings.

Checklist: ways of being vigilant

1) *Looking (Passive)*
Noting changes whilst going about one's everyday business – to the shops/work/school/leisure activities. Such changes could include: draglines at work on river banks, tree felling, hedgerow removal, dumping of litter, vandalism, new buildings, roads, etc., cattle trampling on ancient monuments, empty listed buildings, smashed windows, fallen slates, people picking/uprooting wild flowers, surveyors at work, paint on trees, the sound of chainsaws, the ploughing of previously unploughed land, new holes in walls and hedges, road casualties (animals), bad smells emanating from polluted streams and rivers, infilling of ponds, large vehicles parked in fields.

2) *Looking (Active)*
A deliberate attempt to look for changes within your parish/village. This is best achieved by regular walks along a set route. Many useful surveys can be made in this way. They are particularly useful if done over a long enough period because the geographical and seasonal changes of wild flowers, birds, reptiles and amphibians and butterflies, for example, can be noted. Look for fragments of pottery etc. which can be uncovered after ploughing. Take a note or sketch book or camera and look at the same things day after day, week after week.

The Suffolk Preservation has recruited vigilantes in each parish to report on any damage to footpaths, hedges, ponds, old meadows, marshland or wild life habitats.

Monitoring
Vigilance means not only looking for changes but also finding out about proposed changes *before* they happen. It is vitally important to know about an idea or proposal when it is at the planning stage so that you or your group can influence the decision.

Newspapers Local, regional and national (e.g. *The Times, Financial Times, Guardian, Daily Telegraph*) should always be scoured for information. Think about the implications of national policies with regard to your locality. Arrange for a number of reliable people to monitor different newspapers and to keep cuttings files as this can be a time-consuming and costly business.

Look out for news about parish, district and county council meetings and *planning applications*. They should appear in the main local paper – but are often so boringly presented that everyone misses them. They should also appear on lamp posts or even trees near to the site, and be sent to the local library as well as to the parish council whose notice board should display them. *But* you are given only twenty-eight days in which to make alternative proposals or if necessary to object.

Parish, district and county councils The clerk to your parish council, if you have one, can be sent the *planning applications* for your area. Make sure you keep in touch with him/her and go to the planning department of the district council to look at the planning applications. If you have formed a group ask the district and county planning departments if you can be added to their mailing list for consultation of local plans etc.

The county council and district council Yearbooks, available from your *library*, are invaluable: they list the councillors and committees, and give times and dates of meetings. Your library should have the minutes of the parish, district and county council meetings and the times and dates of meetings – if they don't *ask* them to. All parish council meetings should be attended. Make sure there is a 'democratic half-hour' in which the public are allowed to speak before the meeting. Try to go to some relevant district and county council meetings as well.

Radio and television Local radio and regional TV news programmes are also sources of valuable information. If you know someone who has the radio or TV on for long hours ask them to note things down – there is nothing worse than half-remembered pieces of information.

Checklist: essential information
Make your own list of the *listed buildings* in your locality.
The list is maintained by the planning department of your
district council.

Also find out about *TPOs, felling licences, conservation
areas, open country maps, local plans* and *minerals planning
permission* from the district and county councils.

Get a copy of the *definitive map* showing footpaths and
rights of way, and map of roadside verges (which may be
managed in conjunction with the county naturalists' trust)
from the highways or surveyors department of the district
council or county council.

Find out about *scheduled ancient monuments* from the
county archaeologists (at the county planning department
or the county museum).

Find out about the general policy towards landscape,
nature conservation and the conservation of ancient
monuments and buildings from the county structure plan
(for sale from planning department at county hall). There
will probably be other publications on individual topics
such as *Saving Old Farm Buildings – Hampshire's Heritage*. The
district council too will have all kinds of interesting studies
available. Is your parish in a national park, green belt,
AONB, AGLV?

Your local library is a wonderful repository of
information about current events and the history of the
locality, as well as holding the publications of county and
district councils.

Local amenity societies (such as CPRE, FOE and civic
societies) are well informed. Contact them. Join them if you
can. But remember that their time is valuable and they are
always short of funds – they need your help as you may
need theirs. Try to exchange information. Rural community
councils will also offer information and advice.

The regional office of the Nature Conservancy Council
should give you the exact location of *National Nature*

Reserves and *Sites of Special Scientific Interest* (SSSIs) in your area. (Their position may be only roughly noted on county structure plans.) The countryside department of the county council's planning department should have detailed maps showing them. They will also have maps/lists of the *Local Nature Reserves* (LNRs), which they designate.

Keeping an ear to the ground
Many activities which can bring about dramatic change do not need planning permission – and not everyone thinks to apply for it. The clerk to the parish council should be informed about any major schemes in the parish, but minor, routine maintenance works are often more insidious and can sometimes be just as damaging as larger schemes which require planning permission. Remember that forestry schemes (apart from felling licences), agricultural, and water authority works lie outside planning control, so you may have to find out about these activities from other sources; although in theory the local authority should have been notified if not consulted.

Government agencies and nationalised industries
These, generally speaking, are exempt from having to get planning permission for their activities. Under s.11 of the Countryside Act 1968 ministers, government departments and public bodies are given the general duty to 'have regard to the desirability of conserving the natural beauty and amenity of the countryside' in the exercise of their functions relating to land. However, the blandness of this clause makes it almost meaningless.

With all large publically owned organisations there is a difficult balance between efficiency and being accountable to the general public. None of the statutory undertakers are renowned for their public accountability. The Forestry Commission and some water authorities can be particularly unhelpful. This is deplorable since it is the public's money that they are spending, and they are supposed to be working in the public interest. Electricity and gas boards are empowered to undertake their work under a mass of legislation. When the local gas board workers (or contractors) smash up the old York stone paving stones in your road in the course of their work, who do you contact? There are regional and area gas and electricity consumer consultative councils to which the public can complain. Local authority members are appointed to the regional councils and they are also ex-officio members of their area councils reporting to the regional body. Contact can be maintained with the statutory undertakers through this local authority link. Find out the names of the relevant district councillors in the district council Yearbook or telephone the information office of the district council.

Encourage all these agencies to manage their land with the conservation of wild life and landscape in mind or persuade them to let the parish council or group manage it for them. The ten regional water authorities alone own over 321,000 acres of land excluding the areas covered by water – nearly 1 per cent of rural England and Wales.

If you have good contacts with someone who works for any of these agencies back them up and build up a relationship with them. For example, Robin Wardrope in Sharpness managed to get the local water authority to give him some trees to plant along a river bank which had been subjected to a flood prevention scheme, and local firms to contribute £400 to plant trees around the nearby docks. Ways in which you can approach water authorities, IDBs and the Forestry Commission are given on pages 75 and 104

How to gain influence

Knowing your patch

There is no substitute for knowing what you are talking about! One of the best ways to achieve this is to research and produce a *parish book*. (Many WI groups produced wonderful village scrap books to celebrate their Golden Jubilee in 1965. *The Living Village* published by Hodder & Stoughton in 1969 is a selection of scrap-book entries chosen by Paul Jennings. If your area has already been covered these could be added to and updated.) The idea of a parish book is to get a picture of what your parish contains now and how it evolved. As well as helping to put your locality in context geographically and historically it will also be of use to future inhabitants. It could involve many people, each being responsible for one chapter, with one person taking on the job of editor. The book could include subjects such as the history of the parish, its area, land use and population, a survey of the buildings, archaeological remains, wild life and so on. It could be illustrated with maps, photographs, literature and artwork (see Chapter 13).

Heyshott Parish Council in West Sussex produced a map showing all the trees of amenity and wild life value in the parish. Each was graded as to its importance. The parish council knows what proportion of oaks it has to ash etc. It also knows all the trees with TPOs on them so it can take immediate action if one is threatened. This kind of knowledge and research enhances people's awareness and it gives a good impression. The parish council should know much more about the trees in its patch than a visiting official.

You will lose credibility if your surveys and reports are not thorough or are incorrect. Make sure they are carefully presented, without being lavish.

Knowing the right contacts
If someone is about to cut down your favourite tree or dig up a field monument you won't have much time to find out which official to telephone, so find out *now* who is responsible for doing what, so that you are prepared. The rural officer of your rural community council or the countryside department of the county council may already have a list of who is responsible for what in the country. If they do not have one, offer to compile one for them to publish.

Checklist: contacts

Make a list of the names, addresses and telephone numbers of the following. Add organisations/contacts not listed which are relevant to you.

1. *Local Government*
Parish Council
Parish Councillors(s)
        Clerk
        Chairman

District Council
i) *Officers*
Chief Planning Officer
Other Planning Officers
Tree Officer
Buildings (Conservation) Officer
Archaeologist
Highways/Surveyors Department
Person responsible for management
    of roadside verges – Surveyor/Highways Dept
Footpaths Officer (Definitive Map)
Leisure and Recreation Officer

ii) *Members and committees*
Councillor(s)
Chairman of Amenity Committee
Chairman, Planning and Transportation Committee
etc.

County Council
i) *Officers*
Chief Executive
Chief Planning Officer
Countryside Officer
Tree Officer
County Archaeologist
Heritage Coast Officer
Listed Building Officer
Footpaths Officer
County Archivist
Environmental Health Officer

ii) *Members and committees*
Councillor(s)
Chairman of Planning and Transportation Committee
Library and Leisure Services etc.

2. Statutory Bodies
Agricultural Development Advisory Service (ADAS) of MAFF
Officer
Countryside Commission
Regional representatives
Electricity Board
District Council Representative
Consumer Council
Forestry Commission
Regional Office
Gas Board
District Council Representative
Consumer Council

National Park
Warden(s)
Nature Conservancy Council
Assistant Regional Officer
Warden(s)
Regional Arts Association
Director
Arts Officer etc.
Water Authority
Chairman
Divisional Land Drainage Engineer
Fisheries Department
Water Quality Department
Local Water Bailiff
Local Authority Representatives on the Regional
Recreation and Conservation Committee

3. *Voluntary Bodies*
Amenity/Civic Society
Secretary/Chairman
Council for the Protection of Rural England (CPRE)
County Office
Local Office
County Landowners' Association
County Branch Secretary
County Naturalists' Trust
Conservation Officer
Administration Officer
Warden(s)
Farming and Wildlife Advisory Group (FWAG)
County Officer
Friends of the Earth (FOE)
Local Group Secretary
National Farmers' Union (NFU)
County Branch
Ramblers' Association
County/Local Branch

RSPB
County/Local Branch
RSPCA
Local Inspector/Group
Rural Community Council
Rural Officer
Womens' Institute (WI)
County Office
Local Office

4. *Media*
Local Newspaper(s)
Editor
News Desk
Reporter
Local Radio Station
News Editor
Programme Organiser (BBC)
Programme Controller (ILR)
Regional Television Station
News Desk
Reporter/Presenter

5. *Local Contacts*
Police Department
Fire Brigade
Vet
Landholders

6. *Others*

If you know the names of all these people and what they are responsible for – you are very well informed! The important thing is knowing the right person to contact in the district council, water authority or whatever over specific problems. So much valuable time can be wasted finding the person who can make a decision. Don't spend all your efforts lobbying someone who can't influence the decision.

Make sure you know which council committees and sub-committees deal with the issue which concerns you. Find out the names of the council members and the chairman of the committee from your district/county council yearbook. (The names of committees and the subjects they cover differ from county to county.)

Councillors are sometimes a little elusive – most of them have full-time jobs as well as being councillors, so they an be difficult to contact. But they will hold regular 'surgeries' – find out when they are. There is also the problem of party politics, local allegiances and the uncertainty of knowing whether your councillor or the chairman of the relevant committee will be sympathetic to your cause. If you are in doubt, contact the council official who should give an impartial view, or a sympathetic group who have had similar problems.

Make a point of meeting your councillors, local journalists (newspaper and radio) and the chairman of the relevant committees as well as the local landholders. Apart from getting to know their views on various issues it is much easier to talk to someone on the telephone about an awkward problem if you know them, and it will help them if they can 'place' you. Be persistent without being pushy.

Knowing the right procedure
Learn who to approach and when. If your problem is serious, then always go to the top person. You are likely to get prompt attention that way. But don't bother busy people with trivialities – next time you may find their attention wandering . . .

Be familiar with the by-laws affecting your locality and the relevant legislation. Ask your library to stock copies of the most useful Acts of Parliament; buying them yourself can be costly and disappointing – their detail and language make them less than exciting reading.

Make a list of who is responsible for what in your locality and circulate it, perhaps via the parish magazine. Include dates and times of parish, district and county council meetings which you think might be of interest. Ask people to correct and update your information. Ask councillors etc. to come and give informal talks about their work to your parish meeting or group. This is one of the easiest ways to meet the people you should know in an informal way.

Individual or group action?

If you dislike meetings and prefer to work on your own, then working with a group might not be your cup of tea. However, there is no doubt that a parish or village group will almost always carry much more weight than an individual. To survive and achieve results as an individual you really need a precise issue or to campaign about a specific place.

Before you form a new group make sure that there is not an existing group in the locality which is doing a similar job. Is the parish council the right vehicle? What kind of members does it have? Is it dominated by unsympathetic people? If so, is it possible to elect 'better' people in the future? Would you be prepared to stand as a councillor yourself? There are many examples where individuals in positions of authority have achieved wonders. (see page 279 for information on how to become a councillor). The proliferation of groups is not necessarily a bad thing provided that they do not waste their energies arguing with each other or duplicating each other's work. There is no reason why groups should not work together if and when it suits them. A letter showing the solidarity of local groups in campaigning over a particular issue can be very persuasive.

There are a number of drawbacks to forming a group: (i) it is very time-consuming; (ii) you have to make sure people are informed and involved; (iii) there are bound to be personality clashes and people who feel left out:

The advantages are: (i) a group has more influence and is more likely to be consulted and taken notice of than an individual; (ii) Doing things together is usually more fun than working on one's own; (iii) there can be a real feeling of community cooperation and achievement; (iv) you can cover more ground. All these can also be achieved by joining an existing group, but if you form your own group (v) you can create your own objectives and mode of action.

Forming a parish/local group

Before you form a group talk to as many people as you can to find out what they think. Test the water. If people's reactions are favourable then find out what they might be willing to do. You will need to ascertain that there will be a number of active people and that you won't end up doing all the work yourself. Have a clear idea of what you hope the group can achieve and why it will be different from existing groups. It should complement their efforts, not compete with them. Can the parish council do the job? – they, after all, are democratically elected. What gives you the right to 'interfere'? – know your answers to knotty questions like these.

Discuss the possibility of holding a public meeting and decide what form it might take and what you want to achieve. Advertise it widely. Put posters in prominent places and distribute leaflets to each household a few days before the meeting. Make sure the leaflets describe the provisional ideas of the group and a rough agenda is included. Send a letter to the local newspaper saying why there will be a meeting and where and when it will be. Telephone your local radio station and see if they will mention it.

With a parish or village group you will have a limited membership. Remember that you are trying to act in the interests of the parish or village as a whole, not one small section of it. If members become bored or they feel left out or not wanted you have probably lost them for ever – and there won't be much 'new blood' to replace them. There will probably be cliques and people are bound to disagree. Discuss these problems openly. Resist the temptation to

empire-build; stay small and flexible. Don't let your group become just a talking shop. If you need a constitution make sure it serves your group: that it is democratic and not restrictive do not become a slave to procedure. For information on constitutions, read Community Action Note No. 3, *Constitutions*, and *Voluntary but not Amateur* by the London Voluntary Service Council.

Make sure that there are a variety of tasks for people to choose from – indoor ones such as fund-raising and research, and outdoor ones involving survey and practical work. Have them and some potential task organisers worked out before the meeting. It may be that your group is small and you will only be able to do one job at a time. It is better to do one job properly than to do a number badly. Don't fall into the trap of taking on too much. People will feel let down and disappointed and you will lose credibility and enthusiasm.

You may be trying to form a group because of some outside threat, and this will dictate your speed of action. The following books/leaflets will give you much more information. Association of Liberal Councillors Campaign booklets: *Parish Politics, How to Get Things Done, Community Campaigning Manual* and *Community Politics Manual*. BBC Grapevine: *How to Form a Group*. Community Action: *Action Notes* and *Starting to Organise*. Jay: *The Householder's Guide to Community Defence Against Bureaucratic Aggression*. Hall: *How to Run a Pressure Group*.

Newletters/parish newspapers/magazines
Newsletters are an effective way of keeping people informed and of maintaining interest. They can be simple one-page notes or small newspapers and they can be a source of excitement and skill-building in themselves.

Simple news sheets – a few A4 sheets stapled together – can be produced with little equipment. Only a typewriter, duplicator, paper, stencils and ink are needed. If you wish your newsletter to look more professional it can be printed by offset litho by a local printer. This process is a little more expensive, but has the advantage that more sophisticated kinds of art work can be included. If money is not a problem, or if you have a lot of information to impart, typesetting will allow you more space per line and will enable you to use different sizes of type.

If your group does not own a duplicator or photocopying machine, you may be able to get your printing done cheaply at a resource centre, or by sharing equipment with other groups. Four parishes in Somerset found that they could reduce the costs of production by sharing equipment. 'By pooling their funds they have bought an electric duplicator, which means that they can duplicate all four newsletters in the area and save a lot of money on commercial rates. A local resident has helped the cooperative venture along by buying an electric stencil cutter which is used to cut the stencils for the newsletters. Both pieces of equipment are available for use by organisations in the parishes.'

West Somerset Magpie Extending the principle of sharing equipment and reducing costs you can also share a newsletter – and reduce your workload as well as your costs. In West Somerset a free monthly news sheet and diary of events has been produced for the whole district. The aim is to let people know about local events and to encourage support for them. The group which produces Magpie hope to encourage local newsletter editors to distribute Magpie with their own newsletters as a supplement. (From *Thatch*, Issue 17, Winter 1983; Somerset Rural Community Council)

The *Welford Bugle* (Northants) is produced monthly, free of charge with a low cost of production. The editor, Geoffrey McAlister outlines how it is done:

'Circulation: Normally monthly, 550 copies. These are distributed to every house in the village (pop. 1,000 approx.) and to local farms. The paper is free, and we have agents for distribution for each estate, area, etc.

Make-up of *Bugle*: We invite the local public to write of their experiences, holidays, travel, anything of interest, and have a strict rule to remain non-political and non-sectarian. The majority of local activities are printed, also forthcoming events i.e. drama, cricket, football, dances, meetings etc.

Cost: We rely on donations and advertising for survival. The A4 paper we have been using has cost us £3 per ream bought locally, but we have now discovered a supplier (Discount Stat. Supplies, Crawley, West Sussex) for a minimum order of 48 reams, £2.06 per ream. We have been paying £5 for a tube of ink, and 15p for stencils, but hope to reduce this by ordering from the aforesaid suppliers. The *Bugle* Office headquarters are rent-free supplied by the Church.

Production: My wife is the Editor and I am the printer; we have a pool of typists. The printing machine is an electric Roneo duplicator, bought by public subscription in 1975, likewise the electric typewriter. We also enjoy the services of a Treasurer and advertising agent; both are very necessary. The cost of each production varies, but is normally in the region of £30. We generally print 6 or 8 sheets both sides per copy.'

There are many different styles and methods of producing newspapers/news sheets. Some books/guides are listed in the references section.

Parish library

Your group will find that there are a number of essential books it will need to buy for reference and information on management techniques. You could either persuade your local library to stock them or buy them yourselves for use by your group and others in the locality. If your nearest bookshop is a long way away there are a number of organisations which will supply books on conservation by mail order. These include Conservation Books 228 London Road, Reading, Berks RG6 1AH (0734 663281) and the Schumacher Society Book Service, Ford House, Hartland, Bideford, Devon. (023 74 293)

How to influence your parish/district/county council
Your parish council should be influenced by your knowledge of the locality and the presentation of your arguments but it may feel threatened by your existence, so tread carefully. If you write a report for the parish, district or county council make sure the facts are correct and it is well presented.

Remember that you will be providing councillors and officials with research, information and ideas which are not available through official channels, so they should be grateful for your contribution. Beware they do not exploit or divert you – your way and theirs may be different. There are a number of useful guides on writing reports: Community Action, Action Notes No. 4, *Writing a Report*; Directory of Social Change, *Campaigning and Lobbying* and *Campaigning through Research and Publications*.

There are three other main factors which are of importance to councillors in their reaction to amenity groups. (i) The composition of the membership of your group. The reality often is that, if it includes a chairman of high standing in the community, then you may be half-way there. (ii) The nature of your demands – the more radical they are the more difficult it will be. (iii) The style – the manner in which your demands are communicated. Have you gone through the accepted procedures (e.g. direct contact with the councillors/committee chairmen) or gone straight to the press with a shock-horror story? Research has shown that councillors dislike flamboyant, aggressive and publicity-conscious demands! But, circumstances must influence the style of your action, and experience may be gained through other groups. There may be such a groundswell of sympathetic opinion that you have councillors eating out of your hand.

But it is your dedication and enthusiasm which will probably count for more than anything else. If you have good ideas and are enthusiastic and personable than your battle will be half-won. You must be seen to be reasonable and able to see other people's points of view. Not all development is bad and some can be modified to good advantage. Several parishes have altered housing developments by incorporating playing fields and village greens they might never otherwise have gained (see page 158).

Cooperation with landholders

If you live in a rural area it is likely that most of the land in your parish will be agricultural land, over which there is no planning control unless it is designated in some way. This land is a part of our everday experience – we look at it, travel and walk through it and, as Richard Mabey says in his book *The Common Ground*, we feel that it belongs to us through our familiarity with it. When our favourite landmarks disappear (hedges ripped out, trees cut down, etc.) we feel a sense of personal outrage. 'How could they do that to *our* trees!' Well, we have to understand that they are not *our* trees any more than St Paul's Cathedral is *our* building; yet the same sense of outrage is felt by visitors to big cities if one of *their* favourite buildings is demolished. But these things are a part of our national and local heritage and *we* have a *right* and *duty* to try to save them for ourselves and for future generations. Landholders have rights but *duties* as well – and, as with any group, some are responsible and caring and some are short-sighted and greedy.

If your local landholder is not a cooperative person and is chairman of the parish council and various committees of the district and county council you are in trouble! He might be cooperative about everything, or willing to cooperate on some things but not others. What is important is to show local landholders that *their* land, which is *your* view, *your* local walk, *your* place of play is of value to you and that you cherish it and would be very unhappy if anything drastic was to happen to it.

Start by asking the landholders if you can take a close look at trees, birds, archaeological remains or whatever interests you – on their land. Don't trespass, because you may never be given a second chance. Always report back to say what you've found and that you will send them a report of your findings. Offer to help with the maintenance of features you are fond of, such as renovating ponds, laying hedges, mowing field monuments, keeping footpaths signposted, etc. If this approach is successful, offer, with the help of local schoolchildren, a WI or parish group, to 'adopt' a site such as an ancient monument, pond or wood on a longer-term basis.

The ideal solution would be for landholders to talk over any major changes on their land with the local residents, parish or parish group. Both sides would be given the opportunity to give their views. The landholder would feel the strength of people's feelings and the group could ascertain the landholder's economic (or otherwise) justification for the proposals. It could be that the landholder had overlooked the wild life or amenity value of the piece of land in question.

Presentation
There are two ways in which all inhabitants (large landholders and others) of the parish/locality could be made more aware of the interesting features in their parish:

Parish maps can be situated outside the village hall or church or on the village green and show various features on a large-scale map of the parish. They could include: all designated sites, all ancient monuments and buildings of interest – listed or not – old hedgerows and green lanes, footpaths and other rights of way, farm trails, picnic sites, etc. Many people think that people should not be told where SSSIs and scheduled ancient monuments are in case they are robbed of their rarities. But if people are intent on collecting the rare, they will find out where they are anyway. It may be better to let people in on the 'secret' to give them an opportunity to have pride in these places and help to keep vandals away. Many parish councils display village maps, but there are few maps of whole parishes. (See also pages 267-9).

Parish open days are a similar exercise to beating the bounds, but instead of going around the parish, an annual journey can be made to all the places on the parish map to ensure that they are in good order. It might deter someone from obliterating a field monument if he thought he'd have to be answerable to the parish on one hot summer's day!

How to mount pressure when voluntary cooperation fails

There are a number of tactics at your disposal:

1. Using the facts – as incorporated in your report or campaign document.
2. Getting the support of influential people, local and otherwise, and "experts".
3. Lobbying – the protagonist, local officials, your MP etc.
4. Getting public support via public meetings, petitions etc.
5. Eliciting media support.
6. Making use of demonstrations.

The following gives the bare bones of an action guide. For more detailed information read Chris Hall's *How to Run a Pressure Group* and Anthony Jay's *The Householder's Guide to Community Defence Against Bureaucratic Aggression*, Friends of the Earth's *Countryside Campaigners Briefing Sheet*, Des Wilsons *Pressure: The A to Z of Campaigning in Britain* and other booklets on individual topics mentioned at the end of this chapter.

Using the facts

Gathering the facts should lead you to the originator of the proposal for information (e.g. district council planning department) to see the plans for yourself. Do not rely on second-hand information. Call in expert advice if necessary, e.g. a friendly solicitor, planner or architect. Make your report as succinct and brief as possible. It should contain background information, establishing why there is a problem, how it arose, and your solution, with a summary of recommendations at the beginning. It should also say a little about your group.

Influence

Try to get as many influential people and experts as you can to back your case, either with you or in their own right. Sometimes complementary pressure from different directions works better than a single group standing alone.

Lobbying

Before you make a public statement, try to meet the protagonist, to find out his/her side of the story – there may be a way in which he/she can change his/her mind without losing face. Do not be aggressive, but polite and firm. Don't be tempted to be taken into his/her confidence so that you can't report back to your group everything that has been said. Write down what has been said and agreed – and follow up with a letter to make sure all of the points are known to both parties.

Lobby officials who have the authority to make decisions. Whether you are trying to alter policy or details of administration will determine who you approach. If it is policy, then it should be your councillor, relevant committee chairman, the media, your MP. If administration, then the local authority officer, and as a last resort the ombudsman (if the local authority has failed to do its statutory duty). However, there is a great deal of overlap as local authority officers do make decisions and determine policy as well as councillors and others. Be well prepared. Enlist the support of your MP if necessary. Don't be intimidated by officialdom. For information on lobbying see Community Action Notes No. 5, plus *Campaigning and Lobbying* (Directory of Social Change).

Public support

This is important and should be demonstrated to the decision-makers. This can be done by petitions which give you or members of your group the chance to see people and talk to them; add to this leafletting, posters and public meetings. (For help with leaflets and posters see Community Action Action Notes No 14.) Chris Hall's book *How to Run a Pressure Group* has a good section on how to conduct a public meeting. Petitions carry little weight with officials – it is much better to ask people to write letters. Letters should be individually written, well informed, concise and polite. Do not underestimate the power of a good letter. An advantage is that dialogue can start as it will usually necessitate a reply.

The media

Press releases. Your press release should be on one side of the page if possible and double spaced. Use your headed writing paper and put PRESS RELEASE in large type at the top. Date it and give the name of someone reliable who knows more and who can be contacted by telephone. Give the times when he/she will be available. Write short, punchy sentences. Be brief and to the point. Give facts rather than opinion.

Your report campaign document should be sent out with the press release for further information, should it be needed. Send copies of your press release to relevant community groups and amenity societies as well as the local newspapers, local radio and TV stations. If you feel your story merits national or regional coverage then send it to a favourite journalist on the national newspapers as well as topical radio news programmes such as 'Today', 'The World at One' and 'The World Tonight' and ITV and BBC TV and radio newsdesks.

For further information on how to write a press release, read the excellent pamphlet *Dealing with the Media* by Pat Healy in the Directory of Social Change's pack. Also, *Press, Radio and TV: How to handle publicity* by Mike Oborski (ALC Campaign Booklet No. 11).

Newspapers You should have a list of contacts and know the time of day and week when it is best to contact them. For example, it is no good trying to interest a journalist in your story if he/she is trying to write his/her piece (for daily newspapers this is between about 3.30 and 7.30). You should also know the copy date deadlines, and picture deadlines. You should have identified and met sympathetic journalists. Letters to the Editor can be influential.

You can never guarantee that the paper will be sympathetic, and unless the journalist reads the story back to you, you can never be sure that the story will be correct or favourable to your case. You have to weigh up if it is better to use your own publicity mechanism (leaflets etc.) over which you have control and which can reach whom you choose. This is why it pays to get to know local journalists so that a mutual interest and trust can be built up.

Try to give journalists 4-7 days' warning of a story or an event. If you are sending out press releases, send them to the news editor as well as your contact. If the 'event' is photogenic, then send one to the picture desk as well. They may like to send their own photographer, but in any event, ask a competent photographer to take photos for you – they will always be useful as a record of what happened.

Local radio It is wise to make use of your local radio station as well as your local newspaper because you will reach different audiences. Radio has an immediacy which a weekly newspaper does not have, and with radio it is possible to go into issues in more detail. It is especially useful for advertising events and for appealing for volunteers for specific projects (although this can be a drawback if the response is too 'successful').

Who to approach? Listen to your local radio station and analyse their programmes – you will discover which slot to aim for and which presenters might be sympathetic to your cause. If you wish to get a news item broadcast, then approach the news editor. If you would like a programme made about your group or an issue you are promoting, you could either approach the programme organiser (BBC) or Programme Controller (independent local radio) or an individual presenter or producer.

Most radio stations have open days or will arrange to show groups around the station to show how it works. Take advantage of these opportunities. Don't be afraid to contact your radio station – after all, they rely on local people for information and news.

Examples of what local radio stations can do
BBC Radio Manchester has its own weekly natural history programme, 'The Outsiders', which deals with the wild life in and around Greater Manchester. It is broadcast every Friday evening from 6.30 to 7.00 p.m.
Pennine Radio, Bradford, recorded the play *Echoes from the Valley* written by Garry Lyons. Not many small radio stations have the courage to support local playwrights.
Radio Cornwall runs Helpline – a kind of volunteer bureau on the air jointly with the rural community council and local volunteer bureau. Anyone in difficulty and requiring practical help can call the radio station where trained receptionists deal quickly and effectively with each call. Members of the public wishing to volunteer their services to the community can do likewise.
Radio Solent broadcasts a Sunday morning 'Location Quiz'. Cryptic clues are given about a place in the Radio Solent area and people ring in with their ideas of where it is. This is an excellent way of extending one's knowledge about a locality and of whetting people's interest in it.
Radio Northants every morning puts on a two-minute resumé of 'Village News' repeated once later in the morning. The material for this is derived from a network of 150 voluntary 'Village Correspondents'. The information they provide ranges from what's on in a certain parish, to worries about over-zealous tree pruning. Particular items may be picked up as full news stories. The idea has proved so successful that the breakfast programme now also broadcasts a twice weekly 'Around the

Houses' slot featuring information from town housing estates correspondents.

Radio York has a similar network of village correspondents and news slot.

The best source of information on local radio is 'The Local Radio Kit' by Keith Yeomans and John Callaghan. It comprises a small book, a cassette on how to be interviewed, how to take part in phone-in programmes and on how to improve your performance; and a card game which gives information about 'what kinds of programmes are broadcast, what kind of people make them . . . ' Also: Community Action Notes No. 16, *Community Radio*; Grapevine, *How to use your local Radio Station*; and *Dealing with the Media* by the Directory of Social Change.

Local TV Get to know the regular slots where news material is needed, and the producers responsible for them. Ring a contact in the news room at least a week before your event takes place and follow up with a press release. If relevant, stress the 'picture merit' of your story.

Demonstrations

Successful demonstrations usually take a great deal of organising, involving much time and manpower. It is better not to have a demo at all than to have one which is a flop. Don't promise things – such as hundreds of participants – if you can't deliver. Think carefully before committing yourself. If the problem you are concerned with is not visual it would be just as well to issue a press release or report. If you are saving a wood or tree then a gathering of people would be very appropriate. If you have the ability to determine the timing of your event then make sure it doesn't coincide with something else which is likely to steal all the media coverage – such as the budget! Don't put all your eggs in one basket – a strike by the local press could wreck months of work and be a real blow to morale. Find someone who can draw/cartoon/photograph/write slogans/ make posters – much can be done by catching the eye. Make placards interesting, amusing and punchy. Try to get a 'personality' along to help get more coverage. It is wise to contact the police before you arrange your gathering to ensure that you are not planning anything which is illegal, such as blocking the public highway.

Spontaneous direct action, like sitting in a threatened tree, may be your last resort – the extent to which you feel justified in putting yourself in danger or breaking the law must be carefully thought through.

Action brings results

Many groups are formed to fight a motorway proposal or other development, and then continue after the case has been won or lost. Many of these large-scale proposals cannot be anticipated, but the insidious, everyday ones such as road widening, new roundabouts, the building of out-of-character houses etc. can be stopped or modified at the planning stages. If you dislike the changes which are going on around you, you and your local group *can* do something about it.

If you lose a local landmark before you have had a chance to do anything about it, do not give up, write letters to relevant local authority officials, the local newspaper, your MP. Ask others to do likewise. Bring the matter to the attention of the parish council. Only by knowing the strength of public feeling can local authorities and others with influence prevent similar things happening in the future. The two examples which follow show the rewards to be gained from different approaches and various committment to a place.

The history of a successful campaign:Donyatt Cutting, near Ilminster
South Somerset/West Dorset FOE is a small group, spread out over a wide area. Donyatt Cutting was once the deepest railway cutting in Somerset, now disused and known as a local beauty spot. Its three varied habitats — open grassland, wetland, semi-mature woodland — are host to more than 55 species of birds and over 176 species of plants, as well as many animals and amphibians.

The five-acre site is owned by Somerset County Council, which after eighteen months of opposition from the Somerset Trust for Nature Conservation, the RSPB and Yeovil District Council, besides local residents, granted itself planning permission to use the cutting as an industrial waste dump (27 April 1982).

Why was the campaign lost at this stage?
Lack of co-ordination between protesting groups, and local people. Poor research, no lobbying of councillors; small petition; no poster campaign; no public meetings; very little press coverage.
The FOE campaign
Because of the status and confidence of the other organisations involved, no one had thought to involve FOE until after the battle appeared to be lost. Our campaign began in April 1982. We distributed 400 A3 posters (+ information and petition forms to 120 local members and supporters), executed detailed research, including botanical listings and insect and butterfly surveys commissioned from the local branch of the British Naturalists Association. We interested the press, local radio and TV, achieving a number of front-page leads and regular campaign reports.

Major points in the campaign
– 7 June 1982, referred County Council's decision to the Ombudsman. (He decided no maladministration involved, but the action was very good publicity.)
– June 1982, BBC Local Radio interview.
– 19 September 1982, 92 people joined FOE bike-ride/picnic (including a local farmer and his family, and a local GP) to fund the campaign – good publicity.
– September 1982, petition of over 2,000 signatures (TV and radio); all county councillors involved in the decision written to and telephoned; meeting with all three local parliamentary candidates
– 1 November 1982, public meeting at Donyatt; councillors present as well as 82 local people. Local FOE, accompanied by Charles Secrett, given one hour to present the case for preserving the site; informed of the support of MP J. Peyton (Con.); Liberal Paddy Ashdown (now MP) said he would join a site occupation.
– 16 November 1982, campaign featured on national BBC 'Today' programme, marking start of FOE's national Countryside Campaign.
– 17 November 1982, Somerset County Council announced cancellation of its plans to dump in the cutting at Donyatt, bowing to 'the views of local people and conservation interests'.

Results of the campaign

Donyatt cutting has been preserved as a valuable wildlife habitat; FOE have been invited to consult with Somerset Trust for Nature Conservation to draw up a management plan to run the site as a nature reserve. The County Council is furnishing funds to maintain the quality of the natural assets of the cutting, and we hope that the area will ultimately be designated a Local Nature Reserve. The cutting has been transferred from the County's Estates section to the Countryside section, and now appears on the County Structure Plan as C3 (site of ecological importance).

FOE has gained a great deal of credibility and popular support locally, resulting from the success of the campaign, and the extensive media coverage (70+ mentions in the local press). New members have joined FOE as a direct result of the campaign. Our requests from local societies to give talks on wildlife and the countryside have increased considerably.

The Donyatt Campaign forms the centre-piece of our educational programme; we gave our fifth school talk at the beginning of July 1983, and have standing repeat invitations. Our presentations has been added to the Environmental/Personal Responsibility curriculum at several secondary schools.

The Somerset Trust invited FOE to feature the Donyatt campaign in a travelling exhibition on caring for the environment, along with the RSPCA, World Wildlife Fund, etc.

FOE have accompanied small groups of school students to the cutting, to introduce them to the wealth of plant and animal lie harboured there. (Ron Frampton, Co-ordinator, Piers Rawson, Conservation Officer, for South Somerset/West Dorset FOE Old Owls, Easthay Lane, Thorncombe, Chard, Somerset TA20 4QN)

Yalding and Nettlestead Protection Society

The Society was formed in 1974 for the purpose of 'maintaining and enhancing our attractive village.' Its aims are set out fully below.

The Aims

1. To encourage a greater interest in and understanding of the local environment.
2. To guard against unsuitable development, protect historic buildings and conserve the character of the village.
3. To oppose the abuse of the ancient bridges and the country lanes by unsuitable traffic.
4. To protect and plant trees, hedges and woods and to encourage a varied flora and fauna.
5. To conserve the rivers, streams and ponds.
6. To secure the clearance of litter and rubbish.
7. To further the maintenance and promote the proper use and establishment of public footpaths and bridleways.
8. To research into local history.
9. To safeguard common land.
10. To promote the recycling of waste products.

List of Activities

Each activity has a group leader who forms the main committee together with our chairman, secretary, treasurer and two members for funding raising and publicity.

Footpaths
1. Cleared, sign stoned (more than 100) and way marked all the footpaths in this parish and many in some adjoining parishes.
2. Have for the past ten years held regular monthly walks in and around the parish.
3. Published four sets of walk cards (5 cards in each set) of this and surrounding areas.

4. At present involved in the preparation of Kent section of long distance footpath. We are surveying Yalding, Nettlestead, Hunton and Linton section.

Natural History
1. Conducted a tree survey of this parish.
2. Conducted a habitat-based flower survey of Yalding and Nettlestead Parish over period of one year.
3. For six years had waste paper collection (monthly) to raise money for trees.
4. Planted about 900 trees in both parishes. After care until established.
5. Had Tree Preservation Orders put on some important trees and tree surgery. Encouraged parish council to do same.
6. Pond clearing.
7. Take local schools on nature walks. Adult nature walks too.
8. As Yalding is designated a Conservation Area we keep a close eye on our trees and hedgerows and have on a number of occasions managed to stop trees being felled. We have a good relationship with the borough council and some trees have been doubly protected by them following intervention.

Planning
1. Watch local planning applications. We receive weekly planning list. Attend inquiries and site meetings if it is felt necessary.
2. We study local structure, countryside and mineral subject plans etc.
3. At present working with parish council on revision of Conservation Area, which will be put forward to the local planning authority.

Local History
1. Research into local history.
2. Survey old building especially those in danger of being demolished or converted. Recently applied to have an old granary listed which was in danger of demolition. This was accepted by the DOE and it is now a grade II building. We recently did a photographic survey and research into a large farm complex to be converted. Local schools helped on this project.
3. At present working on a 'Village Guide'. Also doing research into our old grammar school for where there is an appeal to raise money to re-roof the building. We have also raised £100 to help re-roof the village lock-up. Which has now been done by the Parish Council.

Litter
1. We sometimes have litter clearing days because dumping is a problem in this area. Also we often have to empty bins locally as our dustmen fail

to do the public ones most weeks. We are very conscious of the litter problem but find it difficult to get anyone to do anything positive about it, Borough Council etc.

Newsletter

Since our inception in March 1974, we have sent out a regular newsheet, but have recently published a proper newsletter. We felt the need to communicate more fully with our members, keeping them better informed of our activities and those of various other bodies – Parish Council etc. It was also a way of involving some of our less active members. Our aim was monthly but unfortunately this proved to be impossible due to other commitments, but it is fairly regular, either every second or third month. We try to report our activities and meetings, also the parish council meetings and planning matters on a regular basis. We encourage people (not necessary members) to write articles on a variety of subjects and although many are diffident at first the quality and content has always been good. The artwork is done by one of our members. He is a professional and very enthusiastic. Without his work the presentation would be much less attractive. We also have a very helpful typist and access to the local school photocopier. We aim to involve as many people as possible because it makes the content more interesting, and we hope that by involving other members they will be interested enough to take on this project if the editor ceases to do it. Subscriptions cover most of the cost of the newsletter and any additional costs are covered by the regular income we receive from the sale of our four sets of Walk Cards. I feel that if you are an active society an interesting newsletter is a must – but only if you have someone able to devote their time and energy to it.

Nature Reserve

To say we have a Nature Reserve is perhaps an overstatement. But, we do look after a pond and some adjacent land (on which we hope to plant some trees), the responsibility of which was given to us by a local farmer who intended filling it in. This pond has been cleared of rubbish with the help of a group of 'A' level students from a local comprehensive school. About twelve boys and girls came one day a week for two terms and helped to reinstate the pond to something like its former self as part of their extra-curricular studies. Their master is a geography teacher and keen environmentalist and has continued to bring students each year. We also try and care for a small pond on some common land just outside the village. Adjacent to it we have planted a copse of about 45 trees consisting of willow, wild service and ash together with ground cover of field maple, guelder rose and spindle. The willows surrounding the pond were pollarded some years ago to let more light into the pond and this was done with the help of the British Trust for Conservation Volunteers and young people locally. This is now quite an interesting area as the land has a high water table and there is some interesting flora.

Our society is quite small – we have about seventy members. The parish has a population of about 2,750 people and most of our members come from in and around the village – a few come from Nettlestead and surrounding villages. Yalding itself is designated a 'Conservation Area' with a wealth of very attractive buildings, a large percentage of which are timber framed. We are fortunate to live in such an attractive farming area and hope that we can help to retain its special character.

NB We had to obtain permission from the Parish Council to clear the pond and plant trees on the common land which is part of Yalding Lees. (Ann Kyne, Secretary, YNPS)

Useful contacts

The following organisations work nationally and at a local level through a network of autonomous or affiliated local groups. (A useful description of voluntary organisations is given in Crisis and Conservation – conflict in the British Countryside by Pye-Smith and Rose, Penguin, 1984).

Civic Trust
This is 'is an independent charity which encourages the protection and improvement of the environment.' Over 1,000 local amenity societies and buildings preservation trusts are on the national registers maintained by the Civic Trust. They do not pay a registration fee or subscription to the Trust and they remain completely independent, but they do receive advice from the Trust and it 'articulates their concerns nationally and seeks to increase recognition of their work'. Associate Civic Trusts have been set up in North-West England, Wales, in the North-East and in Scotland. The Trust issues an excellent bi-monthly magazine, Heritage Outlook. Address: 17 Carlton House Terrace, London SW1Y 5AW. Tel (01) 930 0914.

Council for the Protection of Rural England (CPRE)

Works at a national and county level. The branches fight their own battles, 'calling on national office help where needed . . . Branches appear at public enquiries; they check the local lists of planning applications; they contribute forceful views on local plan-making. CPRE maintains a small expert office to monitor central government and its agencies, encourage legislation to protect the countryside and to amend legislation which may be harmful.' CPRE's journal Countryside Campaigner is issued quarterly. CPRE, 4 Hobart Place, London SW1W 0HY. Tel. (01) 235-9481. For addresses of Council for the Protection and Rural Wales (CPRW) and the Association for the Protection of Rural Scotland (APRS)'see Chapter 18.

Friends of the Earth (FOE)

Part of an international network covering 28 countries. The FOE office in London coordinates campaigns on wild life and the countryside, pollution, transport, nuclear waste and energy and provides information and advice to 250 local groups and 100 countryside action groups which are either new groups or are formed within or around existing local FOE groups. Countryside action groups keep watch over SSSIs and other important sites and campaign when they become endangered, carry out surveys, lobby MPs and councillors, arrange talks and meetings set up exhibitions. FOE members receive a newspaper which is published four times a year. Contact FOE, (377 City Road, London EC1. Tel. (01) 837 0731) for the telephone number/address of your nearest FOE group.

National Association of Local Councils (NALC)

'Together with the 44 County Associations, NALC exists to serve and assist member councils to represent the general interests of all the parish, town and community councils at county or at national level . . . The Association holds conferences and training days to inform councillors (and clerks) about their roles.' Local Council Review is its informative quarterly journal. The address and telephone number of your county association can be obtained from

*NALC, 108 Great Russell Street, London WC1B 3LD Tel. (01)
637 7305).*

County Naturalists' and Nature Conservation Trusts

*Each County Trust (and the London Wildlife Trust) promotes the
conservation of nature and wild life habitats in its area by
purchasing and managing reserves, education and liaison with
landholders, local government and statutory undertakers. 'All
members of the 44 Trusts are associate members of The Royal
Society for Nature Conservation which is the Trusts' national
association.' Members receive newsletters from the Trust and
Natural World, the magazine of the RSNC published every four
months. WATCH is RSNC's junior branch. Contact RSNC, The
Green Nettleham, Lincoln LN2 2NR. Tel. (0522) 752326 for the
address of your local trust.*

Rural Community Councils

*Independent voluntary organisations funded by the Development
Commission and local government. They receive advice, support
and information from the Rural Department of the National
Council for Voluntary Organisations (NCVO). RCCs are
concerned with the needs and interests of rural communities.
RCCss are in contact with 'parish councils, village hall committees
and other local groups, for whom they provide information and
advisory services. (In almost every county, the RCC provides the
secretariat for the Parish Councils Association, and in many cases,
also for the Playing Fields Association.) RCCs seek to encourage
local community initiatives in the fields of transport, recreational
facilities, the environment, community care and employment
(working closely with CoSIRA) . . . RCCs employ countryside
officers to develop such activities, to encourage villages to carry out
"appraisals" of local needs and potential, and to promote public
participation in the planning process at county, district and village
level.' RCCs also run annual Village Ventures Awards for
interesting local initiatives. Contact The Rural Department,
NCVO, 26 Bedford Square, London WC1B 3HU. Tel. (01) 636
4066 for the address of your RCC.*

Women's Institutes

The WI is an independent voluntary organisation. It comprises over 9,000 WIs which are affiliated to both the National Federation of Women's Institutes and to a County Federation. 'Each County Federation has a headquarters and is run by an Executive Committee, elected by all WIs in that particular Federation. This works through a number of sub-committees to further the aims of the movement by organising meetings, activities, classes and conferences of all kinds.' WIs promote issues such as the World Conservation Strategy and the provision of services in rural areas, and undertake surveys of habitats and churchyards. Look up the address of your county federation in the telephone directory or contact the WI Federation Secretary, NFWI, 39 Eccleston Street, London SW1W 9NT. (01) 730 7212.

References and further reading

Association of Liberal Councillors Campaign Booklets: *Parish Politics*, 20p; *How to Get Things Done*, 50p; *Community Campaigning Manual, Community Politics Manual*, 25p; *Press, Radio and TV*, 75p; *The Theory and Practice of Community Politics*.

BTCV, *Organising a Local Conservation Group*, 1983.

The Commission for Local Administration in England, *Your Local Ombudsman* (21, Queen Anne's Gate, London SW1).

Community Action, *Investigators Handbook*.

Community Action, *Constitutions*, Action Notes No. 3. *Lobbying*, Action Notes No. 5. *Starting to Organise*, Action Notes No. 10. *Organising a demonstration*, Action Notes No.11. *Writing a Report*, Action Notes No. 4. *The Propaganda Battle*, Action Notes No. 6. *Leaflets*, Action Notes No. 14.

The Conservation Foundation, *The First Conservation Annual*, 1982. *The Second Conservation Annual*, 1983 (£1.95 + 45p p&p).

Department of Transport, *Public Inquiries into Road Proposals*, 1981.

Directory of Social Change, *Campaigning and Lobbying*, 1978.

Grapevine, *How to Form a Group*, BBC, 1982.

Hall, C., *How to Run a Pressure Group*, 1974.

HMSO, *Which Ombudsman?*, 1982.

Jay, A., *The Householder's Guide to Community Defence Against Bureaucratic Aggression*, 1972.

Jennings, P. (ed.), *The Living Village – A report on rural life in England and*

Wales based on actual village scrapbooks, 1969.

King, A., *Paradise Lost? – The Destruction of Britain's Wildlife Habitats*, Friends of the Earth, 1980.

London Voluntary Service Council, *Voluntary but not Amateur – A guide to the law for voluntary organisations and community groups*, LVSC, 68 Charlton Street, London NW1 1JR, £3.00.

National Association of Citizens Advice Bureaux, *The Citizens Advice Bureau Service* (110 Dury Lane, London WC2B 5SW).

Northamptonshire Rural Community Council *et al.*, *Nature Conservation in Your Village* (leaflet), 1983.

Nottinghamshire County Council *et al.*, *The Living Village* (leaflet).

Rural Resettlement Group, *Rural Resettlement Handbook*, 3rd edition, 1984.

Shell, *Shell Better Britain Campaign Information Packs* (available from the NCC, Northminster House, Peterborough PEI IUA).

Shoard, M., *The Theft of the Contryside*, 1980.

Wilson, D., *Pressure: The A to Z of Campaigning in Britain*, 1984.

Newsletters, newspapers, etc.

Avon and Somerset Community Council and BAIE, *Newsletter Folder*, £1 incl. p&p (Community Council for Somerset, St. Margaret's, Hamilton Road, Taunton, Somerset).

Community Action, *Print*, CA Notes No. 19.

Country Air, *Guidelines for Producing a Newsletter*, Yorkshire Rural Community Council, May 1983.

Directory of Social Change, *The Community Newspaper Kit*, 1981, £1.50 + 45p p&p.

Lowndes, B., *Making News – Producing a Community Newspaper*, (National Federation of Community Organisations, 8-9 Upper Street, London N1 0PQ, 1982, £2.50.)

NCVO, *Community Newspapers – how to produce them*.

NCVO, *Communicating for your Organisation – a Practical Guide*, parts 1 and 2.

Treweek, C., Zeitlyn, J. and the Islington Bus Company, *The Alternative Printing Handbook*.

Westcott, R. *countryprint – community newspapers and magazines – how to produce them*, Leominster Marches Project.

The media

Community Action, *Community Radio*, Action Notes No. 16, 1982.

Directory of Social Change, *Dealing with the Media*, 1978.

Grapevine, *How to use your Local Radio Station*, BBC, 1983.

MacShane, D., *Using the Media: How to deal with the Press, television and radio*, 1979.

Yeomans, K. and Callaghan, J., *The Local Radio Kit*, National Extension College, 1981 (National Extension College, 18 Brooklands Avenue, Cambridge CB2 2HN).

If you are interested in the future of wild life and the countryside and in working for better legislation, the following are recommended: *The Countryside Campaigner's Briefing Sheet* by Charles Secrett of Friends of the Earth, *Proposals for a Natural Heritage Bill* (1983) and *sites of special scientific Interest: 1984 – The failure of the Wildlife and Countryside Act*, July 1984 @ £1.95 also published by FOE.

River Walk Malmesbury

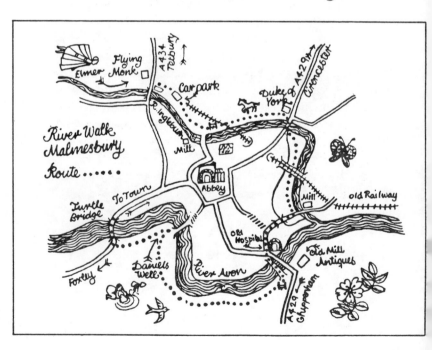

River Walk
Malmesbury
Route ......

15
Gathering, Using and Presenting Information

Happy are those who see beauty in modest spots where others see nothing. Everything is beautiful, the whole secret lies in knowing how to interpret it.

Camille Pissarro, 1893

When you know what is in your parish and where it is, there is less likelihood that it will be mislaid. This chapter gives some practical ideas for gathering information about past and present, different methods of using it and presenting it to others.

Unless you are the sort of person or group that has a single passionate interest, we suggest that before embarking on any research the practical uses of your work should be carefully considered. What would be most useful? What are the most pressing problems? Is there anything in your locality which is about to disappear which needs documenting quickly? This highlights the importance of being prepared. If surveys were to hand and research had been started it might have proved possible to encourage the development or activity in a less sensitive place.

INFORMATION GATHERING

There are five main reasons for gathering information about your place:

1. To document something which is about to be lost

(archaeologists and photographers are used to seeing something for the last time).

2. To gain information quickly about something which is threatened in order to argue for its protection.

3. To provide information about an area or subject in order that any changes promoted may be taken in the full knowledge of what will change and who will lose and gain from it.

4. To gather information for its own sake – for the enjoyment of it.

5. To then communicate to others and excite them with new views of the locality.

Field survey and documentary research

Many kinds of research are possible, from simple surveys involving mapping trees and hedgerows or drawing barns to ambitious, complex research projects covering habitats and all the buildings of the village. Decide upon the reasons for doing the study, write down some objectives. Have some idea who you are doing it all for and what final presentation will be appropriate – do you want to produce a map, a book, an exhibition, a heap of paper? If there is no urgency, begin by looking at the topics which most interest you – put together a list of things you already know and people who might be useful.

Never forget that although for ease of understanding and working it may be tempting to compartmentalise your locality into discrete areas of interest such as buildings, land, wild life and archaeology, these things have strong interrelationships and it is easier to protect a place if its collective richness can be demonstrated.

Research is a messy business, with no hard and fast rules. Even if you have a careful list of objectives, an easy method of finding things out and a straightforward way of documenting findings, you will find that you are always changing the objectives a little, discovering your own way of doing things. Never be ruled by your first ideas or your filing system!

Find out what others have done: in the past, in other places, at County Hall etc. It can save lots of time. There are many different ways of recording landscape, habitat, buildings and so on and it is clearly helpful when it comes to comparing and interpreting survey results if there are consistent methods of information gathering and recording. The survey may already have been done, or survey forms may be available for you to use.

Always note things down carefully: the names and telephone numbers of good people to contact; the author, title, publisher and date of useful documents and books, together with the pages you find helpful/relevant; where particular things are on the map; any other sources of information and where you found them – you never know when they will prove useful again.

The following example is intended to give you an idea of the range you could cover and the sorts of information available which make different approaches appropriate. To do just one of the things mentioned may be very useful and enjoyable.

Research on old buildings
Significant buildings of historic and architectural interest will probably already be known to you – listed buildings (see page 145) should be mapped and details recorded. But your locality is more than likely full of barns, terraced cottages, mills, old shops and farmhouses which on a more modest level reflect the local traditions and building materials, and provide a wealth of interest and information about the economy and social relationships of the past. A study of vernacular architecture may tell you more about the history of your parish than the church or manor house. Try a close look at the building details of the locality – the windows, chimneys, types of brick, lamps, man-hole covers – small things, but they add to the richness of the place.

Find out from any local civic society, vernacular buildings group or archaelogists what surveys have been done and ask if they have any aspirations for survey work in your locality. Make friends with the country-based conservation officer – he or she may be interested in all kinds of buildings, not simply those which are more special. Two main types of survey are possible: (i) recording the physical elements of the building at first hand – field study or survey; (ii) documentary evidence search amongst historical records, old photographs, etc.

Field study

1. You may decide it it is more urgent or helpful to concentrate on one particular area, one period of time or one type of building (barns, shops, etc.). At any rate, have some clear reasons and objectives written down. Think too of what final method of recording and presentation you may wish to use.

2. Purchase a Ordnance Survey map – 2½ inches to the mile, and other scales if needed later, a note book and sketch book.

3. Begin somewhere convenient or threatened (always ask permission from the occupier). Record the address and note its grid reference in your note book, give the building a reference number, note its position on the map.

4. Note the ways the front door faces to give its aspect direction (check with the map or a compass).

5. Note the main building materials of roof, walls, windows, fences, etc.

6. Note the shape of the building and the plan (with any out-builds and ruins).

7. Note any dates inscribed (these may be a clue to the date of the whole building, but beware of later additions or repairs). Note any similarities to other buildings.

8. Sketch and photograph the buildings and details of windows, building construction, roof, chimneys, mouldings, etc.

9. In a really detailed survey you may wish to do measured drawings of the interior and exterior of particular buildings or representatives of certain types.

10. Note the condition of the building and its present uses.

Historical and other documentary information
1. Details of changing ownership may be available if the title deeds are held by the owners or local solicitors. The County Record Office should have title deeds, records of the Courts Baron, Estate maps, county directories, Glebe terriers and other unlikely-sounding archive material which may help trace ownership, occupancy, use and condition of the buildings and land.

2. Tithe maps, if they exist, dating from the early nineteenth century, show the parish in great detail and include layouts and even portraits of buildings.

3. For the seventeenth, eighteenth and nineteenth centuries probate inventories may exist which could give clues to the use of the buildings – they are held by the records office or diocesan registries. The Board of Agriculture County Reports from the late eighteenth and nineteenth centuries give comments on buildings as well as crops, implements, workers. Travellers like William Cobbett, Celia Fiennes and Daniel Defoe may have passed your way and described activities and buildings of your locality.

4. Early building accounts give details of construction and sometimes plans – estate agents or the county record office will hold any in existence.

5. Old maps, paintings, sketches and photographs should be sought and scrutinized – but they may not always tell the truth. . .

Often your powers of deduction will be stretched and help will be needed to patch together the fragments of information. The county archivist, local architects, engineers, archaeologists and vicars are always worth approaching for help. It is worth learning a little about architectural styles and becoming sensitive to the demands that local climate and old activities have had on the position and shape of buildings.

The best specific source of encouragement and information is R. W. Brunskill, *The Illustrated Handbook of Vernacular Architecture*. D. Baker, *Living with the past* includes useful information on the buried and the built environment. See also J.R. Ravensdale, *History on your Doorstep*; D. Iredale, *Discovering your old house*; the Victoria County Histories. Approach the county planning office for information on listed buildings. The Vernacular Buildings Group, their journal and *Current Archaeology* are full of useful samples of individuals and groups who are documenting vernacular buildings. The Society for the Protection of Ancient Buildings has many helpful leaflets, for example on barns.

Oral histories

. . . my father's mother, who is now
Blest with the blest, would take me out to walk.
At such a time I once enquired of her
How looked the spot when first she settled here.
The answer I remember. 'Fifty years
Have passed since then, my child, and change has marked
The face of all things. Yonder garden plots
And orchards were uncultivated slopes
O'ergrown with bramble bushes, furze and thorn:
That road a narrow path shut in by ferns,
Which, almost trees, obscured the passer-by.'

Thomas Hardy, 'Domicilium'

There are probably a number of older people in your parish who have lived in the locality all their lives and who can remember what it was like 50–70 years ago and can sometimes pass on the recollections of their parents and grandparents as well. Unless this wealth of information is recorded it will be lost. One of the most effective ways of recording these memories is with a tape recorder; not only does it provide us with valuable information, but a greater sense of the personality of the person, regional dialects, local sayings and words are also captured. It is a marvellous way of making history 'come alive'.

There may well be an active oral history group in your locality. Ask your librarian or local history society for information or the National Sound Archive/or the Oral History Society. If you would like to learn more about possibilities and techniques there are a number of helpful books available – see references.

Decide upon the final form of presentation before you embark on a project. Will your tapes by played on local radio, and/or will they be transcribed for a local newspaper or magazine, will they go towards a local book or play? Much information about the wild life in your area can be gleaned from local gamekeepers, water bailiffs, foresters, local authority workers and others who have spent their working lives out of doors. From their observations you can piece together a picture of what changes have happened over the years.

Contact your local *Help the Aged* branch. Many of them are doing oral history projects. You would also involve parish group, WI group, local school, WEA evening class.

Ideas for projects include people's memories of: farming methods in the early 1900s in the parish; wild life in first half of the century in the parish; local characters and their activities; wild flowers; changing landscape/woodlands/roads and tracks.

The County Archivist may be interested in keeping the tapes. Alternatively, ask the Oral History Society (they publish the *Directory of Oral History Collections*) if an oral history archive exists near you which would be pleased to accept your material.

Junction 28 Community Arts Project, South Normanton, Derbyshire
The most obvious examples of this work are the books published by PostMill Press (named after a local landmark) the first of which was the

result of taped reminiscences of a local woman, Nora James, titled *A Derbyshire Life*. A companion volume to this was *A Derbyshire Town Remembered*, featuring old South Normanton. Both were compiled and edited by Rib Davis (working two days per week as resident writer with the project). Again the basis of the book was taped reminiscences, this time from a variety of local people. A further book, *A Derbyshire Street Remembered*, is in preparation, and is concerned with a now demolished street which was essentially a community.

Exploring Living Memory Group
This group came together in 1981 to coordinate information about the many reminiscence projects which have sprung up in London over the last ten years and to extend this kind of popular history in local communities.

In 1984 the ELMG put on a three-day festival of reminiscences at the Royal Festival Hall. The exhibition contained photographs and mementoes from popular history and reminiscence groups throughout London. Events included practical workshops, archive film, videos, reminiscence theatre, and music hall.

North West Sound Archive, Clitheroe Castle, Clitheroe, Lancs.
The North West Sound Archive was formed in 1979 in response to the need to record and preserve the oral culture and traditions of the North West. The Archive regularly records oral history on a wide variety of subjects, especially where little information has survived.

The Archive has access to around 12,000 recordings including many newstapes and programmes.

The growth of interest in tape recording oral history has meant a close involvement in the setting up of a North West oral history group. The archive is regularly involved with local authorities, especially in the training and formation of local groups to tape record local history. Such groups include those at Bolton, Sefton, Wigan, Manchester, Milnthorpe and the Liverpool Dock History Survey.

Photography

Photographs can be used as documentary material (of prize cattle, the cricket team), technical evidence (cracks in the bridge, oil in the stream) for aesthetic effect and artistic expression (early morning mists, skies full of seagulls).

So many people have cameras now, and photography can be a very good way of exploring interest in the locality. Cameras can be shared or borrowed. The expensive part of photography is the cost of the film and its processing, enlargements, captions and mounting for exhibition use. It is wise to cost any potential project carefully before embarking on it. But photography is a marvellously versatile tool and one which anyone can use to very good advantage.

If you are taking black and white photos, access to a dark room can cut costs considerably. Local photography clubs and colleges with photographic courses might be able to help. Some towns have resource centres/community print shops where darkroom facilities and courses are available. The placement of an advertisement in your local newspaper may reap rewards in the form of second-hand equipment. Rural Community Councils or the photography officer of the Regional Arts Association may be able to help with advice on other aspects such as funding, facilities, events and technical workshops.

If you want to keep photographic records of the area or some aspect of it, black and white photos are cheaper, especially if you will need copies for the district council/ civic society or whatever. Colour slides are best for giving talks.

Photographs can be used to great political effect: communicating far more effectively than hundreds of words. Bad housing conditions, polluted waterways, and the plight of oiled birds can all be shown more forcefully with photos. Care must be taken not to invade people's privacy, but the recording by photograph of an illegal act or one you feel strongly about, (such as the cutting down of a protected tree) can be very helpful.

BBC Grapevine produced a useful pamphlet called *Photography* in 1982. *Community Action* magazine (No. 40, 1978) covered many technical points in 'Photography in Action'.

Projects
Photography is one of the most effective methods of recording things – events, people or landscape. Every

parish should be encouraged to set up its own photographic library which could include old photos of the area and a continuous collection of the best photographs taken each year by the inhabitants and visitors. Local newspapers and local magazines can also be a valuable source. (See p. 199 for artistic ideas.)

In order to collect photos on a wide variety of subjects a different theme could be taken each year or the same themes repeated, e.g. people and their work in the parish; buildings in the parish; landscape of the parish; flowers/woods of the parish; and so on. A competition could be mounted each year and the best ones could be exhibited. (Grants may be made available for enlarging, mounting and captions.) Try a pinhole project (see p.200).

It is important to document the features in the locality which are likely to disappear – old houses, old people, wild life habitats, (woods, wetlands and so on), listed buildings/ancient monuments/SSSIs.

Parish books. Photographs should be an important component of a Parish Book. (See page 270).

Parish photographers. Ask the Parish Council to pay the expenses of a resident photographer to take photos of the locality over one year. The best 50/100 photos could be exhibited in the village hall, raising money to cover some of the costs.

Close looks e.g. at an industry in your parish – this includes farming!; the wild life in your garden; your local allotments.

Collecting photographs – local photographic societies may help. 'Old photos can be copied with an Single Lens Reflex Camera, using extension tubes if need be to bring the lens close enough to the subject, or with other cameras using supplementary close-up lenses. Even quite simple cameras can be used for this purpose, though an SLR yields the best results. Some societies buy Polaroid cameras so that in the event of emergency (the unauthorised felling of a protected tree, for example) a photograph is instantly available.' (*Understanding our Surroundings* – Civic Trust.)

Isle of Portland
The keeping of photographic records is encouraged by the Town Council, by giving small funds to an enthusiastic local photographer to take photos of the locality, unusual events and to collect old photographs. The collection provides a fascinating and evocative look at the history of stone quarrying and relationships with the sea as well as much about local people, their forbears and their landscapes.

Batcombe Photographic Report, Somerset
In Batcombe, local residents have been especially interested in local history since *A History of Batcombe* was published in 1970. That publication also made them realise just how unreliable their own memories could be and how important accurate records of places, people and events are to the local historian. From this came the idea that one of the greatest assets which parishioners could hand on to future generations would be an accurate pictorial record of the parish in the twentieth century, to be lodged in the County Records Office.

Backed by the Parish Council, a small working party was set up to produce a record using profits from *A History of Batcombe*. Photographs of the village taken since the turn of the century were collected from villagers for the record, but the difficulties involved in that made it clear that a record of contemporary photographs would be more useful and so it was decided that this should be produced.

In 1980 work began. All households were asked for the history of their house and by using other sources a brief history of the 180 buildings in the parish was produced and a photograph of each was taken. All the buildings were shown on a map of the parish contained in the record and referenced by a number. An aerial photograph of the village completed the record.

All the work was undertaken by the working group but especially by the two people on it who were responsible for photography and for the building histories. The Batcombe team advise that other projects should enlist more volunteer workers, for the task is greater than it might at first seem. The costs involved are also greater than they at first seem, for the photography proved expensive, and fund raising during production of the record was necessary to complete it. This was focussed on the record itself with an evening devoted to showing villagers progress on the project. It, and the record itself, enjoys the support and interest of the entire village, so much so that a duplicate copy is to be made and kept in the village. The fund-raising evening also evoked interest in the photographs of old Batcombe which had not been used, and so for their next project the parish is considering how these can best be used. It is hoped that another more recent local history may be produced, written and portrayed from the view of the people who have lived there.

(Community Council of Somerset)

USING INFORMATION

Many people now agree that it is important to look at the locality as a whole if we are to understand the intricate relationships of people to place and place to wild life, and to protect them.

Parish appraisals

Parish appraisals are a very useful way not only of finding out what there is in your parish, but also what the inhabitants feel about the place and its facilities and what improvements they would like to see. The appraisal will have no legal standing, but is an excellent way of informing the local authorities of your views and wishes, of finding out more about your own locality and involving people in the future of their area. It can cover a wide spectrum of interests, from provision of housing, employment, transport, education and shopping facilities to the history of the locality and its natural history and landscape features.

County, District and Rural Community Councils can give you a great deal of help and advice about how to conduct a Parish Appraisal and will sometimes assist with the production and printing of questionnaires. There are no hard and fast rules about how you should do an appraisal – there are so many possibilities. The easiest way is to set up a group and get going.

Parish landscape and wild life appraisal – how to set about it.
1. Find out from county and district, countryside officer what documents (structure plans, district plans) and what

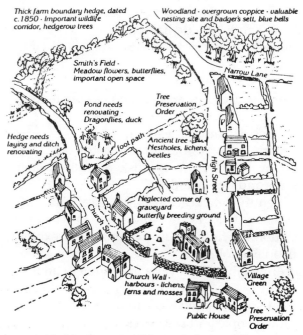

Thick farm boundary hedge, dated c.1850 · Important wildlife corridor, hedgerow trees

Woodland · overgrown coppice · valuable nesting site and badger's sett, blue bells

Smith's Field · Meadow flowers, butterflies, important open space

Narrow Lane

Pond needs renovating · Dragonflies, duck

Tree Preservation Order

Hedge needs laying and ditch renovating

foot path

Ancient tree Nestholes, lichens, beetles

High Street

Neglected corner of graveyard butterfly breeding ground

Church Street

Church Wall · harbours · lichens, ferns and mosses

Village Green

Public House

Tree Preservation Order

Encouragement in Northamptonshire to do it yourself

policies exist for landscape and habitat protection locally, E.g. designations such as: AONB/AGLV/NP/Green Belt/ NNR/LNR/SSSI.

2. What other policies might have implications for landscape and wild life. What studies are in progress – mineral working, settlement and transport, recreation/ amenity, agriculture and forestry, nature conservation and landscape.

3. What planning permissions exist for buildings and mineral working which have not yet been taken up.

4. Discover what ways the district, county and rural community and council have of helping you to help yourselves. Approach the county naturalist trust, county archaeologist etc.

5. Decide on the aims of your appraisal, e.g. one or more of the following:

to locate the important factors/elements of the local landscape and wild life habitats;

to identify changes of recent years and any prospective change;

to work out local conservation ideas;

to prevent loss of woodlands, trees, hedges, walls, historic features, views, landmarks and footpaths, wild life havens, streams and so on;

to work out ways of enhancing the landscape of the parish by cleaning up rubbish dumping, landscaping eyesores and tree planting;

to identify practical tasks for local authority parish council, landholders and volunteers to accomplish;

to publicise findings in meetings and exhibitions, to get people involved;

encourage further review from time to time.

6. Decide on how detailed an appraisal you can make, given time, people and resources.

7. Consider how to organise the work, what deadlines to give yourselves, who is to do what, and the kind of map or report you finally want to produce to influence whom.

8. Decide how to involve others – remember you need the permission and goodwill of landholders. Contact WEA, schools, WI, etc.

9. List people who may be able to give advice and funds (the parish council, the county council, local businesses).

10. Decide on the ways in which to collect information, what maps to use as a base, how to record and keep information and then how to analyse it.

11. List potential sources of information – apart from the landscape itself, the county records or aerial photographs, local books, the county and district planning offices.

12. Begin field survey, map work, documentary survey, questionnaire survey of local attitudes.

13. Sort out the findings.

14. Decide on possible actions:

exhibition of findings and meetings to involve local people;

preventative measures to be taken to save woodlands, trees, ponds, meadows – e.g. TPOs, sapling tagging, management ideas;

improvement of eyesores etc. – tree planting, rubbish clearance, wild flower seeding;

enhancement of local distinctive and well-loved features – trees, streams, hilltops;

discussions with district and county countryside officers to explore mutual help.

Conservation policy and strategy proposals

The parish of Otford in Kent set itself the ambitious task of producing an *Environmental Conservation Proposal*. This 60-page report, produced by a coopted member, describes Otford, its natural environment and the relationship to the community; it then goes on to make policy guidelines and management proposals. Specifically it covers: location, topography, geology, meteorology, descriptions in detail of six constituent areas, prescriptions – policy and strategy – for each area, administration needs, and ideas for involvement of residents. It includes many maps and provides a strong basis from which the Parish Council have been able to encourage action ranging from footpath maintenance and creation to possible purchase and management of woodland open spaces.

Parish treasures

More modest ways of using information can be very effective. Jersey, Hampshire, Dorset and other counties collected information on the natural and man-made features which people value in their own parishes.

In Dorset at the instigation of the Dorset Federation of WI, Dorset Naturalists' Trust and Dorset Association of

Local Councils, information was collected over a number of years by research assistants under various Manpower Services Commission (MSC) schemes on natural treasures and man-made treasures – monuments and memorials in rural areas and allusive treasures, i.e. sites of historic events, sites of literary or artistic connections, sites of local traditions, sites of local industries, current and obsolete, historic buildings not yet listed and green lanes. Survey forms were sent to volunteer field correspondents recruited by parish chairmen/clerks.

The results have been published by Dorset County Council in two volumes for each District (Purbeck, North Dorset, Wimborne and West Dorset). The introduction to the volumes says:

'This survey lists for the first time what is judged by local people to be of special interest in their locality. It gives the County and District Councils a record of this judgement while to the people of Dorset it provides a guide by local people of their own parishes. However, the inclusion of an item in this list as a treasure confers no protection on it except the protection of recognition and recorded knowledge. The list merely informs the local authority that an item is valued locally and gives reasons for its inclusion. . . . It is hoped that volunteers will continue to act as watchdogs on Treasures located in their Parish. . .'
Owners approval and assistance should be sought before any action is taken.

Each Parish could undertake its own Treasures Survey. Coordination should be sought from the County Council/ Rural Community Council or Association of local councils, so that a standard survey form for the county can be prepared. This may become part of the parish map – certainly the information should be available locally and in visual as well as written form.

Parish maps

Information and insights collected as part of the Parish Treasures survey should be visually portrayed in map form. A large-scale base map (6 inches to 1 mile) with information on natural and man-made things of importance in the locality could be fixed in a prominent place. Apart from simply informing it will provide a focus for people's comments, additions and musings. You could overlay information about landscape changes and planning applications when appropriate.

We are walking (approximately once a month) round different sections of the village boundary. We have had four walks so far and think we shall complete it in six walks. We are then going to draw the map on a large (8 ft x 4 ft) sheet of melamine which is being hung in the coach house – a small room adjoining the Methodist Chapel. We are keeping it simple, just marking lanes, fields and properties with a code. Then we are keeping all the information in books with everything we can find out about our own 'plot' e.g. old field names, original function of buildings, characters who lived there, as well as modern usage and plants, butterflies etc. For example, I have found that my cottage was once thatched, the barn was used for storing the horse bus into Truro on a road which has now turned into a bridle path. My field was used for the village 'tea treats' every Cornish feast day, when the children had races and buns and the whole population danced through the village behind the local band. We are trying to make a complete historical record of the village and involve as many people as possible.

(Ann Bailey, Rose Village Community, Cornwall, 1984)

Parish Map: possible inclusions and sources.

	OS Map	Other sources (apart from local observation)
Parish Boundary	1, 2, 3, 4	Tithe Maps county Record office
Old tracks/green lanes	2	County Archaeologist
Disused railways, bridleways/footpaths farm trails	1	Victoria County Histories, local NFU branch
Rights of way	1	Definitive map 6" County Surveyors Office, Ramblers' Association, Open Spaces Society
Commons	2	Co. Planning & Co. Surveyors Office, Open Spaces Society
Field boundaries, field and other local names	2, 3, 4,	Tithe map, Co. Library & local old folk, Co. Records office/ farmers, Enclosure Award Estate and farm plans
Ancient monuments (scheduled or not)	2, 3,	County Sites and Monuments Record, County Archaeologist, Victoria County Histories, Archaeological Society, Aerial photographs
Historic buildings (listed or not) Conservation areas	2	Co. Conservation Officer, Civic/Amenity Society
Parkland/orchards	2, 4,	NCC, Estate plans
Flooding water meadows and old meadows	2	Local Water Bailiff, Regional Water Authority, Nature Conservancy Council
Ponds, streams, rivers	2, 3, 4	Local Water Bailiff, Regional Water Authority, Internal Drainage Board

Quarries, old and working, old industrial workings	2, 3, 4	Local Industrial concerns Industrial archaeology societies.
Woodlands, decidous and coniferous, Ancient woodland	2, 3	NCC, Forestry Commission County Naturalists' Trust
SSSI/Nature Reserves		Structure and Local Plan survey reports, NCC/CNT.
AONB/NP	1	Co/ District Planning Office structure and local plans
Picnic sites, Recreational areas		County and District Council Planning/Amenity and Recreation Depts.
Parish boundary stones, old stones, milestones	1	Tithe maps
Sites with historic events	1	Local books, oral history, library, local history societies
Sites with artistic/literary connections		Books, Library, County Museum, Regional Arts Assn.
Land ownership		Local people, Local Authority for statutory bodies.

Key:
1 – 1:50,000 OS Map (about 1 inch to the mile)
2 – 1:25,000(about 2½ inches to the mile)
3 – 1:10, 000 (about 6 inches to the mile)
4 – 1st Edition or other old OS Maps

Sources of information and help

Bedfordshire County Council has produced an excellent pack *Parish Appraisal Package – Bedfordshire landscape and wild life* which gives information on how to do parish landscape and wild life habitat surveys. *Landscape Action in Hertfordshire – A guide to getting things done* contains very useful information on landscape action, and local landscape appraisal, and some loose-leaf information and action notes. *Nature Conservation in your village* is a leaflet published jointly by Northamptonshire Rural Community Council, the County Council and the Northants Trust for Nature Conservation.

These guides can be translated for use in any county, but first approach your local rural community council, county and district to see if they have produced helpful booklets.

PRESENTATION

Information presented to others not involved in its gathering can be illuminating and provocative or so dull and boring as to put people off. If you wish to communicate your findings well you must decide:

1. What to communicate and why. Is it interesting background information? Is it vital to help save, for example, the old barn? Is it to explain things, to encourage awareness, to interpret?

2. What audience you wish to reach – the local planning officer, developers, residents, visitors, children or adults.

3. How to communicate: notice boards, plaques; books, posters, leaflets, film; town crier/guides; meetings; events: plays, festivals.

4. Where to communicate: in a central place; in scattered places; at the vulnerable place.

5. How much you can afford in time and money to do it, and how to find both.

Information can be presented in a wide variety of ways: in books, leaflets, on panels, with maps; in museums, heritage centres; on site – on trails/walks and by use of drama, music, recordings, photos, slides, etc. It can be permanent or transitory. The following examples give an indication of what can be done:

Books

Culmstock – A Devon Village produced by the local history group is a collection of information and essays including a walk around the parish boundary, local flora, national policies on the poor, the village doctor's dispensary, local expressions and dialects, fifty years of farming, vernacular architecture. The result is a fascinating mixture of social, economic and natural history simply researched and written in different lively styles.

In Herefordshire the local WEA Research Group produced a spirally bound book on *Ewyas Harold Common*. It documents the origins, social and economic evolution of the common and commoners, the water supply, diggings, plants, birds and butterflies. It plots a history of resilience and vulnerability of a very specific place.

Guides/trails and walks

Meltham Civic Society (West Yorkshire) sell for £1.00 'Countryside Guides' which are maps showing public footpaths, bridleways, roads and bus routes with places of interest marked. The back of the maps provides information ranging from planning a walk, to local history, water supply, geology and natural history. The local authorities and Countryside Commission gave financial assistance.

More modest cyclostyled maps of local paths are often locally available from the sub-post office having been produced by parish council or local groups.

The Kinver Civic Society (Staffordshire) have produced a variety of leaflets including an A4 folded sheet describing and mapping a circular footpath walk in their locality. They hope to do some research into the old green roads of the parish.

A similar modest A4 leaflet describes the *Dower House Farm Trail*, a three-mile walk near Uckfield in E. Sussex. The farmer, Desmond Gunner (Farming and Wildlife Advisory Group representative), explains in it what is produced on the farm as well as what has been done to encourage wild life and improve visitors' enjoyment of the countryside.

Ludlow Civic Society has started an ambitious project to place over 100 plaques around the town describing the history and architecture for residents and visitors. A guide, *Ludlow Walks*, shows three different journeys around the town.

Museums and heritage centres

The John Moore Museum Tewkesbury

This tiny museum is housed in a medieval half-timbered cottage, part of a row carefully restored in the late 1960s, the time of John Moore's death. In his broadcasts and novels John Moore had done much to champion the concerns of the countryside. The museum displays are based upon quotes from *Portrait of Elmbury* and other books and include farm implements, displays about rivers and wild life and recordings of birdsong. The importance of conservation is emphasised within the museum and indeed in the building itself. With its neighbours it demonstrates how local initiative activated by a development proposal from Woolworths as early as 1935 started the purchase of Abbey

Cottages as a protective measure. By the 1960s the dilapidated row was soon to be demolished but the local surveyor for the Victoria County History called in the Society for the Protection of Ancient Buildings, realising that behind the layers of façade lay a rare medieval row of shops and houses – 24 of them! Apart from the John Moore Museum, one of them has been taken back to its probably original style, with medieval furnishings; several are let as bookshop and offices and some are lived in.

Information centres and meeting places

The Shoreham Society centre
The Darenth Valley in Kent is used by many visitors, especially in the summer – school parties, ramblers and day trippers. The Society is negotiating with British Rail for use of part of the local station under lease. Various facilities are envisaged: displays about local history and natural history, maps for walkers and the sale of literature, lavatories, and refreshments. The station is still in use; the centre could therefore provide information and interest where many people arrive and depart.

Celebrating the locality

Through festivals, books, drama, photography, film, painting and music attention can be drawn to the features of the locality which we important to you. The arts can provide potent means of communication. See chapter 13.

Sources of information and help

Information leaflets, museum displays, viewpoint signs, plaques, guides are just some of the ways in which history and environment can be described for residents and visitors. Interest in encouraging people to discover more from their surroundings through these *interpretation* techniques has grown dramatically.

The Countryside Commission has published a variety of useful booklets on Countryside Interpretation in their Advisory Series – eg. No. 2 Interpretive Planning, No. 4 Guided Walks, No 9 Self Guided Trails, No 12 Audio-Visual

Media in Countryside Interpretation, No 14 The Public on the Farm.

The Civic Trust has produced an excellent book, *Understanding our Surroundings – a manual of urban interpretation*, which is useful for rural areas too.

The Society for the Interpretation of Britain's Heritage was formed in 1975 to 'provide a forum for discussion and exchange of ideas on the interpretation of Britain's heritage, both urban and rural; disseminate knowledge of interpretive philosophy, principles and techniques; promote the value and role of interpretation to those involved with recreation management, conservation, education, tourism and public relations in national and local government, charitable bodies and private organisations'. Membership Secretary: 12, Bakers Furlong, Burghill, Hereford.

The Heritage Education Group, Civic Trust, was set up through the DOE in 1976 'to encourage initiative in heritage education, to diffuse information about relevant aspects of environmental education, and to nurture long-term developments stemming from specific activities. . . It believes a better understanding of environments, new as well as old. . . . – will lead to more effective participatory planning. . .'

References and further reading

Field survey and documentary research
Baker, D., *Living with the Past*, 1983.
Brunskill, R. W., *The Illustrated Handbook of Vernacular Architecture*, 1978.
Copson, P. *The Warwickshire Countryside – an ecological evaluation*, Warwickshire Museum Service, 1980.
Current Archaeology – journal.
Iredale, D., *Discovering your old house*,1982, and *Discovering local History*, 1973-80.
Ranson, C., *The Parish – A Guide to Surveying its Landscape and Wildlife*,

NCC (Essex).
Ravensdale, J. R., *History on your doorstep*, BBC, 1982. Rowley, T., Villages in the Landscape, 1978.

Oral histories
Blythe, R., *Akenfield*, 1969.
Evans, G.E., *Where Beards Wag All*, 1970.
Howarth, K., *Living Memories – a practical guide to tape recording the past*, Pennine Heritage Network, Birchcliffe Centre, Hebden Bridge HX7 8DG, 1984, £2.95.
Humphries, S., *The Handbook of Oral History: Recording Life Stories*, The Inter-Action Creative Community Project Series, 1984.
Thompson, P., *The Voice of the Past*, 1978.

Photography
Community Action, *Photography in Action*, CA No. 40, 1978.
Grapevine, *Photography*, BBC, 1982.

Village and parish appraisals
Bedfordshire County Planning Department, *Parish Appraisal Package – Bedfordshire Landscape and Wildlife*.
Burns, P. (ed.), *Do It Yourself Nature Conservation*, Avon Community Council.
Derounian, J., *Village Appraisals in Devon*, Community Council of Devon.
Dorset County Council Planning Department, *Countryside Treasures in Dorset*, 1978.
Hertfordshire Association of Local Councils *et al.*, *Landscape Action in Hertfordshire – a guide to getting things done*, 1981. (Available from the Countryside Initiatives Officer, Hertfordshire Council for Voluntary Service, 2 Townsend Avenue, St Albans, Herts at 50p incl. p&p.)
Hooper, N., *Your Village in the Future – Carrying Out a Village Appraisal*, Community Council of Devon.
Northamptonshire Rural Community Council *et al.*, *Nature Conservation in Your Village* (leaflet), 1983.
Nottinghamshire County Council *et al.*, *The Living Village* (leaflet), 1983
Parsons, M., *Conserving the Yorkshire Heritage* (booklet), Yorkshire Rural Community Council, 1981.

Presentation
Bailey, K. V., *Past, Present, Future*, Heritage Education Group/Civic Trust, 1982.
Civic Trust, *Understanding our Surroundings – A Manual of Urban Interpretations*, 1979.

Cook, N., *Local History Exhibitions: How to Plan and Present them*, The Standing Conference for Local History, 1970.

Countryside Commission, *Interpretive Planning*, Advisory Series No. 2, 1979; *Guided Walks*, Advisory Series No. 4, 1977; *Self-Guided Trails*, Advisory Series No. 9, 1981; *The Public on the Farm*, Advisory Series No. 14, 1981; *Audio-visual Media in Countryside Interpretation*, Advisory Series No. 12.

Dymond, D., *Writing Local History – A Practical Guide*, Bedford Square Press, NCVO, 1981.

Harley, J. B., *Maps for the local historian – a guide to the British Sources*, Standing Conference for Local History, 1977.

Hoskins, W. G., *Local History in England, 1980; Fieldwork in Local History*, 1967 and 1982.

Richardson, J., *The Local Historian's Encyclopaedia*, 1981.

16

How local government works

Local councils

Of all the tiers of democracy the most accessible should be the local council. As the smallest unit of local government it has enormous potential. The local council can:

Assess local problems and points of view.

Advocate local views to other organisations.

Act on its own and in cooperation with local groups, voluntary organisations and local authorities.

What are they?

In the English shire counties there are 10,000 civil parishes (these are separate from ecclesiastical parishes). All have a *parish meeting* in early summer each year where everyone (all electors) can have their say on local issues. 7,800 parishes have *parish councils* which meet at least four times a year and in many cases, once a month. Notices about meetings must be in a conspicuous place three days before meetings. All meetings are open to public and press (unless the council decides that public discussion on a particular issue is not in the public interest).

Councils can hold a 'democratic half-hour' before each meeting so that members of the public can ask questions and raise ideas. After that, the public can observe but not speak in the meeting itself. The parish council can be convened outside the regular schedule of meetings by six members of the public, two parish councillors, or the chairman.

In Wales, the equivalents are *Community Meetings* and *Community Councils*. There are 900 communities, with 750 councils. The powers and duties are the same as for parish councils. In Scotland, there are about 56 *Community Councils*, but they, have no statutory powers and cannot raise money through the rates.

How are they formed?
In England, it is the duty of district councils to establish a parish council in all parishes of 200–20,000 electors. In towns over 20,000, new parishes can be formed by the district council, if there is sufficient public demand. Newark and Penzance have created new town parishes. On the Isle of Wight nine parishes are in process of creation or re-establishment. Parishes under 200 have parish meetings (which do not have powers or duties like parish councils), but the district council can group small parishes or communities together to form a *common council*. In Scotland community councils may be formed where there is demand for them.

The Local Government Boundary Commission receives reviews from district councils suggesting alteration of boundaries, formation and abolition of parishes. In large urban areas it has generally been left to voluntary groups to build up neighbourhood councils which have no statutory powers and no ability to raise rate money. In towns with populations of less than 20,000 the parish or community council may choose to call itself a *town council* and elect a town mayor, but its powers and responsibility are the same.

How are they elected?
Local councils must have at least 5 councillors (usually 1 for 500 inhabitants). Elections are held in May every four years; most elections were last held in 1983. Vacancies between election are filled by by-elections (if demanded) or otherwise by co-option. Electors are the same as for any

election (from parish to national elections), i.e. you can vote if you are over 18, a British subject or citizen of Ireland, and your name is on the register prepared by the *district council* by 10 October each year and published by 15 February the following year.

How to become a councillor

You will need to be committed and energetic as well as over 21, a British subject or Irish citizen either (i) living in the parish or community (or within three miles of it) for the last year, (ii) working or (iii) having land there. You cannot become or remain a councillor if you work for the local council, become bankrupt or are sentenced to three months or more in prison within five years of the election.

How can you stand? You will need a proposer and seconder who must *live* in the parish or community. Nomination papers may be obtained from the returning officer at your district council office after the publication of the notice of election.

How do councils operate?

The councillors elect a chairman. Special tasks may be allocated to individual councillors or committees, for example to receive information on planning applications from the district council and decide whether an application should be discussed by the whole council. Committees can be formed with outside advisors who are not on the council. Often this is a useful way of dealing with big issues, organising special projects, or running 'village appraisals' to survey local problems and views.

The day-to-day work is done by the Clerk who writes agendas and minutes, receives information from other organisations and circulates it to the councillors, and deals with correspondence. Council minutes may be inspected by local electors (copies of town council minutes are usually held in the local library).

Local councils are often accused of being 'parochial' but

their greatest strength is the ability to take a detailed look at local issues, yet some councils suffer from isolation. Any issue is different in detail in any locality, but is the same general problem being discussed next door? Where parishes have kept each other informed, even joined forces in campaigning, they can less easily be ignored. There are several forums through which wider contacts can be made, in particular the Association of Local Councils. The national association has a branch in nearly every county of England and Wales (they share address and facilities with the Rural Community Council). They hold meetings several times a year. Some councils do not bother to send representatives, but these county meetings can be used to compare local problems and tactics and to keep in touch with county-wide and country-wide issues in which local councils are involved. Often parish councils have found it useful to invite their ward county and district councillors to attend parish meetings. This keeps those councillors informed, especially if there is a 'democratic half hour' to raise local issues. These councillors can often provide information and advice on how to approach their authorities with issues. It is quite common for the same person to be on the local as well as district or county council.

Increasingly, candidates for parish council elections are standing with a party affiliation. Once elected, however, detailed parish issues rarely cause divisions along party lines. Councillors' affiliation to parties and their political aspirations should be noted, however, as these networks can be useful in publicising issues.

Powers of parishes and communities

Local councils may raise money through the rates by precepting on the district council rate – usually 1p or 2p in the pound is requested. In towns this can raise tens of thousands of pounds, but the return is usually more modest. For example, in 1983-4 these Dorset parishes raised:

Blandford Forum	£5,028
Fontmell Magna	£507
Melbury Abbas	£216
Woolland	£49

Money may also be raised by public lotteries, letting halls, open spaces, etc., through claiming grants of various kinds and by borrowing. The money should be spent upon legitimate expenses for running the council and anything in the interests of the area and its people. This offers immense possibilities to the creative council.

Powers exist to help in the provision of many amenities including:

Allotments	Litter bins
Boating facilities	Orchestras
Burial grounds	Parish halls, dance halls
Camp sites	Parks and playgrounds
Car parks	Public bridleways and footpaths
Exhibitions	Public conveniences
Grass verges	Recreational facilities
Lighting	

In addition the local council can clear up ponds and ditches, maintain old graveyards, support local arts and crafts, repair rights of way; it can set up capital funds, give grants and donations.

The district (and county) council if so requested must notify the local council of all planning applications affecting the parish and must represent the views of the local council to the district planning committee.

Parish councils do not *have* to do a great deal, but they *can* be very active and full of initiative. They can of course give enthusiastic if not financial support to local ventures and can assist voluntary organisations by giving them money and by arguing their case at county or district level.

What can I do?

Some local councils are unadventurous, petty and run by age-old cliques, others, as we have seen, are active,

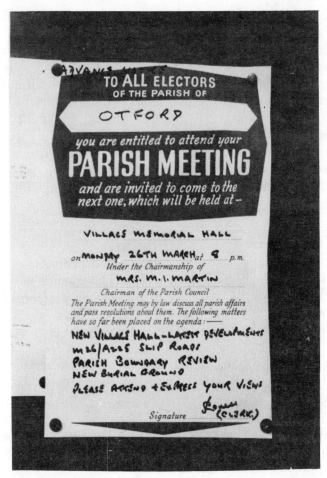

TO ALL ELECTORS
OF THE PARISH OF

OTFORD

you are entitled to attend your

PARISH MEETING

and are invited to come to the
next one, which will be held at –

VILLAGE MEMORIAL HALL

on MONDAY 26TH MARCH at 8 p.m.
Under the Chairmanship of

MRS. M. I. MARTIN

Chairman of the Parish Council
The Parish Meeting may by law discuss all parish affairs
and pass resolutions about them. The following matters
have so far been placed on the agenda:—

NEW VILLAGE HALL – LATEST DEVELOPMENTS
M26/A225 SLIP ROADS
PARISH BOUNDARY REVIEW
NEW BURIAL GROUND
PLEASE ATTEND & EXPRESS YOUR VIEWS

Signature (CLERK.)

creative, supportive, willing to question and offer new proposals when local actions or even national policies are likely to have unacceptable local repercussions.

Stand for the council. Seats on the local council are not always contested – but democracy needs elections; one candidate per seat offers no choice.

Even if you do not wish to stand as a parish councillor there are ways of provoking dormant councils into greater activity. There are growing demands for enhancing the grass-roots democracy which we take for granted. As a start you could:

go to council meetings or at least keep an eye on the council minutes to see what goes on;

find out how much the local council raises in rate money and how it spends it;

find out what the council could do and what it has done in recent years;

suggest, through councillors, that the activities be increased, and the rates too if necessary – an extra penny may enhance village life and environment considerably;

ask about the receipt of planning applications from the district and county councils – encourage councillors to inform people and solicit opinion as widely as possible;

encourage councils to have half an hour at council meetings when the public can discuss issues and ask questions;

encourage the council to join the National Association of Local Councils for ideas and information;

encourage everyone to go to the annual parish meeting to discuss important local matters.

County and district councils

How do they work?
Many powers and responsibilities for the wellbeing of the community and the environment reside with the district and/or county councils.

Both district and county councils are elected. Formally almost all decisions are taken by councillors in committee meetings and/or full council meetings.

Press and public have a right to listen to full council and committee meetings (but not sub-committees); generally, confidential items are taken at the end of meetings and press and public are asked to leave.

Minutes are open to local electors; copies and extracts may be taken from them; sometimes agendas are accessible too.

The frequency of full council meetings varies between

one every three months to one every six weeks; committee meetings are held more frequently.

The structure of district and county councils can vary a good deal as can the range of committees and their powers.

County Hall and the district council offices are full of paid staff whose job it is to serve the elected members and to cope with the day-to-day running of council activities. The officers (paid staff – not elected) of the council have usually organised themselves into departments which directly shadow or serve the committees of the council. The chiefs of section will be called the county/district planning officer, education officer, environmental health officer and so on. Below them there will be various sections with their leaders and teams. It is important to find out the structure and the influential people involved. In practice, of course, many of the decisions to be made in council or committee are discussed between elected councillors and the officers before council meetings, and given that the officers' full-time jobs are to collect information, perform day-to-day tasks and present ideas for future activities, much power lies with them. They may choose to miss things off agendas, or to push a favourite cause.

Responsibilities of county and district councils
(England, non-metropolitan, and Wales)

	County	*District*
Housing		*
Planning		
Structure Plans	*	
Local Plans		*
Development Control	*	* most
National Parks	*	
Areas of Outstanding Natural Beauty	*	
Heritage coasts	*	
Country Parks	*	*
Tree Preservation	*	* most
Building Preservation	*	*
Ancient Monuments	*	*

	County	District
Conservation Areas		*
Derelict Land	*	*
Acquisition and Sale of Land	*	*
Mineral Planning	*	
Local Nature Reserves	*	
Transportation		
Footpaths and Bridleways		
Rights of way – definitive maps	*	
Surveys	*	
Maintenance	*	
Protection	*	
Signposting	*	
Creating/Diversion/Extinguishment	*	*
Maintenance of road verges	*	
Transport planning and Coordination	*	
Highways	*	
Traffic regulation	*	
Parking	*	*
Road Safety	*	
Footway Lighting	*	*
Museums and the Arts	*	*
Libraries	*	
Airports	*	*
Fire Service	*	
Police	*	
Social Services	*	
Education	*	
Leisure Services		
Swimming baths and Playing Fields	*	*
Parks and Open Spaces	*	*
Small holdings	*	
Allotments		*
Environmental Health		
Animal diseases	*	
Slaughterhouses		*
Factories and farms		*
Refuse Collection		*
Refuse disposal	*	
Clean air	*	*

Coastal Protection   *
Consumer Protection   *
Building Regulations   *
Cemeteries   *
Markets and Fairs   *
Nuisances (smells, etc.)   *

Find out who the leading officers are as well as the chairman of particular committees; both may be very powerful. It is important to have both officers and councillors on your side if you can.

Information on committee structure, organisation of officers, names of councillors, committee members and chief officers and dates of committee and sub-committee meetings is in the *council's Year Book*, which should be available in local libraries, or through the public information office of the council; sadly, these are not usually for sale. If this cannot be found look in the *Municipal Year Book* which lists councillors over the whole country.

Planning
Strategic and day-to-day concern for the environment rests with the local authorities. The county council structure plan, the district council local plans and their supporting survey volumes will show areas designated as having high landscape value, scientific and historic interest and will describe policies for conservation and more stringent development control. Many counties and districts have undertaken special countryside and landscape studies.

The planning departments of county councils usually have a countryside section. They are responsible for the overall protection of the countryside, the planning and management of heritage coasts and country parks, including the planting of trees, the establishment of local nature reserves, picnic areas, the management of council-owned land. Officers may include a county ecologist, a landscape officer and a tree or forestry officer, a county archaeologist, a building conservation officer.

Some county councils employ their own management teams who will do physical work as well as surveys and planning. Hertfordshire County Council has set up five 'management areas' of about 100 sq. km. 'each with their own specialist Countryside Manager, who discusses problems and opportunities directly with the public'. 'The Countryside Manager trains and operates a Ranger Service of full-time, part-time and volunteer personnel to lead and carry out practical conservation work and visitor assistance, and through this service he can take quick and positive action to resolve small scale conflicts and problems. . .'

In recent years many of the decisions affecting the countryside have been devolved to the District Councils. They too will have a countryside section within their planning or technical services department which will deal with local plans, most planning applications, felling licences, TPOs, conservation areas and so on.

Buildings and other forms of 'development' require *planning permission*. 'Development' can include works in, on, over or under land and includes changes in the use of buildings and some land. Agricultural activities, including afforestation, are exempt from the demands of development control – only new large farm buildings need permission. All but major applications go to the district council. Permission is not witheld or given at the whim of councillors informed by planners, but is intended to reflect a careful decision which takes many environmental, social and economic factors into account. Applications for planning permission are assessed in the light of the statutory plans for the area, informed by the politics of the day. Refusals (but not granting) of permission can be appealed against, to the Secretary of State for the Environment and Wales.

Structure plans are drawn up by the *county planning authority* and approved by the Secretary of State: they include generalised maps and policy statements which suggest control of certain developments in some areas and encouragement to develop in other areas. These are based on published studies of population, employment, countryside and so on which may give you all kinds of useful descriptive information about your area.

Local plans (district or action area plans) for particular places and plans about specific topics (subject plans) are usually made by the *district planning authority* which also oversees most of the development control/planning permission process. These plans are more precise and include detailed maps as well as written statements of policy.

From background studies, subject plans, and the structure and local plans you can gain a good deal of information about your area and sort out the ideas which the authorities have for it. All of the reports and plans should be available through your local library; they can be bought or consulted at the county and district offices. It may be too late to comment on or object to the plans, but there are ways of voicing objection or encouragement for individual applications for planning permission if they affect you or your locality. The usual way is to write to the chief planning officer of the district council and to get in touch with parish and district councillors. You must ring and write without delay since the law dictates very short periods for public comment. Local planning authorities are not obliged to inform anyone affected by planning applications, but they advertise them in local papers and in the vicinity. The parish council should receive copies of all local planning applications and you have a right to consult the *planning register* (which includes all the planning applications) at the district offices.

Complaints: local ombudsman
There are three commissions for local administration, one each for England, Wales and Scotland. Each has a number of local commissioners (ombudsmen) who are responsible for different areas.

They investigate citizens' complaints of *maladministration* by county or district councils, London authorities or the regional water authorities, but *not* parish or community councils. They can only investigate maladministration (e.g. if the council/water authority etc. have gone about doing something the wrong way or have used bias or unfair discrimination) or failed to take relevant matters into account. They cannot do anything about the merits of the authorities' decisions.

Complaints are normally channelled through councillors of the offending authority but they may be placed directly with the ombudsman. Local authorities cannot be forced to give compensation to a complainant if his/her case is upheld, but most do so and put the system right for future cases.

Members of Parliament

Central Government acts as both initiator of policies – through laws, circulars and so on – and as place of final appeal in the case of major planning projects etc. It also provides a proportion of the money to run district and county councils through the Rate Support Grant. Although you may not have the Secretary of State for the Environment, Transport or Agriculture in your locality, you do have an MP and if your councillors are not interested in your cause, you may find rapid action possible through this route. The local library will be able to tell you his or her name and address.

References and further reading

Association of Liberal Councillors Campaign Booklets esp. *Parish Politics: A Liberal Guide*, Booklet No. 5, 60p.
Byre, T., *Local Government in Britain: Everyone's Guide to how it all works*, 1981.
Derounian, J., *Planning – A Guide for Devon People*, Community Council of

Devon/Devon Association of Parish Councils, 1982.

DOE, *A Voice for your Neighbourhood – the Neighbourhood Council*, HMSO, 1970.

Grapevine, *Parish Councils*, BBC.

Hargreaves, D., *The Parish Councillor's Handbook*, The Municipal Group, 1979, £1.00.

HMSO, *Local Government in Britain*, COI Reference Pamphlet 1, 1980, £2.50.

The Labour Party, *Local Government Handbook – England and Wales*, 1981.

Meek, M. and Patmore, C., *The Planning System – A brief guide for Parish Councillors in North Yorkshire*, Yorkshire Rural Community Council and Yorkshire and Cleveland Local Councils' Assn, 1981.

Municipal Yearbook.

National Association of Local Councils, *The Role of Local Councils, Powers and Constitution of Local Councils*, NALC, 1979.

Arnold-Baker, C. and Clark, J., *The Role of Local Councils*.

NALC, *Local Council Review* – journal.

Nottinghamshire Association of Local Councils, *Parish Council Clerks: Manual of Guidance*.

17
Money and help

FINANCIAL HELP

It is paradoxical that many voluntary/community groups often have to spend more time and effort on fund-raising than on achieving the goals they set themselves.

However, many small local groups do not need to raise large amounts of money as they do not employ full-time staff or need to pay for premises. Here fund-raising to pay for printing costs etc. can be an enjoyable task, involving different members of the group and attracting new ones. Coffee mornings, jumble sales, barbecues and so on require good organisation and publicity to be successful. *The Community Organisations Survival Kit* 1982 gives lots of ideas on how to raise funds within the local community as well as from charitable trusts and industry. It is available from the National Federation of Community Organisations, 8-9 Upper Street, London N1 OPQ at £1.50.

Local businesses and trusts

Local businesses will often respond to requests for funds and they will often offer practical help – equipment, people, their products for prizes. You may also be able to sell them advertising space in your newsletter or report.

Business and Charitable Trusts often prefer to give to local causes. Look in the *Directory of Grant-making Trusts* (published annually by the Charities Aid Foundation) in your library for the trusts which give money in your area and for your kinds of activities. Most charitable trusts will only give money to charities. For advice on whether it is worth your group becoming a charity consult *Charitable*

Status – A Practical Handbook by Andrew Phillips and Keith Smith published by Inter Action 1982 £2.50. (15 Wilkin Street, London NW5) and the Charities Aid Foundation, 48 Pembury Road, Tonbridge, Kent TN9 2J0, who provide information and advice. The Charity Commission, 14 Ryder Street, St James's, London SW17 6AH and the Charity Commission (Northern Region) Graeme House, Derby Square, Liverpool LZ 7SB, will give information on how to register as a charity. It can take a long time.

Before writing to a company or trust, telephone the public relations office or appeal secretary to find out the correct procedure for making an application and to ascertain if it is worth your while writing. Practice on someone least likely to give you money to build your style and confidence. Ask what more information is needed. You will need to know the correct time in which to send your application (some trusts only meet a few times a year) and the name and title of the person to send it to. In your letter, try to point out the reasons why the company or trust should be interested in your project and why the project needs to be done. State your objectives' clearly, enclose a budget for the project and a leaflet or prospectus or annual report which gives background information about your organisation. Keep it short and simple. If you are receiving funding from another organisation, say so. Most trusts and companies prefer to give small amounts to many groups and are happier if you are not dependent on them alone for funding. Look in the *UK Kompass Register of British Industry and Commerce* (which should be available in any large library) for the names of the director/board members of the company you are thinking of approaching and in the *Directory of Grant-making Trusts* for names of trustees. You are much more likely to be successful if your group can make a personal approach to a board member or trustee of a charitable trust.

Many books, booklets and articles have been written on the art of fund-raising. Some of these are listed below. The best way to learn, however, is by experience, and much depends on the character of the fund-raiser. Someone who is personable and enthusiastic and who has an easy telephone manner and who can write a good letter is ideal.

Useful books and leaflets

Fund-raising by Grapevine. BBC. Free leaflet.
Voluntary but not Amateur – a guide to the law for voluntary organisations and community groups London Voluntary Service Council, 68 Charlton Street, London NW1 1JR £3.00.
Government Grants: A Guide for Voluntary Organisations NCVO 1983 £3.50.
Fundraising and Grant Aid for Voluntary Organisations – a guide to the literature Compiled for NCVO by Susan Bates Nov. 1981 £1.50 26, Bedford Square London WC1B 3HU.
Raising money from trusts Directory of Social Change 1981 £2.95. 9 Mansfield Place, London NW3.
Raising money from industry Directory of Social Change 1981
Raising money from government "
Raising money through Special Events "
Raising money for the Arts "
Fund Raising: A Comprehensive Handbook by Hilary Blume
Accounting and Financial Management for Charities Directory of Social Change 1980.

National agencies, trusts and companies

A number of sources of money for environmental and arts projects are listed below:
1. *Department of the Environment*, Room C15/11, 2 Marsham St., London SW1P 3EB (01-212-3515) offers a variety of grants (described in a free leaflet) which must be matched from non-government sources.
(i) The Special Grants Programme is intended to help national and regional voluntary organisations.

a)   Management/administrative   grants   for organisations involved in practical conservation of the natural and man-made environment, education, advisory and coordination services.

b) The Projects grants are for practical innovatory or experimental work in the environment.

c) The Urban Initiatives Fund is for rehabilitation work of disused or under-used urban land and buildings. It helps the RIBA provide a community architectural service for local voluntary groups for self-help projects. The RIBA will match the grant (Community Architectural Service, RIBA, 66 Portland Place, London W1.).

ii)   Urban conservation and historic buildings

Grants are available for repair of buildings of outstanding historic or architectural interest (usually grade I or II* listed buildings).

'Conservation Area Grants are available for buildings in conservation areas (which are designated by local planning authorities) and are made for works which will make a significant contribution to the "preservation or enhancement of the character or appearance of a conservation area".'

iii)   Ancient Monuments – grants are available for the owners for the management of scheduled ancient monuments, for excavation costs, to any person, society or group to help with the acquisition, preservation, management maintenance or even removal to a safe place of an ancient monument.

Applications for ii) & iii) should be made to the Historic Buildings & Monuments Commission, 23/25 Savile Row, London W1X 2HE.

2. *Countryside Commission*, John Dower House, Crescent Place Cheltenham, Glos. GL50 3RA (0242-521381) /8 Broad Street, Newtown, Powys. (0686-26799) /CC for Scotland, Battleby, Redgerton, Perth (0738-27921).

1)   Development Grants for voluntary organisations to

help establish or extend activities in conservation, recreation or access (max. 75 per cent).

2) Grants to public and private organisations for practical schemes of conservation and access (up to 50 per cent). The range includes management and conservation of important landscape features, amenity tree planting, woodland management, creation and management of footpaths, environmental interpretation voluntary management agreements, purchase of outstanding landscape and important recreation areas, employment of countryside advisers and schemes which involve volunteers in practical conservation and recreation provision. The Regional Offices should be approached in the first instance.

3) The Groundwork Resource Unit helps in the creation of local trusts promoting urban fringe improvements in the North West of England.

Countryside Commission Regional offices:

Eastern
Terrington House
13 Hills Road
Cambridge CB2 1NL
0223 354462

South East
30/32 Southampton Street
London WC2E 7RA
01-240 2771

Midlands
Cumberland House
200 Broad Street
Birmingham B15 1TD
021-632 6503

Northern
Warwick House
Grantham Road

Newcastle upon Tyne NE2 1QF
0632 328252

North West/Groundwork
184 Deansgate
Manchester M3 2WB
061-833 0316/9950

South West
Bridge House
Sion Place
Clifton Down
Bristol BS8 4AS
0272 739966

Yorkshire & Humberside
8A Otley Road
Headingly
Leeds LS6 2AD
0532 742935

3. *Nature Conservancy Council*, Grants Section, Northminster House, Northminster Peterborough, Cambs. PEI IUA (0733 40345) gives grants or loans to single projects or purchases for nature reserve management, practical species conservation, increasing awareness and understanding of nature conservation also the small grants scheme gives up to £500 for small projects. Send for their leaflet *Advice to Applicants* or an application form from the NCC's Grants Section or from any NCC office.

4. *Arts Council* of Great Britain, 105 Piccadilly, London W1V DAU (01-629-9495) offers revenue, project, bursary and capital grants for the arts – but you are better to approach –

5. *Regional Arts Associations*: They offer advice, revenue and project funding for drama, music, photography, film, dance, literature, visual arts, community arts etc.

Scottish Arts Council
19 Charlotte Square

Edinburgh EH2 4DF
031-226 6051

Welsh Arts Council
Museum Place
Cardiff CF1 3NX
0222 394711

Eastern Arts Association
Cherry Hinton Hall
Cherry Hinton Road
Cambridge CB1 4DW
0223 215 355

East Midlands Arts
Mountfields House
Forest Road
Loughborough
Leicester LE11 3HU
0509 218292

Greater London Arts Association
9 White Lion Street
London N1 9PD
01-837 8808

Lincolnshire and Humberside Arts
St. Hugh's
Newport
Lincoln LN1 3DN
0522 33555

Merseyside Arts
Bluecoat Chambers
School Lane
Liverpool L1 3BX
051-709 0671

Northern Arts
10 Osborne Terrace
Newcastle upon Tyne NE2 1NZ
0632 816334

North West Arts
12 Harter Street
Manchester M1 6HY
061-228 3062

Southern Arts Association
19 Southgate Street
Winchester
Hampshire SO23 9D4
0962 55099

South East Arts
10 Mount Ephriam
Tunbridge Wells
Kent TN4 8AS
0892 41666

South West Arts
Bradninch Place
Gandy Street
Exeter EX4 3LS
0392 218188

West Midlands Arts
82 Granville Street
Birmingham B1 2LH
021 631 3121

Yorkshire Arts Association
Glyde House
Glydegate
Bradford
West Yorkshire BD5 0BQ
0274 723051

   6. *Crafts Council*, 12 Waterloo Place, London SW1Y 4AU
01 930-4811 – grants and loans are available to crafts
organisations, groups or individuals for special projects –

e.g. mounting exhibitions, for setting up workshops, training bursaries and craft commissions. The quality of craft skill must be to a high standard.

7. *Tourist Boards.* Applications should be made to the appropriate Regional Tourist Board. They offer 50 per cent grants and loans for schemes in specific areas which would improve or provide tourist facilities. English Tourist Board, 4 Grosvenor Gardens, London SW1W 0DU (01-730-3400). Development Department, Welsh Tourist Board, Welcome House, Llandaff, Cardiff CF5 2YZ (0222-567701). Development Division, Scottish Tourist Board, 23 Ravelston Terrace, Edinburgh EH4 3EU (031-332-2433).

8. *Development Commission* is one of the sponsoring bodies of the Rural Community Councils. It will give grants for projects which benefit the rural economy if no other funding can be found. Grants for village halls and community buildings are available in Rural Development Areas, CoSIRA – the Council for Small Industries in Rural Areas – is also funded by the Development Commission. It grant-aids schemes for the conversion of redundant farm and rural buildings for any employment creating uses in Rural development Areas. For information, contact your CoSIRA County Organiser. Development Commission, 11 Cowley Street, London SW1P 3N1 (01-222-9134) /Welsh Development Agency, Treforest Industrial Estate, Ponypridd, Mid Glamorgan (044-385-2666) /Scottish Development Agency, 120 Bothwell Street, Glasgow (041-248-2700) CoSIRA 141 Castle Street, Salisbury, Wiltshire SP1 3TP (0722 336255)

9. *Forestry Commission* administer a Forestry Grant Scheme, the main aim of which is timber production. This includes grants for broadleaved trees and native pinewoods in Scotland. Forestry Commission, 231 Corstorphine Road, Edinburgh EH12 7AT (031-334-0303).

10. *Architectural Heritage Fund administered by the Civic Trust* provides low-interest loans to Building Preservation

Trusts to restore listed buildings and buildings of local importance and interest. Civic Trust, 17 Carlton House Terrace, London SW1Y 5AW (01-930-0914).

11. *Historic Buildings Council Conservation Grants* administered by *The Civic Trust* financed by the DOE, allocates repair grants to historic buildings in conservation areas.

12. *Heritage Interpretation Programme* funded by the Carnegie United Kingdom Trust is designed to encourage local amenity societies to undertake interpretive projects. Fifty per cent grants are given to approved schemes by societies registered with the Civic Trust.

13. *Shell Better Britain Campaign*, NCC, Northminster House, Northminster Peterborough, Cambs. PEI IUA (0733 40345) Ask for the Information Pack which is full of useful information. Grants of up to £500, advice, campaign workshops and Achievement Awards are available for voluntary groups undertaking environmental projects which benefit the whole community. The Campaign is a partnership between BTCV, NCC, Civic Trust and Shell Oil.

14. *World Wildlife Fund* Panda House 11-13 Ockford Road, Godalming, Surrey GU7 1QU (04868) 20551. 'Ninety per cent of the funds raised are used in support of organisations purchasing areas of land of national importance. The balance of ten per cent has in the past been applied to one-off management projects very often on sites purchased with our help, research projects which result in a direct benefit to conservation and occasionally educational projects.'

15. *The Tree Council* has limited funds but can give 50 per cent of a tree planting scheme. The Tree Council, Room 101, Agriculture House, Knightsbridge, London SW1X 7NJ (01-235 8854).

16. *Regional Water Authorities.* The Welsh Water Authority and some others give small grants for conservation projects. Ask your regional water authority for information.

17. *Inland Waterways Association* gives grants towards voluntary restoration of waterways. They also offer a range of insurance cover to affiliated groups. Inland Waterways Association, 114 Regents Park Road, London NW1 (01-586 2556).

18. *Prince of Wales Committee* is a charity which helps voluntary and non-profit-making groups to improve the Welsh Environment for the benefit of the community as a whole. The Committee can provide grants towards materials and equipment needed by a project. Address: 6th floor, Empire House, Mount Stuart Square, Cardiff CF1 6DN.

19. *Regional Television Company Trusts* may offer grants for projects which benefit communities in their area.

20. *Local Authorities* vary a good deal in the interest they take in voluntary organisations' work. Many support local projects through loan or grant aid, provision of premises, rate rebates, equipment and labour loan and so on. The rural community council or local council for voluntary service will be able to advise on the help available and whether the county, district or parish council should be approached. It is helpful to seek advice and help from local authority officers and then to seek support from councillors in whose area the project will be and those who sit on the relevant committees.

i) *Town Schemes.* 50 per cent grants offered by DOE and County and District Councils for the repair of buildings in some conservation areas where there are concentrations of historic buildings.

ii) *Buildings.* County & District councils can make grants for any building of architectural or historic interest.

iii) Free tree schemes are offered by some district and county councils.

21. *Trusts.* Many charitable trusts give to other charities small or large – look in the Charities Aid Foundations' *Directory of Grant Making Trusts* in your local library.

22. *The Ecology Building Society*, 43 Main Street, Cross Hills via Keighley, W. Yorks BD20 8TT. 'Advances shall be made

to persons or on properties which in the opinion of the Board, are most likely to lead to the saving of non-renewable resources, the promotion of self-sufficiency in individuals or communities, or the most ecologically efficient use of land.' The Society is willing to lend to communities and cooperatives as well as individuals.

23. *Competitions* can be a good source of extra funding or publicity. With a little extra effort – usually a write-up of your work and a photograph – you may attract newspaper/radio coverage or a few hundred pounds for your project. Look out for local and national competitions. A few examples follow.

i) *Village Ventures Competitions* are run by community councils and cover anything from pond restoration to organising a study of the parish.

ii) The *Henley Award* for high-quality restoration or conversion of old farm buildings is organised by the CLA and CPRE/CPRW.

iii) The *Britain in Bloom* competition is run on a regional basis by the British Tourist Authority.

iv) *Pride of Place* is an annual competition run by the Civic Trust. It aims to encourage societies to work on local environmental improvement projects. The competition highlights different regions each year. In 1983 the prize money totalled £6,750.

v) *Conservation Awards* run by Ford of Britain and the Conservation Foundation. In 1983 £20,000 sponsorship was divided into cash prizes and trophies in six categories Heritage, Environment, Reclamation, Industry, Young People and Conservation Engineering. Contact The Conservation Foundation, 11a West Halkin Street, London SWIX 8JL (01 235 1743) for details.

vi) An annual award jointly offered by the Countryside Commission and CLA has a different theme each year – contact them for details.

vii) *Carnegie Interpret Britain Award* run by the Society for the Interpreting of Britain's Heritage and administered by the Centre for Environmental Interpretation.

PHYSICAL HELP

How to find help

Parish groups should be encouraged to gain the knowledge to manage their own wild life and amenity areas. Advice on management is readily available from the county and district planning departments, county naturalists' trust or local conservation volunteers.

The following *national and county groups* can be approached for physical labour, specific advice and general help:

The British Trust for Conservation Volunteers is the main source of physical help in the countryside. The BTCV will do a wide variety of tasks from pond clearance and footbridge building to drystone walling and fencing. There are over 300 local conservation groups affiliated to the BTCV. If you require their help, contact your nearest local group, Regional Office or the headquarters at 36 St Mary's Street, Wallingford, Oxfordshire (0491-39766). The charge for each volunteer ranges from £1.00 a day for local work to £3.50 a day for residential work.

County Council Countryside Departments may employ their own rangers and run training sessions in countryside management techniques. Officers and rangers can offer advice and help.

County Naturalists' Trust members are also a source of voluntary advice and help. They often involve local schools, borstals, Girl Guide and Boy Scout groups as well as MSC people in management projects.

The Inland Waterways Association, The Waterways Recovery Group and local branches of the IWA are very active in restoring waterways to navigation. The IWA can provide addresses of the Waterways Recovery Groups and local

Waterway societies. IWA, 114 Regent's Park Road, London NW1 (01-586 2556).

Local branches of the *Ramblers' Association* are active in footpath clearance and waymarking. Contact your local group or the national headquarters: Ramblers' Association, 1-5 Wandsworth Road, London SW8 2LJ (01 582-6878).

Volunteer Bureau. The 281 Volunteer bureaux throughout Britain recruit, interviews, train and place volunteers. The *Volunteer Bureau Directory* lists all the centres. It is available from the Volunteer Centre, 29 Lower King's Road, Beckhamsted, Herts. HP4 2AB. (04427-73311) at £2.00.

Young Farmers' Clubs are open to *all* young people with an interest in the countryside. They are involved in many environmental tasks in their localities. Contact your local club or the National Federation of Young Farmers' Clubs, YFC Centre, National Agricultural Centre, Kenilworth, Warwickshire (0203 56131).

Manpower Services Commission Schemes. It may be possible for your group or the parish council to employ some people under an MSC scheme. Contact your local MSC area office (see telephone directory) for information on youth training schemes, the community programme, voluntary projects programme. The Community Schemes Unit at the NCVO, 26 Bedford Square, London WC1 (01-636 4066) will give you information too. Don't forget the Scouts, Guides, school children, students, YHA, youth clubs, WI and armed forces who may be able to offer a hand.

Further information on sources of help is contained in *Volunteers in the Countryside*.

How to get experience and training

There are many opportunities: the Countryside Commission organises sponsored rangers' courses; the BTCV runs many courses in management and a national programme of residential tasks; the National Trust organises Acorn Camps weekend work for young volunteers on National Trust properties; and many County Councils help to train volunteers as well. (Acorn Camps, National Trust, The Old Grape House, Cliveden, Taplow, Maidenhead, Berks SL6 6HZ 062-86-4228).

Shell Better Britain in conjunction with the NCC, Civic Trust and BTCV run training workshops. Information for workshops in your region can be obtained from Shell Better Britain Campaign, NCC, Northminster House, Northminster, Peterborough, Cambs. PE1 1UA (0733 40345)

Useful publications: *Insurance Protection – a guide for voluntary organisations and for voluntary workers.* Edited by Paula Pedlar, NCVO 1983.

Volunteers in the Countryside Advisory Series No 11, 1980 by the Countryside Commission.

18

Organisations and Addresses

Statutory

Arts Council of Great Britain, 105 Piccadilly, London W1V DAU. (01 629 9495)

British Tourist Authority, 64 St. James's Street, London SW1 (01 629 9191)

British Waterways Board, Melbury House, Melbury Terrace, London NW1 6JX (01 262 6711)

Charity Commission, 14 Ryder Street, St. James's, London SW17 6AH

Countryside Commission, John Dower House, Crescent Place, Cheltenham, Glos. GL50 3RA (0242 521381). 8 Broad Street, Newtown, Powys SY16 2LU (0686 26799). Battleby, Redgerton, Perth PH1 3EW (0738 27921)

Crafts Council, 12 Waterloo Place, London SW1Y 4AU (01 930 4811)

Department of the Environment, 2 Marsham Street, London SW1P 3EB (01 212 3434). Directorate of Rural Affairs, Tollgate House, Houlton Street, Bristol BS29 DJ (0272 218811)

Development Commission, 11 Cowley Street, London SW1P 3NA (01 222 9134)

English Tourist Board, 4 Grosvenor Gardens, London SW1W ODU (01 730 3400)

Forestry Commission, 231 Corstorphine Road, Edinburgh EH12 7AT (031 334 0303)

Historic Buildings & Monuments Commission, 23 Savile Row, London W1X 2HE (01 734 6010)

Manpower Services Commission, Moorfoot, Sheffield S1 4PQ (0742 753275)

Ministry of Agriculture, Fisheries and Food, Whitehall Place, London SW1A 2HH (01 233 3000/5550)

Nature Conservancy Council, Northminster House, Northminster, Peterborough, Cambs. PEI IUA (0733 40345)

Nature Conservancy Council (Scotland): 12 Hope Terrace, Edinburgh EH9 2AS (031 447 4784)

Nature Conservancy Council (Wales): Plas Penrhos, Penrhos Road, Bangor, Gwynedd LL57 2LQ (0248 55141)

Royal Commissions on Ancient and Historical Monuments,
England: Fortress House, 23 Savile Row, London W1X 1AB (01 734 6010)

Scotland: 54 Melville Street, Edinburgh EH3 7HF (031 225 5994)

Wales: Edleston House, Queen's Road, Aberystwyth, Dyfed SY23 2HP (0970 4381)

Scottish Arts Council: 19 Charlotte Square, Edinburgh EH2 4DF (031 226 6051)

Scottish Development Agency: 120 Bothwell Street, Glasgow G2 7JP (041 248 2700)

Scottish Office, New Street, Andrew's House, St. James Centre, Edinburgh EH1 3SX (031 556 8400)

Scottish Tourist Board, 23 Ravelston Terrace, Edinburgh EH4 3EU (031 332 2433)

Welsh Arts Council: Museum Place, Cardiff CF1 3NX (0222 394711)

Welsh Development Agency: Treforest Industrial Estate, Pontypridd, Mid Glamorgan, Wales CF37 5UT (044 385 2666)

Welsh Office, Cathays Park, Cardiff CF1 3NQ (0222 825111)

Welsh Tourist Board, Welcome House, Llandaff, Cardiff CF5 2YZ (0222 567701)

2) Voluntary

Action with Communities in Rural England (ACRE), Stable Yard, Fairford Park, Glos. GL7 4JQ

Ancient Monuments Society, St. Andrew-by-the-Wardrobe, Queen Victoria Street, London EC4V 5DE (01 236-3934)

Anglers' Co-operative Association, Midland Bank Chambers, Westgate, Grantham, Lincs. NG31 6LE (0476 61008)

Apple & Pear Development Council, Unicorn House, The Pantiles, Tunbridge Wells, Kent (0892 20255)

Architectural Heritage Fund, Civic Trust, 17 Carlton House Terrace, London SW1Y 5AW (01 930 0914)

Arvon Foundation: Totleigh Barton, Sheepwash, Devon EX21 5NS & Lumb Bank, Heptonstall Hebden Bridge, West Yorkshire HX7 6DF

Association for Industrial Archaeology, The Wharfage, Iron Bridge, Telford, Salop TF8 7AW (095 245 3522)

Association of Liberal Councillors, The Birchcliffe Centre, Hebden Bridge, West Yorkshire HX7 8DG

Association for Neighbourhood Councils, Kingsway Hall, 75 Kingsway, London WC2B 6TA (01 405 4718)

Association for the Protection of Rural Scotland, 1 Thistle Court, Edinburgh 2 (031 225 6744)

Botanical Society of the British Isles (BSBI), c/o Dept. of Botany, Natural History Museum, Cromwell Road, London SW7 5BD (01 589 6323)

British Agricultural History Society, Institute of Agricultural History & Museum of English Rural Life, Whiteknights, PO Box 229, Reading, Berks RG6 2AG (0734 875123 ext. 475)

British Association for Local History, 43 Bedford Square, London WC13 3DP (01 636 4066)

British Association of Nature Conservationists, Rectory Farm, Stanton St. John, Oxford OX9 1HF (086735 214)

British Butterfly Conservation Society, Tudor House, Quorn, Loughborough, Leics LE12 8AD (0509 412870)

British Hedgehog Preservation Society, Knowbury House, Knowbury, Ludlow, Shropshire SY8 3JT (0584 890287)

British Herpetological Society Conservation Committee, 20 Queensberry Place, London SW7 2DZ

British Historic Buildings Trust, St Michaels Studio, St Nichols Churchyard Derby DE1 3DX.

British Trust for Conservation Volunteers, 36 St. Mary's Street, Wallingford, Oxfordshire OX10 0EU (0491 39766)

British Trust for Ornithology (BTO), Beech Grove, Station

Road, Tring, Herts HP23 5NR (044 282 3461)

Byways & Bridleways Trust, 9 Queen Anne's Gate, London SW1H 9BY (024 974 286)

Charities Aid Foundation, 48 Pembury Road, Tonbridge, Kent TN9 2JD (0732 356323)

Church Information Office, Church House, London SW1P 3NZ

Civic Trust, 17 Carlton House Terrace, London SW1Y 5AW (01 930 0914)

Civic Trust for the North East, 3 Old Elvet, Durham DH1 3HL (0385 61182)

Civic Trust for the North West, The Environmental Institute, Greaves School, Bolton Road, Swinton, Manchester M27 20X (061 794 9314)

Civic Trust for Wales, St. Michael's College, Llandaff, Cardiff CF5 2YJ (0222 552388)

Community Service Volunteers (CSV), 237 Pentonville Road, London N1 9NJ (01 278 6601)

Conservation Foundation, 11a West Halkin Street, London SW1X 8JL (01 235 1743)

Council for British Archaeology, 112 Kennington Road, London SE11 6RE (01 582 0494)

Council for Environmental Conservation (CoEnCo), The London Ecology Centre, 80 York Way, London N1 9AG (01 722 7111)

Council for Environmental Education, School of Education, University of Reading, London Road, Reading RG1 5AQ (0734 875234 ext. 218)

Council for National Parks, The London Ecology Centre, 45 Shelton Street, London WC2H 9HJ (01 240 3603)

Council for the Protection of Rural England (CPRE), 4 Hobart Place, London SW1W 0HY (01 235 9481)

Council for the Protection of Rural Wales, Ty Gwyn, 31 High Street, Welshpool, Powys SY21 7PJ (0938 2525) (see APRS for Scotland.)

Council for Small Industries In Rural Areas (CoSIRA), 141 Castle Street, Salisbury, Wiltshire SP1 3TP (0722 336255)

Country Landowners Association, 16 Belgrave Square, London SW1X 8PQ (01 235 0511)

Directory of Social Change, 9 Mansfield Place, London NW3 (01 435 8171/01 794 9835)

Dry Stone Walling Association, Y.F.C. Centre, National Agricultural Centre, Kenilworth, Warwickshire, CV8 2LG (0203 56131)

Ecology Building Society, 43 Main Street, Cross Hills Keighley, W. Yorks BD20 8TT (0535 35933)

English Folk Dance and Song Society, Cecil Sharp House, 2 Regent's Park Road, London NW1 7AY (01 485 2206)

English Place Name Society, School of English Studies, The University, Nottingham NG7 2RD (Nottingham 56101 X. 2892)

Farming and Wildlife Advisory Group (FWAG), The Lodge, Sandy, Bedfordshire SG19 2DL (0767 80551)

Fauna and Flora Preservation Society, 8-12 Camden High Street, London NW1 0JH (01 387 9656)

Field Studies Council, Preston Montford, Montford Bridge, Shrewsbury, Shrops SY4 1HW (0743 850674)

Findhorn Foundation, The Park, Forres, Soctland IV36 0TZ (0309 30311)

Folklore Society, c/o University College, Gower Street, London WC1E 6BT (01 387 5894)

Friends of the Earth Ltd., 377 City Road, London EC1V 1NA (01 837 0731)

Friends of the Earth Scotland, 53 George IV Bridge, Edinburgh EH1 1EJ (031 225 6906)

The Garden History Society, 12 Charlbury Road, Oxford (0865 55543) and 66 Granville Park, London SE13 7DX

Grapevine, Community Programmes Unit, BBC TV, London W12 8QT (01 743 8000)

The Green Alliance, 60 Chandos Place, London WC1 (01 836 0341)

Greenpeace, 30/31 Islington Green, London N1 8XE (01 354 5100/01 359 7396)

Gwent Badger Group, Elm Tree, Caer Licyn Lane, Langstone,

Newport, Gwent NP6 2JZ (0633 400464)

The Hawk Trust, Freepost, Beckenham, Kent. Birds of Prey Section, Zoological Society of London, Regents Park, London NW1 4RY.

Henry Doubleday Research Association, Covent Lane, Bocking, Braintree, Essex (0376 24083)

Heritage Education Group, Civic Trust, 17 Carlton House Terrace, London SW1Y 5AW (01 930 0914)

Historical Association, 59a Kennington Park Road, London SE11 4JH (01 735 3901/2974)

Inland Waterways Association, 114 Regent's Park Road, London NW1 8UQ (01 586 2510/2556)

Institute of Contemporary Arts, The Mall, London SW1Y 5AH (01 930 0493)

Inter-Action Trust Ltd., 15 Wilkin Street, London NW5 (01 267 9421)

Land Heritage, Wellington, Somerset

London Voluntary Service Council, 68 Charlton Street, London NW1 1JR (01 388 0241)

London Wildlife Trust, 80 York Way, London, N1 9AG (01 278 6612/6613)

Men of the Trees, Crawley Down, Crawley, W. Sussex RH10 4HL (0342 712536)

National Anglers' Council, 11 Cowgate, Peterborough, PE1 1LZ (0733 54084)

National Association of Local Councils, 108 Great Russell Street, London WC1B 3LD (01 636 4066)

National Council for Voluntary Organisations, 26 Bedford Square, London WC1B 3HU (01 636 4066)

National Farmers' Union, Agriculture House, Knightsbridge, London SW1X 7NJ (01 235 5077)

National Federation of Community Organisations, 8-9 Upper Street, London N1 0PQ (01 266 0189)

National Federation of Women's Institutes, 39 Eccleston Street, London SW1W 9NT (01 730 7212)

National Federation of Young Farmers' Clubs, YFC Centre, National Agricultural Centre, Kenilworth, Warwickshire CV8 2LG (0203 56131)

National Society of Allotment and Leisure Gardeners Ltd., Odell House, Hunters Road, Corby, Northants NN17 1JE
National Trust for Places of Historic Interest of Natural Beauty, 36 Queen Anne's Gate, London SW1H 9AS (01 222 9251)
National Trust for Scotland, 5 Charlotte Square, Edinburgh EH2 4DU (031 226 5922)
1984 Committee for Freedom of Information, 2 Northdown Street, London N1 9BG (01 278 9686)
Open Spaces Society, 25a Bell Street, Henley on Thames, Oxon RG9 2BA (0491 573535)
Oral History Society, c/o Department of Sociology, University of Essex, Wivenhoe Park, Colchester CO4 3SQ (Colchester 44144)
Ordnance Survey, Romsey Road, Maybush, Southampton SO9 4DH (0703 775555 X. 436)
Pennine Heritage, The Birchcliffe Centre, Hebden Bridge, West Yorkshire (Hebden Bridge 844 804)
Poetry Society, 21 Earls Court Square, London SW5 9DE (01 373 7861)
Prince of Wales Committee, 4th Floor, Empire House, Mount Stuart Square, Cardiff CF1 6DN (0222 495737/495875)
Ramblers' Association, 1/5 Wandsworth Road, London SW8 2LJ (01 582 6878)
Rare Breeds Survival Trust, 4th Street NAC, Stoneleigh Park, Kenilworth, Warwickshire CV8 2LG (0203 51141)
Rescue – A Trust for British Archaeology, 15A Bull Plain, Hertford, Herts SG14 1DX (Hertford 58170)
Royal Horticultural Society, Wisley, Ripley, Surrey. PO Box 313, 80 Vincent Square, London SW1P 2PE (01 834 4333)
Royal Society for the Prevention of Cruelty to Animals (RSPCA), Causeway, Horsham, West Sussex RH12 1HG (0403 64181)
Royal Society of Arts, 6-8 John Adam Street, Adelphi, London WC2N 6EZ (01 930 5115)
Royal Society for the Protection of Birds, The Lodge, Sandy, Bedfordshire SG19 2DL (0767 80551). 17 Regent Terrace, Edinburgh EH7 5BN (031 556 5624/9042)
R.U.R.A.L., Bore Place, Chiddingstone, Edenbridge, Kent TN8 7AR (073 277 255/708)

Save Britain's Heritage, 68 Battersea High Street, London SW11 3HX (01 228 3336)

Scottish Civic Trust, 24 St. George Square, Glasgow G2 1EF (041 221 1466)

Scottish Field Studies Association, Elie Estate Office, Elie, Leven, Fife KY9

Scottish Wildlife Trust, 25 Johnston Terrace, Edinburgh EH1 2NH (031 226 4602)

Shell Better Britain, Northminster House, Northminster, Peterborough, Cambs PEI IUA (0733 40345),

Smallholder's Association, Tollywood Farm, Bishop's Lydeard, Taunton, Somerset TA4 3BT (0823 432279)

Society for the Interpretation of Britain's Heritage, 10 Priory Crescent, Lewes, E. Sussex BN7 1HP (0273 472970/0273 45400 ext. 722)

Society for the Promotion of Nature Conservation, The Green, Nettleham, Lincoln LN2 2NR (0522 52326)

Society for the Protection of Ancient Buildings (SPAB), 37 Spital Square, London E1 6DY (01 377 1644)

Soil Association, Walnut Tree Manor, Haughley, Stowmarket, Suffolk 1P14 3RS (044 970 235)

Town and Country Planning Association, 17 Carlton House Terrace, London SW1Y 5AS (01 930 8903/4/5)

Town Trees Trust, 11 Gainsborough Gardens, London NW3 1BJ (01 794 2764)

Transport 2000, Walkden House, 10 Melton Street, London NW1 2EJ (01 388 8386)

Tree Council, 35 Belgrave Square, London SW1X 8QN (01 235 8854)

Turning Point, The Old Bakehouse, Ilges Lane, Cholsey, near Wallingford, Oxfordshire OX10 9NU (0491 652 346)

Urban Wildlife Group, 11, Albert Street, Birmingham, B4 7UA (021 236 3626)

Vincent Wildlife Trust (Otter Haven Project), Baltic Exchange Buildings, 21 Bury Street, London EC3A 5AU (01 283 1266)

Watch (Trust for Environmental Education), 22 The Green, Nettleham, Lincoln LN2 2NR (0522 752326)

Waterways Recovery Group, 39 Westminster Crescent, Burn Bridge, North Yorkshire HG3 1LX

The Woodland Trust, Autumn Park, Dysart Road, Grantham, Lincolnshire NG31 6LL (0476 74297)

Workers Educational Association, Temple House, 9 Upper Berkeley Street, London W1H 8BY (01 402 5608/9)

Working Weekends on Organic Farms (WWOOF), 19 Bradford Road, Lewes, Sussex BN7 1RB

World Wildlife Fund UK, Panda House, 11-13 Ockford Road, Godalming, Surrey GU7 1QU (04868 20551)

Youth Hostels Association (England and Wales), Trevelyan House, St. Stephen's Hill, St. Albans, Herts AL1 2DY (56 55215)

More information on the main environmental groups is given in:

Environmental Directory. Civic Trust, 1984 at approx £3.00.

Heritage – A directory published by the British Tourist Authority at £1.00

Directory for the Environment by Michael J. C. Barker, Routledge and Kegan Paul, 1986 £15.95

Shell Better Britain Campaign Information Pack, 1986

Nature Conservation Trusts

Avon Wildlife Trust, The Old Police Station, 32 Jacob's Wells Road, Bristol BS8 1DR (0272 28018)

Bedfordshire & Huntingdonshire Wildlife Trust, Priory Country Park, Barkers Lane, Bedford MK41 9SH (0234 64213)

Berkshire, Buckinghamshire and Oxon Naturalists' Trust (BBONT), 3 Church Cowley Road, Rose Hill, Oxford OX3 3JR (0865 775476)

Urban Wildlife Group Birmingham (UWG), 11 Albert Street, Birmingham B4 7UA (021 236 3626)

Brecknock Naturalists' Trust, Lion House, 7 Lion Street, Brecon, Powys LD3 7AY

Cambridgeshire Wildlife Trust, (CAMBIENT), 5 Fulbourn Manor, Manor Walk, Fulbourn, Cambridge CB1 5BN (0223 880788)

Cheshire Conservation Trust, c/o Marybury Country Park, Northwich, Cheshire CW9 6AT (0606 781868)

Cleveland Nature Conservation Trust, The Old Town Hall, Mandale Road, Thornaby, Stockton on Tees, Cleveland TS17 6AW (0642 608405)

Cornwall Trust for Nature Conservation, Trendrine, Zennor, St Ives, Cornwall TR26 3BW (0736 796926)

Cumbria Trust for Nature Conservation, Church Street, Ambleside, Cumbria LA22 0BU (0966 32476)

Derbyshire Wildlife Trust, Elvaston Castle Country Park, Derby DE7 3EP (0332 756610)

Devon Trust for Nature Conservation, 35 New Bridge Street, Exeter, Devon EX3 4AH (0392 79244)

Dorset Trust for Nature Conservation, 39a High East Street, Dorchester DT1 1HN (0305 64620)

Durham County Conservation Trust, 52 Old Elvet, Durham, DH1 3HN (0385 69797)

Essex Naturalists' Trust, Fingringhoe Wick Nature Reserve, Fingringhoe, Colchester, Essex CO5 7DN (020628 678)

Glamorgan Trust for Nature Conservation, Nature Centre, Fountain Road, Tondu, Mid Glamorgan CF32 0EH (0656 724100)

Gloucestershire Trust for Nature Conservation, Church House, Standish, Stonehouse, Glos. GL10 3EU (045 382 2761)

La Societe Guernesiaise (LSG), c/o Dr T.N.D. Peet, Le Chene, Forest, Guernsey, C.I. (0481 38620)

Gwent Trust for Nature Conservation, 16 White Swan Court, Church Street, Monmouth, Gwent NP5 3BR (0600 5501)

Hampshire & Isle of Wight Naturalists' Trust, 8 Market Place, Romsey, Hants SO5 8NB (0794 513786)

Herefordshire & Radnorshire Nature Trust, Community House, 25 Castle Street, Hereford HR1 2NW (0432 56872)

Hertfordshire & Middlesex Trust for Nature Conservation, Grebe House, St Michael's Street, St Albans, Herts AL3 4SN (0727 58901)

Kent Trust for Nature Conservation, The Annexe, 1a Bower Mount Road, Maidstone, Kent ME16 8AX (0622 53017)

Lancashire Trust for Nature Conservation, The Pavilion, Cuerden Park, Shady Lane, Bamber Bridge, Preston, Lancs PR5 6A (0772 324129)

Leicestershire & Rutland Trust for Nature Conservation, 1 West Street, Leicester LE1 6UU (0533 553904)
Lincolnshire & Sth Humberside Trust for Nature Conservation, The Manor House, Alford, Lincs LN13 9DL (05212 3468)
London Wildlife Trust, 80 York Way, London N1 9AG (01 278 6612/3)
Manx Nature Conservation Trust, c/o A.J. Hopson, 14 Bowling Green Road, Castletown, Isle of Man (0624 87 266)
Montgomery Trust for Nature Conservation, 8 Severn Square, Newtown, Powys SY16 2AG (0686 24751)
Norfolk Naturalists' Trust, 72 Cathedral Close, Norwich, Norfolk NR1 4DF (0603 625540)
Northants Trust for Nature Conservation, Lings House, Billing Lings, Northampton NN3 4BE (0604 405285)
Northumberland Wildlife Trust, Hancock Museum, Barras Bridge, Newcastle-upon-Tyne NE2 4PT (0632 320038)
North Wales Naturalists' Trust, 376 High Street, Bangor, Gwynedd LL57 1YE (0248 351541)
Nottinghamshire Trust for Nature Conservation, 310 Sneinton Dale, Nottingham NG3 7DN (0602 588242)
Scottish Wildlife Trust (SWT), 25 Johnstone Terrace, Edinburgh EH1 2NH (031 226 4602)
Shropshire Trust for Nature Conservation, Agriculture House, Barker Street, Shrewsbury, Shropshire SY1 1QP (0743 241691)
Somerset Trust for Nature Conservation, Fyne Court, Broomfield, Bridgwater, Somerset TA5 2EQ (082345 587/8)
Staffordshire Nature Conservation Trust, Coutts House, Sandon, Staffordshire ST18 0DN (088 97 534)
Suffolk Trust for Nature Conservation, Park Cottage, Saxmundham, Suffolk IP17 1DQ (0728 3765)
Surrey Wildlife Trust, 'Hatchlands', East Clandon, Guildford, Surrey GU4 7RT (0483 223526)
Sussex Trust for Nature Conservation, Woods Mill, Shoreham Road, Henfield, West Sussex BN5 9SD (0273 492630)
Ulster Trust for Nature Conservation, Barnett's Cottage, Barnett Demesne, Malone Road, Belfast BT9 5PB (0232 612235)

Warwickshire Nature Conservation Trust (WARNACT), Montague Road, Warwick CV34 5LW (0926 496848)
West Wales Trust for Nature Conservation, 7 Market Street, Haverfordwest, Dyfed SA61 1NF (0437 5462)
Wiltshire Trust for Nature Conservation, 19 High Street, Devizes, Wiltshire SN10 1AT (0380 5670)
Worcestershire Nature Conservation Trust, Hanbury Road, Droitwich, Worcestershire WR9 7DU (0905 773031)
Yorkshire Wildlife Trust, Third Floor, 10 Toft Green, Off Micklegate, York YO1 1JT (0904 59570)
Royal Society for Nature Conservation (RSNC), The Green, Nettleham, Lincoln LN2 2NR (0522 752326)

Rural Community Councils
Avon Community Council, 209 Redland Road, Bristol BS6 6YU (0272 736822)
Bedfordshire Rural Community Council, The Old School, Southill Road, Cardington, Bedford MK44 3SX (02303 771/ 2)
Community Council for Berkshire, Venture Fair, Lower Padworth, Reading RG7 4JR (0734 713507)
Buckinghamshire Council for Voluntary Service, Walton House, Walton Street, Aylesbury, Bucks HP21 7QQ (0296 21036)
Cambridgeshire Community Council, Cambridgeshire House, 7 Hills Road, Cambridge CB2 1NL (0223 350666)
Cheshire Community Council, 96 Lower Bridge Street, Chester CH1 1RU (0244 22188/23602)
Cleveland Council for Voluntary Service, 47 Princes Road, Middlesbrough, Cleveland TS1 4BG (0642 240651/2)
Cornwall Rural Community Council, 1/2 Victoria Square, Truro, Cornwall TR1 2RS (0872 73952)
Cumbria Council for Voluntary Action, Birbeck House, Duke Street, Penrith, Cumbria CA3 8UG (0768 68086)
Derbyshire Rural Community Council, Church Street, Wirksworth, Derby DE4 4EY (062982 4797)
Community Council for Devon, County Hall, Topsham Road, Exeter EX2 4QD (0392 77977)

Dorset Community Council, 57 High West Street, Dorchester DT1 1UT (0305 62270)

Durham Rural Community Council, Hallgarth House, Hallgarth Street, Durham DH1 3AY (0385 43511)

Rural Community Council of Essex, 79 Springfield Road, Chelmsford CM2 6JG (0245 352046)

Gloucestershire Rural Community Council, Community House, 15 College Green, Gloucester GL1 2LZ (0452 28491)

Hampshire Council of Community Service, Beaconsfield House, Andover Road, Winchester SO22 6AT (0962 54971)

Hereford & Worcester Rural Community Council, Community House, 25 Castle Street, Hereford HR1 2NW (0432 272307) Room 225, County Buildings, St Mary's Street, Worcester WR1 1TN (0905 22384)

Community Council for Hertfordshire, 2 Townsend Avenue, St Albans AL1 3SG (0727 52298)

Community Council of Humberside, 14 Market Place, Howden, Goole, N Humberside DN14 7BJ (0430 30904)

Isle of Wight Community Services, 9 Mount Pleasant Road, Newport, Isle of Wight PO30 1EH (0983 524058)

Kent Voluntary Service Council, 15 Manor Road, Folkestone CT20 2AH (0303 43816)

Community Council of Lancashire, 15 Victoria Road, Fulwood, Preston PR2 4PS (0772 717461)

Leicestershire Rural Community Council, Community House, 133 Loughborough Road, Leicester LE4 5LX (0533 662905)

Community Council of Lincolnshire, Council Offices, Eastgate, Sleaford NG34 7EF (0529 302466)

Norfolk Rural Community Council, 20 Market Place, Hingham, Norwich NR9 4AF (0953 851408)

Northamptonshire Rural Community Council, Hunsbury Hill Centre, Hunsbury Hill Road, Northampton NN4 9QX (0604 65888/65874)

Community of Northumberland, Tower Buildings, 9 Oldgate, Morpeth NE61 1PY (0670 57178)

Nottinghamshire Rural Community Council, Minster Chambers, Church Street, Southwell, Notts NG25 0HD (0636 815267)

Oxfordshire Rural Community Council, The Hadow Rooms, 101 Banbury Road, Oxford OX2 6NE (0865 512488)
Community Council of Shropshire, 1 College Hill, Shrewsbury SY1 1LT (0743 60641)
Community Council for Somerset, St Margaret's, Hamilton Road, Taunton TA1 2EG (0823 81222/3)
Community Council of Staffordshire, 11a Stafford Street, Stafford ST16 2BP (0785 42525)
Community Council for Suffolk, Alexandra House, Rope Walk, Ipswich IP4 1LZ (0473 230000 ext. 4391)
Surrey Voluntary Service Council, Jenner House, 2 Jenner Road, Guildford GU1 3PN (0483 66072)
Sussex Rural Community Council, Sussex House, 212 High Street, Lewes BN7 2NH (0273 473422)
Warwickshire Rural Community Council, The Abbotsford, 10 Market Place, Warwick CV34 4SL (0926 499596)
Community Council for Wiltshire, Wyndhams, St Joseph's Place, Bath Road, Devizes SN10 1DD (0380 2475)
Yorkshire Rural Community Council, William House, Skipton Road, Skelton, York YO3 6WZ (0904 645271)

19
Designations

Information on some designated areas has already been given. For example, TPOs on page 57; Commons and Village Greens on page 42; Conservation Areas on page 149ff and Areas of Archaeological Importance on page 30ff.

Description of some other designated areas are given below:

Nature conservation

Sites of Special Scientific Interest
SSSIs are 'places in the countryside which the Nature Conservancy Council (NCC) has identified as of special interest because of the animals, birds, insects or plants found in them, or because of the interesting rocks or features of the land itself. There are approximately 4,000 (984 being geological sites) SSSIs in England, Scotland and Wales covering an area of approximately three and a half million acres (NCC 1983). They represent the absolute minimum necessary to support viable populations of Britain's rarest and more common wild animals and plants. Together with National Nature Reserves they comprise about 7 per cent of the land area of Great Britain.

Powers to designate areas of Special Scientific Interest (known as 'sites') were given to the Nature Conservancy (now NCC) in the National Parks and Access to the Countryside Act 1949 (section 23).

SSSIs were given added protection under the Wildlife and Countryside Act 1981 because they were being damaged or destroyed at the rate of 10-15 per cent each year.

The 1981 Act 'requires planning authorities to consult the NCC before granting permission to develop land classified as SSSIs, requires Water Authorities to similarly consult with the NCC before carrying out works likely to harm the conservation interest of any SSSI, and requires the Ministry of Agriculture, in consultation with the Secretary of State, to consider objections by the NCC before grant-aiding farm capital works which have harmed or will harm the conservation value of any SSSI. The NCC are required to inform owner/occupiers and the relevant authorities of land classified as a SSSI, and provide a list of damaging operations; in turn owner/occupiers are required to notify the NCC of any intention to carry out works likely to damage or destroy a SSSI. The NCC may appeal to the Secretary of State for a Conservation Order to halt damaging development for 12 months whilst a management agreement is discussed. If no reasonable agreement is possible, and if it is in the national interest to manage the land as a nature reserve, the NCC may acquire the land compulsorily. The NCC may also enter into management agreements with owners or lessees of SSSIs and provide financial support for any work and management practices which contribute to the nature conservation aims on such sites.' (FOE 1983). Further information on the working of the Wildlife and Countryside Act can be obtained from FOE: *Sites of Special Scientific Interest: 1984 – The failure of the Wildlife and Countryside Act* @ £1.95 and from BANC — *Implementing the Act: A Study of Habitat Protection under part II or the Wildlife and Countryside Act 1981* @ £4.45 incl. p & p.

Some SSSIs are costing the taxpayers a great deal of money through compensation payments – e.g. £20,400 p.a. for sixty-five years to protect a broadleaved wood in South East England; £275,000 in 1982 to protect a 5,000-acre upland bog in Scotland; £100,000 p.a. for ten years to protect 1,800 acres of traditionally grazed marshland from cereal cropping in Kent. (Figures from *Proposals for a Natural*

Heritage Bill FOE, 1983). It would obviously be impossible to protect all 4,000 SSSIs in a similar way.

National Nature Reserves (NNRs)

These are areas of outstanding wild life value which are designated and managed by the Nature Conservancy Council. In 1983 there were 193 NNRs covering an area of over 350,000 acres. 'Only 14 per cent by area of NNRs are owned by the NCC, the rest being held under lease or under nature reserve agreement with the landowner' (O'Riordan). 44 NNR agreements are coming up for renewal in the near future.

Local Nature Reserves (LNRs)

The National Parks and Access to the Countryside Act 1949 gave powers to local authorities to establish local nature reserves. By 1983, 61 LNRs had been designated, covering more than 19,000 acres in England, Wales and Scotland.

Many thousands of acres are owned and/or managed by voluntary organisations such as the National Trust, Woodland Trust, county naturalists' trusts and RSPB. For example, the RSPB has established 93 bird reserves covering 43, 728 hectares. The county naturalists trusts and RSNC are responsible for over 1,400 nature reserves covering over 100,000 acres.

Landscape and access

National Parks

Since 1949 and the passing of the National Parks and Access to the Countryside Act 10 parks have been established in England and Wales. The Act demands that each be 'an extensive tract of land which by reason of its natural beauty and the opportunities it affords for open air recreation shall be preserved and enhanced for the purpose of promoting its enjoyment by the Public' (SS 5-14). The land remains in private ownership and all the normal rural activities go on there. (In many other countries National Parks are state-owned and are empty of people, houses and industry.)

A committee of the constituent county councils or a special board governs the park policies and a national parks officer and his team administer the planning and management of the park. Management plans, proposals for conservation of natural beauty and enhancement of public enjoyment are drawn up and powers also exist for acquiring land, providing visitor facilities, rehabilitating derelict areas, arranging access agreements, planting trees and so on. Central government provides 75 per cent of the finance, the rest coming from local rates. More stringent development control procedures apply, for example:

The Landscape Area, Special Development Order (1950) enables National Parks Authorities (NPAs) to regulate the design and appearance of farm buildings, normally exempted from development control, in certain parts of the Lake District, the Peak and Snowdonia National Parks.

But, despite the legislation, areas of moorland and heath in National Parks are being lost (mainly to agricultural improvements and afforestation) at a rate of 12,000 acres a year. Under the 1981 Act the NCC and NPAs are obliged to compensate farmers if grant aid for agricultural improvement is rejected on conservation grounds. It would cost £6 million a year to protect 12,000 acres and this is beyond the means of the NPAs and NCC.

In Scotland there has been considerable resistance to the designation of National Parks and AONBs. There are now over 40 National Scenic Areas extending over almost one third of Scotland. Areas of Great Landscape Value may also be designated by local authorities.

Areas of Outstanding Natural Beauty (AONBs)
Under the 1949 National Parks Act it was also made possible for the National Parks (later Countryside) Commission to designate tracts of land as AONBs in order to conserve their natural beauty. Although not designated

with recreation in mind, these areas are expected to meet leisure demands 'as far as this is consistent with the conservation of natural beauty and the needs of agriculture, forestry and other uses' (C.C.P. 157 A.O.N.B.s A Policy Statement 1983). Agriculture, forestry, rural industries and the needs of local communities must also be taken into account at the same time as the protection and enhancement of natural beauty.

By the end of 1983 England and Wales had 35 AONBs, the management and planning responsibilities being shared by county and district councils. The Countryside Commission is giving advice and grant aid towards the preparation of statements of interest and management plans for these areas. Some areas have special study reports available. Emphasis should be on the conservation of natural beauty and against detrimental development – but the pressures for road, reservoir and industrial development often succeed.

Areas of Great Landscape Value (AGLVs)
Many counties and districts have designated areas of great landscape value or special landscape areas. While having no national status, the presumption here to should be against development, or at least for more sympathetic planning and design of any new buildings or land uses.

Heritage Coasts
Following the start of Enterprise Neptune in 1965 the National Trust now owns and manages over 400 miles of coastline. Protection of the coastline spread as an idea in the 1970s and now local authorities have asked the Countryside Commission to designate well over thirty coastal strips as Heritage Coast. There is no statutory back-up, but the policy commitment is to protect the coastline from incongruous development.

In some of these Heritage Coast Officers working for the County Planning Officer coordinate the work of wardens and volunteers maintaining good relations between landholders and visitors, enhancing access where possible by agreement and careful signing of footpaths, notice boards, car park siting and so on. 25 per cent of the coastline is now designated. In Scotland preferred conservation zones and preferred development zones were designated in response to the oil rush of the early 70s. 60 per cent of Scotland's long coastline falls within the preferred conservation zones. Coast Planning Guidelines were also drawn up by the Scottish Development Department.

Green Belt

As a reaction to the ribbon development and sprawl of towns in the 1930s, the Town and Country Planning Act of 1947 encouraged the designation of green belt areas around towns to prevent further expansion and joining up of urban areas and to protect the special character of historic towns. The idea of using some of this land to complement open space in the city came later. Little building has been allowed within the green belts – but recently there has been much pressure particularly for house building, because of the closeness to the cities and the attractiveness of the green belt areas. CPRE and others have worked hard to prevent this, not only to prevent the erosion of the green belt in this way, but also arguing that revitalisatic of inner city areas will never happen if investment is consistently drawn to the edge of towns.

Abbreviations

Statutory Bodies and Voluntary Organisations

ACA	Anglers' Cooperative Association
ADAS	Agricultural Development and Advisory Service
BTCV	British Trust for Conservation Volunteers
CLA	County Landowners Association
CoEnCo	Council for Environmental Conservation
CoSIRA	Council for Small Industries in Rural Areas
CPRE	Council for the Protection of Rural England
CPRW	Council for the Protection of Rural Wales
DOE	Department of the Environment
FOE	Friends of the Earth
FWAG	Farming and Wildlife Advisory Group
HBMC	Historic Buildings and Monuments Commission
HDRA	Henry Doubleday Research Association
IDB	Internal Drainage Board
MAFF	Ministry of Agriculture, Fisheries and Food
MSC	Manpower Services Commission
NCC	Nature Conservancy Council
NCVC	National Council for Voluntary Organisations
NFU	National Farmers Union
NPA	National Parks Authority
RCC	Rural Community Council
RIBA	Royal Institute of British Architects
RSNC	Royal Society for Nature Conservation
RTPI	Royal Town Planning Institute
RSPB	Royal Society for the Protection of Birds
RWA	Regional Water Authority
SPAB	Society for the Protection of Ancient Buildings
WEA	Workers Educational Association
WI	Womens Institute
WSAC	Water Space Amenity Commission

Designations

AGLV	Area of Great Landscape Value
AONB	Area of Outstanding Natural Beauty
LNR	Local Nature Reserve
NNR	National Nature Reserve
NP	National Park
SSSI	Site of Special Scientific Interest
TPO	Tree Preservation Order

Index

Page numbers in italic refer to examples.